Just Peacemaking

Silence

JUST PEACEMAKING

Transforming Initiatives for Justice and Peace

Glen H. Stassen

Westminster/John Knox Press
Louisville, Kentucky

Translations of excerpts from German-language publications are by Glen H. Stassen.

Book design by Gene Harris

First edition

Published by Westminster/John Knox Press
Louisville, Kentucky

This book is printed on acid-free paper that meets the American National Standards Institute Z39.48 standard. ∞

PRINTED IN THE UNITED STATES OF AMERICA

9 8 7 6 5 4 3 2 1

Library of Congress Cataloging-in-Publication Data
Stassen, Glen Harold, 1936–
    Just peacemaking : transforming initiatives for justice and peace / Glen H. Stassen. — 1st ed.
        p.   cm.
    Includes bibliographical references.
    ISBN 0-664-25298-2
    1. Peace—Religious aspects—Christianity. 2. Christianity and justice. I. Title.
BT736.4.S72 1992
261.8′73—dc20   91-38152

Contents

Preface

Jörg Swoboda, president of the Free-Church Theological Seminary in Buckow, East Germany (GDR), has written:

> As long as I can remember, guests from the Federal Republic have always voiced a particular feeling when departing: they say that for some inexplicable reason they feel very much at home with us, that they will take this feeling home with them as a gift, and finally that they would like to come again—and they do. At first I understood this as merely courtesy, but now I understand their sentiments this way: we in the GDR have had great external pressures, but God kept the ravages of socialism within bounds and created virtue out of our misery. Our congregations have been forced together more closely than those in the west and are much more dependent on one another. So, in our personal relationship, there is much more of value. Our guests feel the intense human closeness and warmth.[1]

Personal relationship, closeness and warmth, Christian community—these are just what I have experienced in East Germany when I have visited. A major part of the stimulus for *Just Peacemaking* came from my remarkable experience of hospitality, community, dialogue, and revolution in East Germany. I want to celebrate and give

thanks for the gift of community, as well as insights and
impetus, from Christian and Annie Wolf, Siegfried
Rosemann, Bernhard Assmann, Stefan Stiegler, Manfried
Preusen, and Jörg Swoboda. In recent years Christian
Wolf especially has given the gift of insight and solidity of
faith, wisdom, ethics, and community. And in what used
to be called West Germany, I am deeply grateful for the
gift of friendship and for much that I have learned from
Bernard Moltmann, Friedhelm Solms, Burkhardt and
Ulrike Scheffler, Angelika Braun, Heinz Eduard Tödt,
Hans-Richard Reuter, Wolfgang Liennemann, Andreas
Zumach, and Volkmar Deile.

My own community, the Crescent Hill Baptist Peacemaker Group, read the book chapter by chapter as it
emerged. Peter Clark won the prize for finding the most
infelicities of expression, and Ruth Ford gave special encouragement for writing narrative chapters, for which
readers may be grateful. Brian Cole added wisdom, and
Amy Smith added precision. All added encouragement—
Laura Ford, Anne Carpenter, Bob and Jane Kenney, Kate
and Michael Westmoreland-White, George Anne Gash,
Eiko Kanamaru, Betsy and Steven Wells, Marilyn Snyder,
Jo Carol and George Walton, Dot Steedly, Betty Cook. If
the book reads like it was written for people, not critics,
and if there is a subtle sense of support, community, and
the gift of grace, thank this good group that has been doing peacemaking together, with some rotation of members, for twelve years.

I also celebrate the community shared among Henlee
and Helen Barnette, Paul Simmons, Bill Leonard, Rick
Axtell, Randall Harvey, Michelle Tooley, Don Yancey,
Aubrey Williams, Joon-Sik Park, Greg Garrison, Bong-Gi
Choi, Henry Mugabe, Rob Sellers, Timothy Madison, and
Greg Brooks—fellow students of Christian ethics. Each
has read a part and/or contributed specific insights. More
important, our study of Christian ethics together is more

than ideas and criticisms; there is a shared feeling of mutual support and solidarity that I deeply appreciate. That community includes my dean, Larry McSwain, who gave me leave to be gone in East Germany during the time of the collapsing of the Berlin Wall and gave the less tangible but more important support of friendship. I have also enjoyed the skilled support and friendship of Wade Rowatt, Melody Mazuk, Andy Lester, and our faculty "Story Group."

I have written with two kinds of community in mind— that among scholars as well as among the broader human community. Much of my involvement is with church members, peacemakers, study groups, and students, so I have tried to write clearly and not abstractly—with real people in mind. I hope I have succeeded. At the same time, the book is not merely a popularization of what other scholars have written. The book is intended as an original contribution. So some dialogue with scholars is going on also. Occasionally I have relegated slightly more technical discussion to the notes in order to avoid slowing down the flow of the text. You may decide whether that discussion has interest for you.

New Testament scholars Alan Culpepper, David Garland, Gerald Borchert, Roger Omanson, and Walter Wink read chapters 2 and 3 and made incisive suggestions. Along with perceptive suggestions they gave what seemed to me to be enthusiastic encouragement. It is hard to convey the sense of community I experienced from what might seem less significant to them; when you crawl out on a limb doing interdisciplinary work, genuine, straightforward feedback from colleagues is an enormous gift.

Christian ethicists Brian Hehir, Alan Geyer, John Howard Yoder, Ronald Stone, Dana Wilbanks, and Jay Lintner, whose work as authors and consultants I celebrate in chapter 9, have been stimulating dialogue partners now and then over the years. They have each read some of what I have written, and I am grateful for their input. Much more, though, I am grateful for the creativity and wisdom of their powerful contributions to the churches' understanding of peacemaking, and I hope this proposal can continue our dialogue and further their excellent work.

Davis Perkins and Harold Twiss of Westminster/John Knox Press have been thoughtful and thorough in their initial encouragement and editing work. We owe them thanks, you and I.

And I owe a belated thank-you to Robert Jervis, Ralph Potter, and the Center for International Affairs of Harvard University for their support for research in perception, misperception, and the theory of international relations. Although I mention Robert Jervis's research at several places, I owe him much more than I have been able to show in this space.

Pat McCullough, for nine years director of the Louisville Council on Peacemaking and Religion, and twice co-chair of the Executive Committee of the Nuclear Weapons Freeze Campaign, said twelve years ago that peacemaking as transforming initiatives was a gift worth nurturing and growing. She has encouraged its development at many steps along the way, and has been a partner in strategizing, a coworker in peacemaking, and a loyal friend for sixteen years. I have learned much in the process. In some places you may hear her voice singing.

Robert Parham and Ken Sehested both have a gift for strategy and for loyal friendship that has lasted over the years. Robert was a cofounder of our church's peacemaker group and a major source of encouragement for "transforming initiatives," which he wanted me to call "surprising initiatives." Ken models putting your body where your words are, and that gives his words a poetry that I can only admire from a distance.

I am grateful for our remarkable family community—

our parents, sisters, brothers, cousins, children. We have much to care about and much to preserve. Like many others, love for our children is one major motive for our involvement in peacemaking.

My paradigm is my sister, Kathleen Stassen Berger—author, teacher, doer of justice, giver of warm support and hospitality. Her books on the developing person are dedicated to shalom for all children. I dedicate *Just Peacemaking* to her and to our parents who gave us our models to grow with.

> Therefore, since we are surrounded by so great a cloud of witnesses, . . . let us run with perseverance, . . . looking to Jesus the pioneer and perfecter of our faith. (Heb. 12:1–2)

1

The Turning: "Everything Is New"

At 2:00 A.M. Friday, November 10, 1989, Siegfried Rosemann answered the telephone. The voice said, "Hey, du! Wir trinken Bier! Komm, trink mit! [Hey, bud! We're drinkin' beer! Come drink with us!]"

"Where are you?" Siegfried asked. They were in a pub in West Berlin, on the other side of the Wall, celebrating, and they wanted Siegfried there, or at least there by phone.

Siegfried grinned as he told his story to the Baptist conference in East Berlin: "Everything is new. Everything!" Others told how their children came home from school surprised by the new, relaxed manner of the teachers and the free discussions without indoctrination. The newspapers were suddenly truthful, and people who had ignored them before were buying them out and reading them one or two hours each day. Soon the government announced free elections, recognized the new, rival parties, promised independent investigation of police brutality, freedom for conscientious objectors, and a dozen other reforms demanded by the people. And we passed traffic jams going west on the autobahns 15 to 20 kilometers long!

A Global Turning

That period was an intense experience of personal re-orientation. The Honecker regime in East Germany (German Democratic Republic, GDR) had resisted change so stubbornly that people in their realism did not allow themselves to expect the Wall could topple in their lifetimes, let alone the whole government, economy, education system, and culture. On the nineteenth of January, 1989, Honecker had proclaimed, "The Wall will remain for two hundred years." One person told me she would lie in bed each morning before getting up, trying to orient herself to the new world being created, only to discover when she opened the newspaper that more dramatic changes had occurred and she still was not oriented.

The opening of the Wall reoriented my own angle of vision on the world. "The Turning" became the symbol of a more widespread global turning. The processes and strategies that brought about the Turning in East Germany have been growing elsewhere as well and may be turning us toward a twenty-first century more peaceful and just than we have dared hope ever since the beginning of the atomic era. I am rooted in the twentieth-century experience of the threat of the mushroom cloud. Starting out as a nuclear physicist and doing research for a while for the Navy and Air Force, I experienced what others also began to sense after Hiroshima and Nagasaki: This threat could spread globally, life could be far more dangerous, war could mean extinction. We had to learn new ways to think and new ways to deal with conflict. But could we, and would we?

I am also rooted in the Christian realism of my teacher, Reinhold Niebuhr. He taught a skepticism about leaps in history that he had learned from the conservative British political theorist Edmund Burke. And he taught me to pay attention less to the hopeful ideals people declare than to their basic interests, loyalties, and power relations, and less to the promises of their high-sounding words than to the pattern of their actions. I have been basically pessimistic about the likelihood that we would develop new patterns of international relations or get rid of the threat of nuclear weapons. At the same time, I knew that if we did not change, we faced a future clouded by the threat of global nuclear holocaust.

Could we learn new ways to think and new ways to deal with conflict? We still are not sure, but we *may* be experiencing a "turning" as we approach the twenty-first century—a turning that needs naming so we can recognize its shape, can develop skills to participate in it, and can sing its song with hope and gratitude.

An Emerging Model of Just Peacemaking

Our post–Cold-War world will be full of changes, and we will face a different set of challenges. The Turning in East Germany symbolizes those changes and challenges. Things really are different. We need a different pattern of responses.

The Turning means the world will no longer be divided between two superpowers. It will not be bipolar but multipolar. Different powers will lead each region—Germany and France in Europe; Iraq, Syria, Egypt, Saudi Arabia, and Israel in the Middle East; and others in other regions. In each region the smaller powers will also have important voices. Some of the larger regional powers could threaten their neighbors. It will not be a world without conflict. Multipolar security systems that can reduce and restrain conflict will have to replace the bipolar system that was formerly imposed on nations. The good news is that we may be seeing a step-by-step turning toward methods of conflict resolution and systems that are functioning to increase global security. Peacemaking will need to be more aware of the valid interests of many different nations. We will need to pay more attention to the United Nations and those regional organizations, like the Council on Security and Cooperation in Europe and the Organization of American States, whose function is to get nations to listen to one another and act in their mutual interest.

That conflict will continue even after the Turning was dramatically illustrated in August 1990. Iraq invaded a neighboring, smaller power, Kuwait, which had not listened to Iraq's interests. The United Nations came through in an unprecedented way with international sanctions against Iraqi trade. Even so, war broke out, with the United States the primary force opposing Iraq. Although many in the United States spoke out in opposition to the war before it started, the nation cheered during and immediately after the war. Then the volume of cheering grew weaker as we began to realize that well over 100,000 persons were killed and the aftermath included bloody and unsuccessful civil wars; spreading disease and inability to provide food, water, medical care, electricity, or sanitary living conditions in Iraq; huge ecological devastation; and deep resentment by millions of Arab people. There was a consensus that we needed to switch from warmaking to peacemaking in the Middle East. (Chapter 10 will discuss the war with Iraq.)

Four days before the bombing of Iraq began, the Society of Christian Ethics (the professional organization of specialists in Christian ethics in the United States and Canada), at its annual meeting, debated what the government should do. The speakers expressed their views with passion, clarity, intelligence, and mutual respect. Some had children in the Marines in Saudi Arabia. All were well trained in the ethics of peace and war. Over the years the society has always come through with insightful and perceptive judgments. The Congress and the nation had a similar debate.

Yet the debate left me feeling deeply frustrated. It reduced the alternatives to making war or simply waiting. Some argued from the ethics of just war theory and others from the ethics of pacifism. Some argued we should make war to force Saddam Hussein and his army out of Kuwait; others argued we should not, but give the sanctions time to work.

A third group, including John Howard Yoder, Charles West, Ronald Stone, and others, argued for conflict resolution efforts, peacemaking initiatives, to try to get Iraq to leave Kuwait and to resolve the conflicts without the killing. I believe this third position represented the strong majority. It included pacifists and just war theorists. The positions held by both of these groups imply the need to take peacemaking initiatives, but their debate with each other reduced the issue to making war versus not making war. The guidance for peacemaking initiatives got lost. The resulting resolution was based on just war criteria and focused on whether we should make war then or not. Ninety-three percent voted no, we should not. The resolution was inarticulate about the guidelines for peacemaking. The Society of Christian Ethics did not urge itself or the people or the Congress or the president to take any clearly defined conflict resolution initiatives. Because we had no clear model of the ethics of peacemaking on which to base our debate, but only the two models of the restraint of war, the points that were made in oral debate about peacemaking initiatives did not have a clear paradigm with which to resonate. Yet precisely here is where I believe the failure in policy lay—the failure to take initiatives to resolve the confrontation.

I came away frustrated that we lacked a third model that we all understood, with something like the seven clear criteria of the just war theory, for judging whether the government is taking serious peacemaking initiatives and for guiding ourselves and the people in our debates and actions about peacemaking. Why do we not have a similar set of criteria and a model for a just peacemaking theory? We cannot get a clear debate on peacemaking alternatives unless we have a model that will focus our arguments. (See chapters 4 and 10.)

Biblical Concreteness and the Lordship of Christ

I want to identify a new model of just peacemaking that is emerging in our time and beginning to show its face in Christian peacemaking strategies as well as in international relations (see chapter 9). It is grounded both in the new reality of our world and in some new biblical interpretation that for complex historical reasons was unavailable to us until recently. Therefore, I have done more original biblical digging than is often expected of a Christian ethicist. I believe new insights are emerging that give us a much stronger biblical base for a new paradigm of just peacemaking. (See chapters 2 and 3.)

Grounded in Realistic Experience

The new paradigm of just peacemaking is also grounded in the historical experience of people who have lived in the face of oppression, violation of their basic rights, and the nuclear threat, and who, together with political scientists, Christian ethicists, and activists, fashioned realistic steps of peacemaking that enabled them to begin living in the time after the Cold War even before the Wall came down. Though oppressed and constricted, they began to live our future.

Because the paradigm is grounded in realistic but persistent hope-creating experience, parts of the book are narratives—historical, realistic, enacted and experienced in public. These narratives include the historical drama of the Turning in East Germany (in this chapter), the agreement to get rid of all the Euromissiles (chapter 5), the discovery of human rights by Richard Overton (chapter 6), and the decision to make war against Iraq (chapter 10).

In making these dramas part of my argument, I have been influenced by the method of James William McClendon's book, *Ethics.*[1] I admire a quality of his method that has not been adequately noticed. Although he opposes an ethic of universal principles detached from their historical roots, he is not merely subjective and is not opposed to principles. He advocates principles—forgiveness, truth, nonviolence, holistic love, inclusiveness, and consent to being—but the principles must be grounded in their rich historical context. He believes in criteria of verification similar to those advocated by H. Richard Niebuhr in *The Meaning of Revelation.* McClendon makes three affirmations: (1) Since the story of our life is biblical and communal, insights are to be tested by biblical exegesis and shared experience; (2) since the story happens not in private isolation but within human history, attention must be paid to what can be learned from critical perspectives external to Christian faith; and (3) since the heart of the story is consent to all God's creating and the practice of forgiveness and love, an ethic is to be tested by its ability to be inclusive rather than to repress important strands of human life or other members of the human community. McClendon's narrative ethics is therapy for abstract ethics that has repressed its own life history and community and thus lost its freedom and energy.

The Power of Nonviolence

We have all known we needed to develop new methods for achieving change without violence. Now we have seen nonviolent revolutions in Iran (where the revolution was nonviolent but not the subsequent regime), in the Philippines, in Argentina, throughout Eastern Europe, and in

the peoples' defeat of the coup in the Soviet Union, and
there is hope for them in South Africa and perhaps Palestine (where parts of the movement are nonviolent, and
other parts are not) and South Korea, Myanmar (formerly
Burma), and China (where the government bludgeoned
the movement to death at Tiananmen Square—for
now—as Erich Honecker wanted to do in East Germany).
The practice of nonviolent action is spreading internationally, and it is turning over unjust regimes. To experience that firsthand in East Germany gave me a much
deeper appreciation of the power of nonviolent direct action, which I had experienced in our civil rights movement but had only read about internationally.

In 1982, at breakfast with workers at Action Reconciliation in West Berlin, I recall Andreas Zumach observing
that Germany has lacked a tradition of nonviolent civil
disobedience and direct action. As a result, demonstrations against expansion of the military/commercial air-
port in Frankfurt turned violent, and the demonstrators
lost.

It could have gone that way in East Germany in 1989,
but the church peace groups had studied Martin Luther
King, Jr., Gandhi, and the civil rights movement in the
United States. At the conclusion of the rally in the Bit-
terfeld marketplace one week after the Wall was opened,
the thousands who were there sang "We Shall Overcome"
(for the first time outdoors—an act of civil disobedience
itself). Suddenly my intense memories of the long struggle
for civil rights in Durham, Williamston, Washington, and
Louisville were fused with the emotion of the achievement
of freedoms long denied in the GDR, as this nonviolent
movement celebrated by singing "We Shall Overcome."

Jörg Swoboda writes:

> Instead of a stone like David they carried candles in their
> hands and moved against the giant Goliath. The govern-

ment officials threatened, defamed, mocked, and ordered the State Security Forces, Special Forces, Emergency Police, State Police, and Army against their own people. The cruel game of fear had worked for years. But now it was played out. Gorbachev's perestroika and glasnost had given the people courage. God had blessed them with unyielding patience and inconquerable nonviolence. They had overcome their fear and found their voice and self-respect again.[2]

Nonviolence was not only a strategy for the people but also a policy to be taught to the government. In our time of nuclear and chemical/biological weapons, nonviolent strategies of conflict resolution must be learned by governments. The Turning symbolizes the newfound relevance of the Sermon on the Mount (see chapters 2 and 3).

The Power of Human Rights

The movement not only refrained from violence. It took the positive action of clearly articulating the human rights that needed to be established. In East Germany and throughout Eastern Europe, the language of public demand and the strongly felt need of the people was neither authoritarian Marxism nor laissez-faire capitalism but human rights. Thus the Turning is a symbol for the power of human rights.

There was much discussion about the future economic order. The consensus was that the Marxist economic system was shipwrecked and should not return. Still, people repeatedly said they did not want to adopt laissez-faire capitalism. A well-informed Catholic leader in a discussion group asked me about the social safety net in the United States. I affirmed there was one for some people but had to tell them of 37 million without health insurance, 1.5 million without homes, drug addicts on six- to nine-month waiting lists for clinics, and five-sixths of poor children eligible for Head Start schooling going without it because its funds had been cut back. They had already read much of this in their newspapers. They found it hard to comprehend that a country so much wealthier than theirs could not afford these basic necessities, which even their nation was providing. Their response caused me to see my own country's ideology from a new angle. They knew, and I knew, that other European nations are doing better on basic needs, and their economies are doing better as well. I asked myself whether the United States too can learn from East Germany and itself come to a time of turning, of repenting for injustices in our system, and change as they are changing. If East Germany could change in the face of authoritarian resistance, why cannot we in our freer democracy? (See chapter 7.)

The Story of the Turning in East Germany

Siegfried Rosemann, responsible for youth ministry in the Baptist Federation of East Germany, invited me to speak in 1989 at about a dozen ecumenical gatherings all over East Germany during the annual Friedensdekade, the ten days of peacemaking emphasis in the churches of East Germany from November 12 to 22. Thus by luck, very clever planning, or God's grace, we experienced "the Turning"—which is what the East Germans call their nonviolent revolution. We began in East Berlin with a conference of the Working Group on Peacemaking of the Baptist Federation, on the weekend before the Friedens-dekade, so it happened that we entered on Friday, November 10, just as the Wall was opening up.

While I was preparing for the trip to East Germany, I had asked my friend, Christian Wolf, lecturer in Christian Ethics and Old Testament in the Free Church Seminary in Buckow, East Germany, what I should say. He said, in effect, "Be biblically concrete. The people in the churches are highly biblical, and they are not vague in their under-

This is Jay T's book

standing of the Bible." They had asked me to speak on the
Sermon on the Mount, on Cain and Abel, and on delivering love in the parable of the compassionate Samaritan, as
well as on the struggle for the INF Treaty[3] and the strategy
of the peacemaking movement in the United States, especially in the churches. These topics were biblical, and they
were practical. I agreed happily. The suggestion gave me
an opportunity to do what I wanted to do, in the spirit of
Dietrich Bonhoeffer—be biblical, practical, and concrete.

My friend also explained that Christians in East Germany had to make a clear decision between the lordship
of a Marxist ideology and the lordship of Christ. Bishop
Albrecht Schönherr had told me about the strong influence of Dietrich Bonhoeffer and his theme of the lordship
of Christ in the churches of East Germany.

John Burgess has written about what I also experienced: Churches in Germany whose habits and self-
understandings still resemble the mold of the state-church
system of the past have lost participants.[4] Overdependence on the state dilutes the gospel and reduces people to
passive receptivity rather than transforming initiatives.
The churches that have not lost members and attendance
seem to emphasize biblical concreteness, Christ as Lord
of all of life, conversion, commitment, and community.
This too has encouraged me to write as I have.

As is well known, the churches were the one place where
opposition groups could meet, discuss freely, and organize. In the two months previous, demonstrators always
met first in churches and then, after a prayer service,
marched around the city with candles. Again and again I
was told that the church context influenced the demonstrations to be disciplined and nonviolent. They preached
nonviolence, prayed for nonviolence, urged nonviolence
on the authorities, and strategized nonviolent action without pause.

Less well known, the churches clarified and made precise

the specific demands that then reached consensus among the people, and thus put well-defined and concerted pressure on the government. For two years, the churches had engaged in an ecumenical "Conciliar Process" of discussion of "Justice, Peace, and the Preservation of Creation," answering a call first issued by Dietrich Bonhoeffer in 1934 and recently reissued by Karl-Friedrich von Weizsäcker.[5] Local congregations discussed draft documents on the three themes and sent their suggestions to coordinating groups in each denomination, and then on to the ecumenical coordinators. This consensus process was crucial to reaching agreement about what changes the people should demand of the government. In the authoritarian society of East Germany, there was no other place than churches where such discussions could be organized, and where their results could be announced and then published.

The document resulting from the discussions has a section titled "More Justice in the GDR," and sections on peacemaking and saving the environment from dangerous pollution and devouring strip-mining. Human rights are emphasized throughout, and specific demands are pressed for rights of democratic participation, with free, secret elections; separation of party from government; freedom of speech and honesty in the media; religious liberty; freedom of the press; freedom of education from ideological indoctrination; freedom from pressure to join the communist youth organization and to take military instruction; freedom to pursue careers without being forced to join ideological organizations; education that encourages independence, responsibility, and creativity instead of conformism; the right to conscientious objection to military service; equal rights for women; the right of judicial review of governmental decisions; freedom of art and culture; freedom of travel; support for childcare and for families; and the right to assembly and organization of independent, voluntary associations.

Max Stackhouse's point[6] about the importance of voluntary associations, and especially church groups, as carriers of the demand for human rights was clearly demonstrated. This powerful experience deepened my conviction that an essential step in "just peacemaking" is the role of groups, churches, and voluntary associations (see chapter 8).

Nine years previously, in Halle, when protesters against the nuclear missiles in Europe were organizing, they began the annual Bridge Worship, something like a liturgical progressive dinner. People gathered at churches on one side of the river for the beginning of worship, and then walked across the bridges to churches of other denominations for the second part of the worship. The bridges symbolized the ecumenical unity between Protestant, Catholic, and Free Churches, and the walking established the right and practice of nonviolent demonstration. The police roared up on their motorcycles and threatened them with arrest: "Don't you know demonstrations are illegal?" The people replied, "We are going to worship; why is that illegal?" After two or three years, thousands were participating. This gave courage and example (and not a little amusement) to people throughout the country. The pattern was followed during the time of the Turning in weekly candle-lit marches through all the major cities and many small ones. Jörg Swoboda titled his book on the nonviolent revolution *The Revolution of the Candles*.

A German folk-saying goes "Steady drops hollow out the stone." For years the people had been steadily, persistently claiming a bit of freedom here and a bit there. Then suddenly, in the space of one month, a notoriously rigid and stubborn government was turned from a decision to wreak Tiananmen-Square violence on demonstrators to a policy of nonviolence; its longtime authoritarian leader, Erich Honecker, was turned out; and the society was turned from the oppression of the Wall to the openness of

the human rights that people had long demanded. It was
like packing the fifteen-year achievements of the U.S. civil
rights struggle all into one month.

November 22, 1989, was the national Day of Repentance, and our last evening in East Germany. We were in a
Methodist church in a suburb of Berlin, and I had given a
message of repentance based on the biblical story of the
two brothers Cain and Abel. Then came dialogue time. A
man rose to remind us that the British and U.S. governments were still saying they planned to install a new generation of short-range nuclear weapons in West Germany,
Wall or no Wall, and the Warsaw Pact was doing likewise.
"Do you expect us to install these missiles and aim them
at our brothers and sisters, like Cain and Abel, against the
very people we are hoping will be our source of help?"

No, I did not. I told the congregation some of the story
of the medium-range Euromissiles (see chapter 5).

The question graphically demonstrated how policy can
lag behind changes in reality. You cannot visit Eastern Europe or the Soviet Union without seeing that reality has
changed dramatically. The Cold War is over. Both Eastern
Europe and the Soviet Union are now looking to the West
as their source of help. They are cutting their troops back
drastically. Their economies are their first concern and
are in great trouble. The economic, social, political, and
religious dislocations are profoundly painful. There are a
host of new perils. My friends tell me unemployment is
likely to reach 50 percent. Persons they know have committed suicide. This is true not only of East Germany but
also of the Soviet Union. Yet at the time of this writing,
years after *perestroika,* the U.S. government is still waiting until reforms are farther along in the Soviet Union
before assisting them. Unlike after World War II, we are
blocking the beginning of a Marshall Plan to help them
recover, while many of our European allies want to go
ahead. Do the Soviet people not need our assistance, step

by step, to learn how to make reforms and to have confidence there will be help in making those reforms? Is this another example of an old policy, the residue of an old enemy image, that has not adapted to the new realities? Are we losing precious time? How much damage has it already caused for the people and the processes of reform and democratization? Will it cause a nationalistic reaction? Or will they reform and develop their economy more quickly and effectively because we held back?

The Turning in East Germany is a symbol that the world really has turned, dramatically. The danger is that we could continue thinking and acting according to our old habits and not adapt to the very much changed world. It really is very different. Here is how free-church pastor Gottfried Zimmerman sees it:

> The GDR citizens have come of age. . . . They can decide on their own to travel in whatever direction they want. The Wall is open. At the border-crossings people are humane. The powerful are dethroned. Captured in the network of their years of lies, they must answer for their abuse of power. The Communist Party's claim to divinity has capsized. . . . The feared buildings of the State Security Forces are conquered. Journalists, whose vocabulary seemed shrunk . . . now can suddenly write in relaxed and interesting ways. Incomprehensible, all this![7]

The incomprehensible change means that economic forces, ecological forces, ethnic forces, and even ethical, cultural, religious, and media forces have become more important. Military forces have become less important, though not totally powerless. The severe economic problems of Eastern Europe and the historical, cultural, and social ties between East and West were too powerful for the armies to keep the Wall propped up. The people of Eastern Europe are not volunteering for their armies, and their governments are reducing forces drastically while

demanding the Soviet Army leave. The armies themselves
are confused about what their purpose should be. The
people are concerned about jobs and unemployment,
building new economic systems, the value of their cur-
rency, and what they can buy. They are concerned about
stopping the damage to the environment—to the air they
breathe, the water they drink, the ground where their children play, the dying forests. They do not think armies can
solve this problem. Peace will require increased attention
to justice and human rights so that diverse ethnic groups
and economic classes will be able to live together.

The Turning to a New Century

The most important forces transcend national boundaries and cannot be controlled by a single nation. Security
will require cooperation. We will need to learn better
skills of affirming one another's valid interests. Significantly, skills of conflict resolution *are* being learned, and
institutions of cooperation *are* steadily growing in
strength. Western Europe is integrating economically, and
politically and culturally as well. The nations of Eastern
Europe seem destined to federate with and eventually join
the common European house.[8] The Turning symbolizes
that we may in fact be learning the skills and building the
institutions that we must develop if we are to survive in a
post–Cold-War nuclear age (see chapter 4).

The Turning also means that "peacemaking" must be
understood in a new way for our new context. First,
peacemaking must be understood holistically. It must include economic justice, human rights, defense of the eco-
structure. It must include positive steps creating the
conditions for well-being, and not only limits on war or
protest against war. It must include a realistic understanding that conflicts will arise, and mechanisms for resolving
those conflicts must be built and used. This is what the

realistic biblical term *shalom* means. Peacemaking after the Turning must be *shalom*-making.

Peacemaking must also include disarming the nuclear threat. At the time of this writing, the two nuclear superpowers (the Soviet commonwealth is still a *nuclear* superpower) still have not agreed to a comprehensive test ban treaty, or to a flight test ban for new missiles. They are still testing and building ever more accurate nuclear weapons, increasingly usable in a Pearl Harbor–like surprise attack. Each side will be tempted to launch if, during a crisis, their radar and computer systems give false warning of an attack. False warnings happen often.

The continued emphasis on nuclear weapons by the two great powers also means their hands are weakened when they try to discourage other nations from going nuclear. The more nations that obtain nuclear weapons, the more fingers there are on the trigger, and the more chances there are to start nuclear war.

Nuclear war is so devastating that it is unlikely to happen intentionally. We are not where we were at the start of World War II, with one side believing they could start a war without the other side being capable of doing it much serious damage.[9] Instead, the danger of nuclear war is more like the start of World War I—that of escalation out of control. We need to get the nuclear weapons under control. That means (1) banning qualitative escalation, (2) stopping proliferation from placing the triggers of nuclear weapons into more hands, and (3) reducing the destructiveness of the arsenals in case they do go off.

Behind the story of the Turning is the story of ridding Europe and the world of medium-range missiles. The peacemaking groups in East Germany that pioneered the demonstrations that blew the Wall down began ten years earlier in the movement to rid Europe of the INF missiles (see chapter 5).

At the end of a head-spinning two weeks of turning in

time, Siegfried Rosemann met us again at Buckow. As soon as he saw the plaque-sized hunk of the Wall that Jörg Swoboda gave me after my lectures at the seminary (far better than an honorary degree), he grinned and said I could break it up in pieces and sell it in the United States for a profit! I replied that although I had already had it for four hours, I had never thought of such an idea, but he had right away. "You're the capitalist, not me!"

On the way back to Berlin, Siegfried told us of his experience the week before. After the Wall opened, he had gotten a visa for himself and Dorothea and asked the children if they wanted to go see West Berlin. Excited, they asked if they could get their own visas too. The government did not issue visas for children. But he could not leave them out of this momentous historical experience. What to do? Siegfried wrote "Ausweis" with a bright purple magic marker on three pieces of paper and put each child's name in their new, homemade visas.

Crossing the border had always been a tense and fear-engendering experience. The guards were impersonal, mechanical, and bureaucratically suspicious. For no clear reason, they could deny your entry, and all your plans would be disrupted. But this time, at the border, the guard actually smiled and seemed relaxed as he stamped Siegfried's and Dorothea's visas with a large, rectangular, official stamp. Then Siegfried presented the three homemade visas. The guard caught on quickly, grinned broadly, and stamped them officially.

That evening, the guard at the return gate did not know what to do. He examined the children's homemade visas back and front, read the bright purple magic marker printing uncomprehendingly, and then examined the rectangular stamp carefully. It was indeed official. What to do? He frowned, scratched his head, and then with an earnest and official set to his jaw, picked up his smaller round stamp with the GDR symbol of a draftsman's compass on it and officially stamped the proud children's historic new visas!

Siegfried now suggested it would not be necessary, as it had been, to walk back through Friedrichstrasse, take the train to the Berlin Zoo, and call Burkhardt Scheffler to come get us. Siegfried and Dorothea could simply drive over to the Schefflers' in West Berlin! But after waiting in line, we were told by the border guard, "Sorry, but they came in by Friedrichstrasse and so they will have to go back through Friedrichstrasse. It's the law." Siegfried smiled and replied earnestly, "Believe me. It's all right. Everything is new." They talked a bit, and then the supervisor came over. "What's wrong?" Two sentences of explanation, and the supervisor smiled broadly and waved. "Go on through. What's the difference?" We laughed, even the guard smiled, and Siegfried held out his hands, palms up, in amazement: "Two weeks ago I wouldn't even have *thought* of raising a question. I could have been punished. No chance of a yes answer. Can you *understand* what it means? Everything is new!"

It is new. We need a new understanding of just peacemaking for our new reality after the Cold War. Yet a lot of the old is still around too. Our new strategy of peacemaking will need a strong dose of realism. But also hope.

Questions for Thought

1. How much of the story of the role of the churches and peacemaking groups in the Turning had you known? Do our news media adequately report the role of the people in bringing about change, or only the outcome when the government finally responds to the pressure?

2. After reading only this introductory chapter, what ingredients would you propose for a just peacemaking model?

3. Why do you suppose both the East German system and the U.S. system are each ecologically unhealthy in their own way, in spite of the contrast in political and economic systems?

4. How serious a problem do you think nuclear weapons are even after the Cold War has ended?

5. How do you answer the questions about helping the Soviet Union organize their economic reform versus holding back?

2

Turning
Toward the Sermon
on the Mount

When we read recent studies of the Sermon on the Mount, we are faced with a triple irony.

First, as the studies point out, many of us praise Jesus' teachings as high ideals and then advocate a way to evade following them.[1] We emphasize how high Jesus' ideals are, how hard his teachings and impossible his demands, as a way of heaping praise on him. The more impossible his ideals, the more praiseworthy his teachings. Then we conclude the teachings are too high and too hard for us to follow, and so instead we should follow some other, more pragmatic ethic.

Gandhi was greatly influenced by the Sermon on the Mount. And he saw through the hermeneutics of evasion: "The message of Jesus, as I understand it, is contained in the Sermon on the Mount. . . . It is that Sermon which has endeared Jesus to me. . . . The message, to my mind, has suffered distortion in the West. . . . Much of what passes as Christianity is a negation of the Sermon on the Mount."[2]

Second, by pointing out that these evasions distort Jesus' clear meaning—that we are to hear and *do* his words—scholars are undermining the evasions they describe as so pervasive. What is pervasive now in New Testament scholarship is the agreement that Jesus' teachings in the Sermon on the Mount were meant to be followed. They were meant not merely for an inner or individualistic realm but for participation in God's rule over all of life. The implications of the Sermon on the Mount are not to be limited to just one part of life, or one class of "super Christians," or a future eschatological dispensation removed from present history, but for God's rule on earth as in heaven. The scholars' very act of pointing out the errors of the hermeneutics of evasion is causing a turning toward the Sermon on the Mount as authoritative for life.

Third, the turning toward the Sermon on the Mount as practical, helpful, and essential for our own living is happening especially in Germany. In Germany, the Lutheran and Catholic traditions dominate—traditions that had fenced off the Sermon on the Mount as applicable only to one realm and not authoritative in normal life or in society.

Medieval Catholicism developed the interpretation that much of the Sermon on the Mount was for monks and special orders, and not binding on lay Christians in the world. Lutheranism developed a different dualism—a sort of inner monastery within each individual. It said the Sermon on the Mount was for the inner, individual self and its motives, not for societal relationships, politics, or economics. Thus the Sermon on the Mount was kept in its place—or in a place assigned to it by an establishment whose response to Jesus was, "Do Not Disturb!"

Ironically, recovery of the Sermon on the Mount in the German churches has been helped by their historic resistance against it. In their resistance, they had established strong limits on how the Sermon on the Mount could be interpreted. Hence new authority for the Sermon on the Mount could be recovered without the threat that we should read the Sermon legalistically as a new set of laws, or that we were about to base Christian ethics on law and works rather than gospel and grace, or that we could expect application to our time without some translation.

The two forms of dualistic double-standard ethics in the historic Catholic and Lutheran resistance were easy targets. They came to be recognized as wrong, and this opened the possibility of hearing the Sermon on the Mount anew. Catholic scholars rejected the false tradition that the Sermon on the Mount was only for monks and "the perfect," and that lay Christians need not follow its teachings. They recognized that in both Matthew and Luke Jesus was teaching the crowds as well as the disciples. Furthermore, *all* Christians are called to be disciples, that is, to follow Jesus, to do his will.[3] Jesus speaks of those who do God's will and enter the kingdom, and those who do not do it and do not enter (Matt. 7:21ff.). There is no separate category for lay Christians who enter in by the narrow gate, without doing the words Jesus taught (Matt. 7:14, 24).

Protestant scholars came to recognize that Jesus was teaching not only about inner intentions but also about doing deeds, and that the point is not merely to be convinced that we *cannot* do them and must repent but to repent and *do* them.[4] "Everyone who hears these words of mine and does not act on them will be like a foolish man who built his house on sand" (Matt. 7:26). It has become clear that efforts to confine the authority of Jesus' teachings about God's will to an inner, private, or individual realm, and to keep them from having any authority in societal or political relationships, are efforts at evasion that contradict Jesus' holistic faith that God is Lord of all of life.[5]

The historic resistance had argued that the Sermon on the Mount was not practical because we have to be realistic about the force of evil in the world. But Germany is the nation that developed *Realpolitik*, that experienced the evil of Hitler, that has had the highest density of nuclear weapons in the world, and that has lived with Cold War divisions running right through its own middle, with the threat of the communist bloc just a hundred yards away across a violently enforced, barren, no-entry area guarded with watchtowers and semiautomatic weapons.

In Germany, faced with the reality of the force of evil in the world and with the need for a realistic politics that could turn the politics of the arms buildup around, it became clear that the Sermon on the Mount was politically relevant.

Similarly, the biggest influences in the recovery of the practical relevance of the Sermon on the Mount in the United States were Martin Luther King, Jr., and the civil rights movement. African Americans have experienced the force of oppression in the world more directly and systematically than most other Americans. King's search for a philosophy of life could not gel until he found an ethic that was clearly practical and effective in overcoming the systemic injustice of racism.[6] Among African Americans, faced with the force of racism and with the need for a realistic politics that could turn around the politics of injustice, it became clear that the Sermon on the Mount was politically relevant.

Central Text for Peacemaking and Justicemaking

In all this irony, there is good news: There is a turning toward the Sermon on the Mount not merely as a high ideal but as authoritative and practical. That is fundamentally important, because the Sermon on the Mount is the central Christian text for peacemaking and justicemaking. It is not the only text; peacemaking and justicemaking are major themes throughout the biblical story. They are essential to the gospel. But as long as we tiptoe around the Sermon on the Mount, our stance is fundamentally weak.

Christians in the first few centuries saw the Sermon on the Mount as the central statement of Christian faith and life; no Scripture was more quoted and referenced by Christian theologians in the period before the Nicene Council in the fourth century.[7] It is the *locus classicus* for Christian peacemaking—the place where Jesus taught most extensively about peacemaking. When Anabaptists and Quakers in the sixteenth and seventeenth centuries recovered and developed the peace-church tradition, they based it most clearly on the Sermon on the Mount.[8] Similarly, much of the centuries-long debate between pacifism and just war theory (see chapter 4) is based on disagreement about the meaning and authority of Jesus' teachings in the Sermon on the Mount. Going back to the Sermon on the Mount is going back to the root of the discussion.

Not Human Striving But God's Transforming Initiative

Interpreting the Sermon on the Mount as a declaration of high ideals toward which we should strive causes resistance. The ideals seem so high that people feel guilty just thinking about them, and they seem impractical in a realistic world. Nevertheless, the language of high ideals, heavy demands, or harsh sayings still sometimes creeps into the interpretation of even the best New Testament scholars, in spite of their emphasis elsewhere on the context of grace.[9] Such language is not faithful to the New Testament context.

The Sermon on the Mount is not about human striving toward high ideals but about God's transforming initiative to deliver us from the vicious cycles in which we get stuck. It has a realistic view of our world, characterized by murder, anger, divorce, adultery, lust, deceit, enmity, hypocrisy, false prophets, and houses destined for destruction. It announces that in the midst of such bondage, there is also another force operating: God is also beginning to rule with justice and peace, like mustard seeds beginning to grow or leaven beginning to spread, as Jesus said in Matthew 13:31–33. The Sermon on the Mount describes specific ways we can participate in the new initiatives that God is taking. They are not harsh demands but methods of practical participation in God's gracious deliverance. "Take my yoke upon you, . . . and you will find rest for your souls. For my yoke is easy, and my burden is light" (Matt. 11:29–30). But the Sermon does not offer a way of cheap grace, a way of vague passivity. God is taking transforming initiatives, and we are asked to participate in what God is doing, imitating God's initiatives.

Just as the Ten Commandments begin with God's gracious delivering action, summed up in the sentence, "I am the Lord your God who brought you out of the land of Egypt, out of the house of bondage," so the Sermon on the Mount begins with the announcement that those who are poor, who are mourning, and who hunger for justice are blessed because God is bringing deliverance.[10] As Christian Wolf puts it, "You belong to the lucky devils who can experience the new world to which God has come."[11]

W. D. Davies, Jacques Dupont, and Robert Guelich point out that *the beatitudes (and the woes in Luke 6) are a commentary on Isaiah 61,* which announces the comforting of those who mourn, inheriting of the land for those who are dispossessed, justice for those who hunger for it, good news for the poor, and the year of God's deliverance. This is the message Jesus read for his inaugural sermon in Luke 4. It is not hard teachings, it is gracious deliverance.[12] Matthew is not giving us entrance requirements that make us feel guilty, but by aligning the Beatitudes with Isaiah 61 is demonstrating "that God was at work in Jesus Messiah accomplishing his redemptive purposes for humankind."[13]

The Reign of God with Forgiveness, Justice, and Peace

Guelich points out that the Sermon on the Mount is "a fulfillment Christology: Jesus came to fulfill the Old Testament prophetic expectations by announcing and effecting the kingdom of Heaven in history." It is both a realized eschatology and a future eschatology in tension.[14]

Jesus is proclaiming that *the rule of God is already happening in history, and that we can be participants*. Schnackenburg puts it nicely: "Only out of the message of Jesus are his demands understandable; only out of his announcement of what God is doing, arises his appeal to humankind. . . . What God inaugurates, people should take part in and what God's power effects and sustains, people should carry through in the earthly-historical sphere, until God finishes it."[15] Furthermore,

> Jesus did not only announce the coming reign of God, but made clear in his message and his actions that the reign of God already was breaking in full of promise and effectiveness, that it was becoming visible symbolically in his own deeds, healings, assurance of forgiveness of sin, turning toward the poor, the disregarded, and the oppressed. The rule of God is already now a discernible reality and places on his hearers of the gospel the urgent appeal to conduct themselves accordingly.[16]

Matthew says "kingdom of Heaven" where other gospels say "kingdom of God," because pious Jews did not want to desecrate the holy name of God by inordinate repetition. " 'The realm of heaven,' then, is not to be found in the heavens; the phrase refers to God's . . . manifest dominion on this earth,"[17] already in process now, and to be finally fulfilled in the future. Christian Wolf writes:

> The theme of the "kingdom of heaven," which means the reign of God, runs throughout the Sermon on the Mount. For Jesus' hearers this resonates with a political overtone. . . . It opposes the reign of Rome in which they actually live.

The old promises of the reign of God were in their awareness: satisfying those who were hungering and thirsting for
justice, caring for the poor and oppressed, giving back the
land and the power to the peaceful and powerless. The reign
of God is coming.[18]

W. D. Davies affirms that the rule of God is already
breaking in, and *it means the fulfillment of the moral content of Old Testament expectations for a new creation, a new
heart and spirit, justice and peace and the presence of God.*[19]
It is described in the announcement of deliverance in many
Old Testament passages, such as Isaiah 60 and 61, that
promise the shining of the light of the glory of God (see
Matt. 5:14ff.); peace among nations; justice-righteousness
and good news for the poor, the blind, and the oppressed;
prosperity; forgiveness; inheriting the land; and that "you
will know that I, the Lord, am your Redeemer."

Another well-known passage is Isaiah 52:7. Notice the
good news is about peace, salvation, and the reign of God:
"How beautiful upon the mountains are the feet of the
messenger who announces peace, who brings good news,
who announces salvation, who says to Zion, 'Your God
reigns.' "

In Isaiah 9:6–7 notice again the themes of peace, justice-
righteousness, and the presence and reign of God:

> For to us a child is born,
>   to us a son is given,
>   and the government will be on his shoulders.
> And he will be called
>   Wonderful counselor, Mighty God,
>   Everlasting Father, Prince of Peace.
> Of the increase of his government and peace
>   there will be no end.
> He will reign on David's throne
>   and over his kingdom,
> establishing and upholding it
>   with justice and righteousness. (NIV)

This is clearly the delivering action of God, not our striving after high ideals. The passage continues: "from that time on and forever. The zeal of the Lord Almighty will accomplish this."

The reign of God (or kingdom of God) is not a place, it is a process—a process of turning and deliverance—a process of peace, justice, and the reign of God. In our language, a better translation is "God's reigning" or "God's delivering" than "kingdom of God."[20]

Jesus announces that the reign of God is already beginning, and he also promises a future grand fulfillment. The key is not to know when; nobody knows (Matt. 24:36, 42–51; cf. Mark 13:32; Luke 17:20). The key is to be ready, which means to be doing the commands Jesus teaches.

Righteousness is central in the promise of deliverance when God's reign comes, and righteousness is a major theme in the Sermon on the Mount. Righteousness means the restoring of just relations among us personally and societally, and with God. It points to God's gracious initiative in delivering us from sin, guilt, and oppression into a new community of justice, peace, and freedom and our obedient participation in God's way of deliverance.[21]

Jeremias observes that the teachings of the Sermon on the Mount point to *participation in God's grace*:

> Every word of the Sermon on the Mount was preceded by something else . . . the preaching of the kingdom of God . . . the granting of sonship to the disciples . . . Jesus' witness to himself in word and deed . . . "Your sins are forgiven". . . . The sayings of Jesus which have been brought together in the Sermon on the Mount are a part of the gospel. To each of these sayings belongs the message: the old aeon is passing away. Through the proclamation of the gospel and through discipleship you are transferred into the new aeon of God. And now you should know that this is what life is like when you belong to the new aeon of God.[22]

Jesus is announcing that God is acting graciously to deliver, and that action is beginning now. He is inviting us to take part in the deliverance. He is also coaching us, explaining how God is delivering so we can see how to participate rather than putting ourselves athwart the flow and coming under judgment and destruction. That is grace.

This means the Sermon on the Mount is not a heavy guilt trip but the happy empowerment of delivering grace.

It also means that peacemaking and justicemaking based on the Sermon on the Mount are not merely a protest against something but grace-filled deliverance. Nor are its teachings merely permission to engage in just war but guidance for participating in peacemaking initiatives. They call not only for *non*-violence or *non*-resistance but also for *positive* participation in peacemaking initiatives.

The Threefold Pattern of the Sermon on the Mount

The emphasis on the grace-filled deliverance of transforming initiatives is seen even more clearly if we notice the threefold structure of each of Jesus' teachings in the body of the Sermon on the Mount. Many people treat the pattern of Jesus' teachings as twofold, or dyadic:

1. You have heard of old, don't kill.
2. But I say don't even be angry.

Carl Vaught writes that the old commandment is "Thou shalt not murder," and the revolutionary new commandment is "You must not be angry with your brother."[23] Jeremias writes, "You should truly not be angry with your brother, you should truly avoid the impure look." He writes of "the heavy nature of the demands which Jesus makes."[24] Sandmel speaks of the extreme rigorism of prohibiting lust.[25] This may be a widespread assumption. But in fact, it is not what Jesus teaches in the Sermon on the Mount.

Jesus does not say, "You must not be angry," or "You must not call someone a fool," or "You must not look at someone with lust." He describes being angry and looking with lust realistically as involving us in a vicious cycle that leads to prison, judgment, adultery. This is a realistic diagnosis. But the Greek verb is not imperative. And this is *not* where Jesus puts his emphasis.

Jesus teaches with a triadic or threefold structure, not a twofold one. The *third* element is where the emphasis falls: If you are offering your gift at the altar and there remember your brother (or sister) has something against you, *go quickly and try to make peace.* If you are on your way to court with your adversary, *try to make peace quickly while there is still time.* This is not a rigoristic, hard saying. It is the way of deliverance from the vicious cycle of anger, resentment, and enmity. It is the way of participating in God's delivering reign, who comes to us when there is alienation between us, talks with us in Christ, and seeks to make peace, while there is still time. We can't *not* be angry. But we *can* try to talk it out and make peace rather than nursing our anger and feeling powerless to do anything. (See table 2.1.)

Similarly, Jesus didn't say, "Don't look at anyone with lust." He said doing so is adultery in your heart. Therefore, *remove the source of the problem*. He speaks with hyperbole, or exaggeration: "If your right eye leads you astray, tear it out." In practical terms, this means "Take away the practice that is firing up the lust." If standing close to a married woman alone at night causes you to look with lust, then tear out the practice. If spying on your neighbor causes it, then stop spying. Jesus understands realistically that some practices lead to lust, and that is a wish to commit adultery, and that is trouble and it can lead to more trouble. He doesn't say, "Keep looking but only with absolutely pure motives." That's impossible. He says, realistically, "Change the practice."

Table 2.1
The Fourteen Triads of the Sermon on the Mount

Traditional Piety	*Mechanism of Bondage*	*Transforming Initiative*
1. You shall not kill.	Nursing anger or saying, "You fool!"	**Go, be reconciled while there's time.**
2. You shall not commit adultery.	Looking with lust—adultery in heart.	**Remove the cause of temptation** (see Mark 9:43–44).
3. Who divorces, give certificate.	**Divorcing— involves you in adultery.**	(Go, be reconciled.)
4. You shall not swear falsely.	**Swearing by anything—involves you with evil/ judgment.**	**Let your yes be yes, your no be no** (see James 5:12).
5. Eye for eye, tooth for tooth.	Violently resisting.	**Turn other cheek. Let him have cloak/shirt.** Go two miles. **Give to one who begs.**
6. Love neighbor and hate enemy. If you greet only brethren . . .	Loving and greeting only those who love you, as tax collectors and Gentiles do.	**Love your enemies, and pray for them.** **Be all-inclusive, as your Father in heaven is.**
7. When you give alms . . .	Sounding a trumpet, as hypocrites do.	Don't let your left hand know what your right gives.
8. When you pray . . .	Praying in public as hypocrites do.	Pray in secret.

Traditional Piety	*Mechanism of Bondage*	*Transforming Initiative*
9. Praying with empty words.	Thinking their much speaking will be heard.	**Pray like this: Our Father . . .**
10. When you fast . . .	Looking dismal as hypocrites do.	Anoint your head and wash your face.
11. Do not invest treasures on earth. (Luke 12:33–34: Sell them and give alms.)	**Moths, rust, and thieves consume, waste, steal, and your heart and eye get divided and darkened.**	**Invest your treasures in God's reign. Your whole self will be light.**
12. No one can serve two masters.	**You'll hate one and love the other. Can't serve God and money.**	**Don't be anxious about possessions, but seek first God's reign and justice.**
13. Judge not.	**By same judgment you'll be judged.**	**Take the log out of your own eye.**
14. If you give dogs what is holy . . .	They'll trample it and tear you to pieces.	**Give your requests to your heavenly Father in prayer.**

Bold text indicates Matthew's saying found in Luke, Mark, or James.

Similarly, if I give to charity *publicly* so others will know how much I gave (6:2ff.) and pray and fast *publicly* so others will take notice (6:5ff. and 6:16ff.), then realistically my motives will be mixed. Deliverance comes not by the impossible ideal of making myself have completely pure motives. Instead, he says, *do it in secret*. And that is hardly an impossible ideal. I may not be a saint, but I can pray secretly, give secretly, and fast secretly.

When we read the Sermon on the Mount carefully with this threefold pattern in mind, we notice that the body of the Sermon consists of fourteen triads. (See table 2.1.)

Noticing the threefold pattern transforms our interpretation: Now we pay attention to the third portion, where biblical triads put their emphasis. We see that the third element is always an initiative, not merely a prohibition. It is always a practical participation in deliverance from a vicious cycle of bondage, hostility, idolatry, and judgment. Each implies living a whole, integrated life in relation to God and points to a way God is fulfilling redemptive expectations promised in the Old Testament. Each moves us away from the "hard saying" or "high ideal" kind of interpretation that has caused resistance, evasion, and a dualistic split between inner intentions in the heart and outer deeds in society. Each moves us instead into participation in God's grace, God's deliverance, God's reign.

The Threefold Pattern Emphasizes Transforming Initiatives

Try as I may, I cannot find anywhere in the scholarly literature where this triadic transforming-initiatives pattern is pointed out.[26] Yet it seems so consistent throughout the body of the Sermon on the Mount, so helpful in illuminating Jesus' meaning, and so supportive of the transforming-initiatives paradigm of peacemaking and justicemaking, that I want to try to establish it firmly, so that it can help "the turning" toward the Sermon on the Mount in our life together on this one, known, still habitable piece of rock and water.

The threefold pattern is confirmed in a number of ways. First, it is remarkably consistent. All three members are present in all fourteen cases, except number 3, and it may be implied there. So much consistency can hardly be an accident.[27]

Furthermore, if we examine the verbs in each column in the Greek, the consistency is even more clearly demonstrated. The first column does not use imperatives but indicatives or subjunctives. There is only one exception—number 11, "Do not invest treasures on earth."

The second column has all *continuous-action verbs,* including participles and infinitives. This supports the suggestion that in the second column, Jesus is not giving harsh commands, but realistically describing the *ongoing process* of trouble that we get ourselves into when we serve some other lord than God.

All the members of the third column are imperatives except the statement in number 5, "Give to the one who begs." Number 6 (Matt. 5:48), "Be ye all-inclusive," is a future used as an imperative.[28] The consistency of the imperative puts strong emphasis on the third column, the transforming initiatives. The commands of Jesus are found here. He does not give us the impossible, idealistic command not to be angry. He commands that we take a transforming initiative: Go, talk, and seek to be reconciled quickly, while there is still time.

This consistency strongly supports the conclusion that Matthew gives us a threefold structure, not a twofold one. The pattern clearly places the emphasis on the third column, the transforming initiatives. That is where the peacemaking happens.

Perhaps scholars have not noticed this triadic transforming-initiative structure because their perception has been dominated by the concept of "antitheses," the dichotomous either/or thinking in much of our culture. I believe Davies and Lapide are correct: We should not call them "antitheses" but "exegeses"—not six antitheses but fourteen triads.

What are we to do with Luke? Luke has most of the same teachings in a different form, many in chapter 6 (the Sermon on the Plain) and others in other passages in his Gospel. Does he also place emphasis on the transforming initiatives? Or is his emphasis entirely different? This is a crucial test.

In table 2.1, the passages where Matthew and Luke (or Mark and James at numbers 2 and 4) say the same thing are in bold print. The conclusion leaps out: Luke emphasizes the third column, the transforming initiatives. This strongly confirms our emphasis on the transforming initiatives. Luke also intensifies the emphasis on justice, almsgiving, lending, and the poor.

There has been a dramatically increased interest among scholars in ferreting out the structure of the Sermon on the Mount as well as of other biblical literature.[29] The studies of the structure of Matthew provide a powerful indirect confirmation of this threefold pattern. They show Matthew has a great love for using threefold patterns—much more than twofold patterns. It makes sense then that he would adopt a threefold pattern for the body of the Sermon on the Mount. So Davies and Allison emphasize "the pervasiveness of triads in the gospel. . . . 5:21–48 clearly divides itself into two groups, each with three members. . . . 6:1–18 treats of three subjects: almsgiving, prayer, and fasting. And 6:19–7:12 contains two more triads, these in perfect parallelism. Matthew, it is manifest, was thinking in triplicate as he composed his first discourse. . . . The Matthean proclivity for the triad just cannot be denied."[30]

They list forty-four triads, not including the triads in chapters 5–7, 10, 13, 18, and 24–25. They suggest that Matthew had a traditional Jewish reason for a three-pillar approach, and that "Jesus, it appears, liked threefold structures."

In Matthew's day, these patterns of numbers were highly symbolic and much emphasized. Fourteen was an especially important number for Matthew, because it was so important to the Pharisaic group with which his group was competing. Matthew wrote the Gospel emphasizing how Jesus fulfilled the Scriptures. The Pharisees claimed that their teachers were descended from a triad of four-teen generations. Hence Matthew showed how Jesus' genealogy was a triad of fourteen generations from Abraham (Matt. 1:1–17). So Finkelstein explains:

> The number, "fourteen," is not accidental. . . . It is clear that a mystic significance attached to this number, in both the Sadducean and the Pharisaic traditions. . . . This may seem a weak argument for the authenticity of a tradition; but antiquity was apparently prepared to be impressed by it. So impressive indeed was this argument, that the Gospel of Matthew, the early Christian apologist, directing his argument against the Pharisees (and also the Sadducees), adopted a similar claim for Jesus.[31]

While there being *fourteen* triads of transforming initiatives is not essential to the arguments for the triadic transforming initiatives, that there are fourteen does give me great aesthetic, if not mystical, pleasure.

Once we see the transforming initiative pattern, we can see the Sermon on the Mount more clearly as grace. Those who thought it offered hard teachings or impossible ideals were misreading the second column as Jesus' emphasis, and as commands. Now we see clearly that was an error. The second column is a realistic description of vicious cycles that engulf us. They are cycles, processes, continuous actions, forms of bondage that lead to hostility, violence, and judgment. The emphasis in the third column is on what God is doing in Christ. Each points to the concrete shape and character of God's gracious delivering action. Each shows us how we can participate in the deliverance. None is an impossible action; each is a practical way of deliverance out of the vicious cycles. We can follow Christ in talking to one who is angry at us, letting our yes be yes, going the second mile, praying for our enemies, praying in secret, and investing our treasures in God's justice. It takes a serious decision to follow, but it is not impossible and harsh. It is the way of deliverance.[32]

Once these commands are seen as ways of participating in grace, they no longer seem legalistic and rigid. They are concrete commands, but they will need translating or transposing into new situations. God is doing new acts of deliverance now. In our day, a Roman soldier does not literally demand that we carry his pack one mile, but another oppressor, demanding something from us, may need an analogous surprising confrontation.

The transforming initiatives in the third column point us to deliverance through participation in God's grace, God's presence, God's reward. For example:

- Matthew 5:24—First make peace with your brother or sister and then come and offer your gift to God.
- Matthew 5:30—It is better to lose one of your members than for your whole body to be thrown into hell.
- Matthew 5:45—Love your enemies so that you may be children of your Father who gives sun and rain to the just and unjust.
- Matthew 5:48—Be all-inclusive as your heavenly Father is all-inclusive.
- Matthew 6:4; 6:6; 6:18—Your Father who sees in secret will reward you.
- Matthew 6:14—Your heavenly Father will forgive you.
- Matthew 6:22—Your whole body will be full of God's light.
- Matthew 6:33—Seek first God's reign and righteousness, and all these will be yours as well.
- Matthew 7:5—Then you will see clearly.
- Matthew 7:7ff.—Your Father in heaven will open it to you and will give good things to you.

Participating in these transforming initiatives is participating in God's grace. This is God's presence, God's ac-

tion, God's deliverance. This is eschatological joy, already
at hand in these mustard seeds!

At the center of the Sermon on the Mount, the Lord's
prayer clearly points to God's grace in delivering us from
cycles of destruction. It has a sevenfold pattern. The first
three petitions—*thy* name, *thy* reign, *thy* will—all ask
God to act to bring about "thy" rule, on earth as in
heaven. The other four petitions ask for *our* deliverance
by God's action—they all have "us" in them. They ask
that God deliver us from the vicious cycles of hunger,
debts, temptation, and evil. Thus the prayer entreats
God's delivering action (God's reign on earth) from alienating processes (hunger, debts, etc.), just as the deliverance theme of all fourteen triads suggests.

The triadic structure illumines the meaning and emphasis of the particular teachings. It puts the emphasis on
the third member, on gracious deliverance and transforming initiatives. So a part of the proof of the structure will
be in examining the specific teachings. To that interpretation we now turn. We shall examine how Paul echoes
Jesus' teaching on peacemaking in his letter to the Romans. Combining Romans 12 with the Sermon on the
Mount will give us a paradigm of peacemaking with seven
transforming initiatives.

Questions for Thought

1. Describe your reaction when the Sermon on the
Mount is presented as high ideals, hard to live up to.

2. Does seeing the Sermon on the Mount as transforming initiatives, participation in deliverance, make you feel
different? Explain the feeling.

3. When the Sermon on the Mount is interpreted as
high ideals, hard to live up to, it calls us to serious commitment, to a decision to follow Jesus. If instead the Ser-

mon on the Mount is seen as participation in God's delivering initiatives, does that make it cheap grace, or does it still call for a serious commitment to following Jesus?

4. Is the threefold (triadic) pattern of the Sermon on the Mount, rather than the twofold (dyadic), clear and convincing? What questions remain?

5. What does Matthew mean when he writes, "the Kingdom of Heaven"? How is this meaning consistent with the transforming initiatives interpretation of the Sermon on the Mount?

6. What do you think of the suggestion in note 27 concerning "Go talk to your sister (wife), and seek to be reconciled, while there is still time"?

7. What does it mean when our English translations have Matthew say, "Be perfect as God is perfect," and have Luke say, "Be merciful as God is merciful"? (See note 28.)

3

Transforming Initiatives in the New Testament

It is striking how many of the transforming initiatives in the Sermon on the Mount are steps in peacemaking: Go talk to your brother or sister and seek to be reconciled; go two miles; give to the one who begs; love your enemies; pray for them; seek first God's reign and justice; judge not, but forgive and take the log out of your own eye.

Sometimes these steps are understood merely as illustrations of a general theme such as love for the enemy. I want to suggest that we take them as concrete steps, each to be taken seriously. When Jesus spoke of going two miles, he was referring to the authority of the Roman soldier to impress a Jew to carry his pack one mile. There was widespread hostility against the Roman occupation, and insurrectionists were fomenting rebellion—which eventually led to the destruction of Jerusalem and the scattering of the Jewish people by the Roman rulers. Surely Jesus meant that we really are to carry the pack a second mile, and pray for our enemy, and talk things over and seek to be reconciled, and forgive and repent rather than judge.

Here are seven reasons why we should be concrete about the steps of peacemaking:

1. Taking Jesus' teachings on peacemaking as *mere illustrations* of a central theme does not adequately represent Jesus' intention in Matthew and Luke. These concrete commands like forgiving, talking, going the second mile, giving to the poor, and praying for our enemy were meant to be heard and done. "Everyone then who hears these words of mine and acts on them . . . " (see Matt. 7:24).

2. Lapide points out that "the rabbis always thought in concrete terms."[1] Hence Jesus taught concretely, and we remember what Jesus taught. We think in general, but we live in particular.

3. Watching Christians rationalize their vagueness in the face of Adolf Hitler and the Nazis, Dietrich Bonhoeffer said Jesus was incarnate not vaguely but concretely: If the church is not speaking concretely, it is not speaking the Word of the living Jesus Christ; it should admit that it has no business speaking some other word, and shut up.

4. In his sociological study of the church's social teachings, Ernst Troeltsch concluded that the church is strong when it is centered in Jesus Christ and speaks the concrete language of ordinary people.[2] Studies of moral reasoning by Kohlberg and Gilligan show that most people think and live concretely, and church-growth literature shows growing churches are concrete in their teachings.

5. In his classic study, *Protestant and Catholic,*[3] Kenneth Underwood shows the weakness of liberal Protestant individualism in working for justice and bringing change, in contrast to the concrete teachings of Catholic churches. We have recognized the strong impact of the Catholic bishops' pastoral letter, *The Challenge of Peace,* with its concreteness and specificity. As Pope John Paul said, speaking at the United Nations, "Peace, like a building, has to be built one brick at a time." Concrete steps are needed.

6. In the New Testament, sin is like addiction; recovery takes more than a vague wish. It takes specific steps of

change, day by day. If Alcoholics Anonymous said the
twelve steps merely illustrate the general point that we
should be in favor of sobriety rather than drunkenness,
and there is no need to follow the steps concretely, they
would be about as effective as sermons saying we should
be in favor of peace rather than war and calling us to do
nothing in particular. When my mother hears a sermon
like that, she comments, "Well, who didn't know that? Ev-
erybody's in favor of peace. What are we supposed *to do*
about it?" The most effective way to drain a principle of
its power is not to deny the principle but to affirm it in
general while refusing to discuss any specifics.

7. Paul understood these teachings in this concrete
sense; in spite of usually not alluding to Jesus' teachings,
he taught the same concrete steps as we see in Matthew
and Luke, though not woodenly and unimaginatively.[4] He
heard them as fresh words of the living Lord in the situation of the churches to which he was writing.

Paul Teaches the Transforming Initiatives of Peacemaking

Though the apostle Paul did point to Jesus' teachings as
authoritative,[5] he seldom mentioned any of Jesus' specific
teachings. It is striking, then, that most of the few ref-
erences Paul does make to Jesus' teachings are about
peacemaking.[6] This emphasis hints at how central he understood peacemaking to be for the gospel of Jesus Christ
and the mission of the church.

Even more striking for our purpose of developing a
model of Christian peacemaking, when Paul teaches most
specifically on peacemaking and the mission of the
church—in Romans 12 through 15—he emphasizes eight
of the same transforming initiatives of peacemaking that
Jesus taught in the Sermon on the Mount and the Sermon
on the Plain (see table 3.1). A careful study by the New

Testament scholar Dale Allison concludes persuasively that Paul was quoting a block of sayings that is the central part of the Sermon on the Plain, Luke 6:27–37.[7] In the previous chapter we saw that Luke and Matthew agree on these transforming initiatives (see table 2.1). Moreover, as we shall see, these eight steps of peacemaking are not merely coincidental; each is deeply grounded in essential dimensions of the gospel.

Table 3.1
The Transforming Initiatives Paradigm

Matthew and Luke	*Romans*
1. Acknowledge your alienation and God's grace realistically.	
Beatitudes, Woes, and throughout Sermons on Mount and Plain	Romans 12:1 and throughout the Letter to the Romans
2. Go, talk, welcome one another, and seek to be reconciled.	
Matthew 5:21–26; Luke 12:57–59 Luke's theme of inclusion of Jews and Gentiles together	Romans 12:18; 15:7 Paul's theme of inclusion of Jews and Gentiles together
3. Don't resist revengefully, but take transforming initiatives.	
Matthew 5:38–39; Luke 6:29–30 Cheek, coat, second mile, give, lend	Romans 12:20ff. Feed enemy, give drink, heap coals of repentance
4. Invest in delivering justice.	
Matthew 5:42; 6:2–4; 6:19–34; Luke 6:30; 11:34–36; 12:22–34; 16:13	Romans 12:13, 16; 15:25ff. Share with needy, identify with lowly, collection for hungry in Jerusalem

Matthew and Luke	**Romans**

5. Love your enemies with actions; affirm their valid interests.

Matthew 5:44–48; Luke 6:27–28, 32–36	Romans 12:15 Rejoice with them when they rejoice, mourn when they mourn

6. Pray for your enemies and bless them; persevere in prayer.

Matthew 5:44b; 6:5–15; Luke 6:28; 11:2–4	Romans 12:12; 14

7. Don't judge, but repent and forgive.

Matthew 6:12, 14; 7:1–5; Luke 6:37–38, 41–42; 11:4	Romans 12:17, 19; 14:1, 4, 10, 13

8. Do peacemaking in a church or a group of disciples

Matthew 5:1; 7:28; Luke 6:17–20a; 7:1 Disciples and crowds	Romans 12:4–8; 14:1– 15:33 One body, church's mission is grace and peace

Allison's careful study concludes that number 3 (don't avenge, but take peacemaking initiatives; see table 3.1), number 6 (pray for your persecutors), and number 7 (don't judge), as well as Romans 13:7 (pay your taxes; cf. Matt. 22:15–22) clearly refer to Jesus' teaching. Käsemann says number 4 (identify with the needy) "corresponds with the prototype of Jesus." Talbert sees number 2 (seek to live peaceably with all) as a quote from Matthew 5:9, and some see it as part of the core teaching in Romans 12:17–18 and 21 that summarizes Matthew 5:39ff. and Luke 6:29, 35. The other half of number 2 (accept one another as Christ has accepted you) refers, of course, to what Christ has done. Numbers 1 and 5 are not direct allusions to specific teachings of Jesus but are in their spirit.[8]

Concrete steps of peacemaking similar to most of these eight also echo throughout the other gospels, Paul's letters, the letter to James, and the Didache, as well as other documents of the early church.

Concrete Steps of Peacemaking

Paul's intriguing emphasis on the same concrete steps found in Matthew and Luke suggests there is a pattern of something like eight concrete steps of peacemaking in the New Testament. Together they form an eight-step paradigm of peacemaking as transforming initiatives.

The steps should not be interpreted legalistically. Jesus speaks concretely with fresh words in our dramatically new context, and we will not all hear them identically. For example, almsgiving was the welfare system of Jesus' day. Our system of almsgiving now includes such things as job-training programs; Women, Infants and Children (WIC) nutrition programs; Head Start; Meals on Wheels; church food pantries; and the like.

Influenced by our own culture and interests, we unconsciously read assumptions into these teachings. To correct for our bias, we need to study the Jewish culture of the time of Jesus, Paul, and Matthew. We also need critical ethical study of our own culture's assumptions. I have found especially helpful the insights of my former teacher, W.D. Davies, who has specialized in the Jewish context of Paul and the Sermon on the Mount; Christian Wolf in the former East Germany, who specializes in Old Testament and in critical ethical studies of our cultural assumptions; Robert Guelich, whose articles several years ago pointed to the importance of the delivering eschatology of Isaiah 61 for the Sermon on the Mount; and more recently the work of German Jewish Orthodox rabbi Pinchas Lapide and ethically critical New Testament scholar Walter Wink. I am seeking to ground my understanding in the best objective biblical and ethical scholarship, and not in hasty leaps to conclusion. The interpretation will be a test of the transforming initiatives approach and will become the basis for a new paradigm for peacemaking in the time of the Turning.

Acknowledge Your Alienation and God's Grace Realistically

The first step is acknowledging the processes of destruction, the vicious cycles in which we find ourselves entangled, and recognizing the grace of God, actively present, that offers a way of deliverance.

The active presence of God, in delivering action, is the theme of the Beatitudes. The Sermon on the Mount is based on God's love, righteousness, reign, sunshine, and caring, all taking place in our midst. It is a call for us to release our anxious efforts to control everything and instead to participate in the initiatives God is taking.

Similarly, Paul begins Romans 12 with "the mercies of God," on the basis of which he beseeches us to be transformed by God's grace and love, and not to be conformed to this age.

There is a realism in the Sermon on the Mount. The second part of each triad in table 2.1 identifies a process of alienation. Acknowledging our complicity and bondage is a key step in peacemaking. Otherwise we spread the disease rather than participate in the cure. We are self-righteous and judging. We perceive others through distorted vision, twisted by the projections of our own defensive need to control our unacknowledged anxieties, guilt, and shame.

Similarly, Paul describes our situation as bondage, captivity, or slavery to processes of self-righteousness, judging, sin, hostility, and violence (Rom. 1:18–3:18; 5:6–21).

The first step in Christian peacemaking is not to change

the enemy. It is to acknowledge realistically our own ill-suitedness as peacemakers. I can become a peacemaker only when I give up my self-righteous judging and controlling and begin to rely on the transforming initiatives of God's grace. This is true of groups and nations as well as of individuals. Reinhold Niebuhr's writings are full of ironic disclosures of the self-righteousness of nations and political leaders. He contended that self-righteousness is more pernicious when it directs the immense power of nations than when it characterizes mere individuals, where it is dangerous enough already.

The process by which Martin Luther King, Jr., came to his strategy of nonviolent direct action was immersion in the realism of Reinhold Niebuhr and then learning how Gandhi's strategy of *satyagraha* overcame racism realistically. The process by which the influential German group, Schritte zur Abrüstung, developed its strategy was a realistic analysis of the vicious cycle of arms buildups, a realistic acknowledgment that neither unilateral disarmament nor mere opposition to missiles could solve the problem, and a realistic advocacy of concrete initiatives. The process by which we come to an honest strategy of peacemaking may also include a major role for themes developed by Reinhold Niebuhr, the Christian realist. This may sound offensive to many. For many Christian pacifists, Niebuhr is the enemy of peacemaking: He attacked pacifism and advocated military strength, within limits. The transforming-initiatives understanding of the Sermon on the Mount does criticize Niebuhr fundamentally, not for his realism but for his missing the delivering dimensions of Jesus' ethic. Ironically, Niebuhr never revised his nineteenth-century idealist interpretation of Jesus' ethic and his cross, except to say they are impossible within history. Niebuhr's students need to carry his realism further, understanding Jesus realistically as well. John Howard Yoder's criticisms of Niebuhr's method and

his arguments for biblical realism have much to teach us.[9]
Recently Duane Friesen, from the Mennonite pacifist
side, and Ronald Stone, from the Niebuhrian realist side,
have been suggesting a new convergence toward realistic
peacemaking.[10] To achieve that end, we need to reexam-
ine the meaning of Jesus' peacemaking in the Sermon on
the Mount.

Go, Talk, Welcome One Another, and Seek to Be Reconciled

Jesus points realistically to the process of alienation that
leads to killing and war. He gives us a threefold description: Whoever is angry with someone, whoever insults
someone, and whoever says "You fool!" is headed for trouble. Similarly, Paul declares our boasting and judging others brings us to judgment (Rom. 2:1–4; 14:10–12).

Clarence Jordan clarifies what Jesus meant by anger:

> He did not mean the occasional fit of temper which might
> sweep over one. The word that he used originally meant to
> teem, or swell, and referred especially to the internal swell-
> ing of plants and fruits with juice. Then it came to be used
> to describe a person who boiled up on the inside until he
> was ready to explode. So he is talking about those who are
> swelling with anger, who have a mounting, growing disposi-
> tion or attitude of anger.[11]

Jordan is describing a process of alienation and bondage
that most of us have experienced, though we would like to
forget it. The anger builds up and leads to trouble, sometimes without our being aware how it torques us out of
tune.

The political scientist Francis A. Beer has summarized
the results of many empirical studies of the causes of war.
Before nations make war, they almost always dehumanize
the other nation, calling them animals, mad dogs (Presi-

dent Reagan about Khadafy before bombing Libya), or worse than Hitler (President Bush about Saddam Hussein before bombing the Iraqi soldiers and economic infrastructure), or the Great Satan (the Ayatollah Khomeini about the United States). Beer speaks of the processes of "locking and hardening."[12] Sam Keen makes the point in a strikingly graphic and visual way in *Faces of the Enemy: Reflections of the Hostile Imagination.*[13] Jesus is pointing realistically to this vicious cycle.

Jesus teaches the simple transforming initiative: Go talk, and seek to make peace. Throughout Luke and Acts, the message is that Jews and Gentiles should welcome one another into the same fellowship and make peace. Paul echoes the theme in Romans 15:7, addressing household churches in Rome who were not on speaking terms: "Welcome one another, therefore, just as Christ has welcomed you." Ken Sehested, in a personal letter, calls what God has done for us in Christ, while we were yet enemies, "God's unilaterally disarming initiative." It means talk together, eat together, and seek to make peace. For example, Mennonites have carried out an effective program of "victim-offender rehabilitation," arranging meetings of perpetrators and victims of crimes where they can talk with each other and work out plans for restitution.

Having described the swelling of anger, Clarence Jordan describes Jesus' antidote in the language of initiative: "When you find yourself getting into this mess, it's time to take immediate action. . . . Take the initiative in getting things put right. You'll be amazed at how much better you and God will get along."[14]

During the time when the United States and the Soviet Union should have been negotiating about the buildup of medium-range INF missiles in Europe, there were long periods when they were not talking. They were only making statements judgmental of each other: "The other side" was building up, and we were only catching up. For five

years, the president of the United States and the leader of
the Soviet Union did not meet or talk with each other,
while the weapons grew ever more accurate, ever more
numerous, ever more dangerous. You cannot solve
problems that way, not without talking together. In a
world that is destroying itself by military buildup, what
Jesus says is not only practical but also necessary for our
survival and our children's.

The admonition to talk, welcome one another, and
make peace sounds like just plain practical common
sense. Simple. But people and nations get stuck in irrational processes. Much of our culture seeks to avoid conflict by not talking whenever there is disagreement. Whole
families and churches live in a state of permanent alienation. The frequency of wars, the enormity of the threat of
the nuclear buildup to us all, and the devastation caused
by spending $1,000,000,000,000.00 (one trillion dollars)
per year on a world-wide military buildup rather than on
feeding, vaccinating, and educating the world's children,
which would cost a few days' worth of that expenditure, is
incontrovertible testimony that we are not acting in our
commonsense interest. When the policy of the United
States was not to talk with Libya or the Palestine Liberation Organization (PLO) or Iran, they sought other means
to get our attention, including terrorism. Not talking per-
petuates a vicious cycle. By contrast, the Fellowship of
Reconciliation has developed a "Crossing the Line" campaign, which sends U.S. citizens into Iraq on a campaign
of conversation and reconciliation.

Don't Resist Vengefully,
But Take Transforming Initiatives

First comes the vicious cycle of alienation: revengeful
or violent resistance. Matthew 5:39 is often translated,
"Do not resist evil." Better would be "Do not set yourself

in revengeful resistance against one who does evil." Paul
put it, "Do not repay anyone evil for evil. . . . Never
avenge yourselves" (Rom. 12:17, 19; cf. 1 Thess. 5:15).[15]
Walter Wink puts it well:

> When the court translators working in the hire of King
> James chose to translate *antistenai* as "Resist not evil,"
> they were . . . translating nonviolent resistance into docil-
> ity. Jesus did *not* tell his oppressed hearers not to resist
> evil. That would have been absurd. His entire ministry is
> utterly at odds with such a preposterous idea. The Greek
> word is made up of two parts: *anti,* a word still used in
> English for "against," and *histemi,* a verb which in its
> noun form (*stasis*) means violent rebellion, armed revolt,
> sharp dissension. Thus Barabbas is described as a rebel
> "who had committed murder in the *insurrection* (Mark
> 15:7; Luke 23:19, 25)."[16]

What is the alternative? Jesus and Paul advocate not
only talk but deeds—strikingly visible deeds that surprise
and confront the adversary's hostility, raising the possibility of a breakthrough in alienation, distrust, and oppression. These are transforming initiatives in action. Jesus
consistently places the emphasis not so much on what we
are *not* to do as on transforming initiatives, the way of
deliverance. He suggests four specific and surprising initiatives.

Turn the other cheek. In the custom of that day, when
someone gave a slap on the right cheek, it meant an insult
by a superior who was taking you as inferior (Job 16:10;
Ps. 3:7; Lam. 3:30; 1 Esd. 4:30). To turn the other cheek
was to stand up and affirm your own dignity as an equal
human person, but without violence. It seized the initiative. In the custom then, the insulter would either have to
recognize your dignity as an equal person by striking you
on the left cheek or would have to back off. This was not a
strategy of passivity but an initiative that asserted your

dignity and confronted the other person nonviolently with his or her antihuman behavior.[17]

Give up your coat. In the teaching of Exodus 22:25–27, Deuteronomy 24:10–13, and Amos 2:8, a creditor who lends to someone who is needy and takes that person's coat as a guarantee must "restore it before the sun goes down; . . . for it may be your neighbor's only clothing to use as a cover; in what else shall that person sleep? And if your neighbor cries out to me, I will listen, for I am compassionate" (Ex. 22:26–27). In Matthew 5:40 the rich person who made you a loan is suing you in court for your shirt as a guarantee for a loan.[18] All you have left is your coat and your shirt. It would not be practical to sue you for your coat because he would have to return it every night, but he gets around the spirit of the law—which intends to safeguard the needs of the poor—by suing you for your shirt instead. (Our English versions use varieties of words to translate the two Greek terms. The point in the Greek is that you are being sued for what you wear next to your skin—your shirt, or tunic, or underwear, or undercoat—and you take the initiative to offer your outer garment, coat, cloak, or mantel as well. Luke puts it the other way around.)[19]

So far New Testament scholars widely agree. Now what does this mean, in its context, to give your coat as well? It means you are standing there naked in front of the one suing you, in law court. In Jewish culture, this is a huge embarrassment for the creditor and everyone else. It confronts the creditor with his or her greed and his or her unjust violation of the spirit of the law if not the letter. And Jesus' Jewish audience would have laughed at the audacity, the embarrassment, and the disclosure of the creditor's greed, exposed for all to see, just as naked as your naked body. Thus you, the poor person, seemingly without power, seize the initiative and confront the injustice, putting great pressure on the creditor to repent and be transformed.

This is no strategy of passivity. It is a transforming initiative. The commentaries agree Jesus' teaching is surprising. Strecker says that "the radical nature of the demand" is based on "the nearness of the kingdom of God."[20] It might also be based on a sense of humor.

Go the second mile. Similarly, Roman soldiers could compel Jews to carry their packs a mile. Lapide describes the vicious cycle entailed in this practice, and then Jesus' strategy of transforming initiatives:

> Mutual enmity was strengthened, so that every day supplied further fuel for the increasing rebellion of the people and the bloody reprisals of the occupiers.
>
> Jesus suggests a third course of action: transforming compulsory service into a voluntary escort after the prescribed mile so that the astounded Roman would be disarmed . . . by graciousness.
>
> Here the initiative is taken away from the superior, evil is repaid with good, and, in all probability, in the course of the second mile a friendly conversation will begin to develop. . . .
>
> That such a disarming love—both in this question of escort and in the matter of clothing and care—was not only preached but actually practiced here and there is shown in the following midrash, which comes out of those difficult times:
>
> Once there was a shipwrecked Roman who, in the time of the heaviest Roman yoke, was washed up naked on the shore of the land of Israel. He hid himself under some rocks and called out from there to a group of Jewish festival pilgrims, "I am a descendant of Esau, your brother. Give me something to wear to cover my bareness, for the sea has stripped me, and I was able to rescue nothing!" They answered him, "May your entire people be stripped!"
>
> Then that Roman raised his eyes, saw Rabbi Eleazar who was walking among them, and called, "I see that you are an old man, honored by your people. You show due respect to

creatures, so help me!" Rabbi Eleazar ben Shammua owned several garments. He took one of them and gave it to the man. He also led him into his house, provided him with food and drink, gave him two hundred denarii, accompanied him for fourteen miles, and showed him great honor, until he had brought the Roman to his house [Midrash Eccl. Rabba 11, 1].[21]

Give to one who begs. These three, along with the fourth initiative, "Give to the one who begs from you," are all a seizing of initiative that can transform oneself, the other person, and the relationship between us. Hans Weder concludes, "Instead of the passivity of patience it is the activity that circumvents the power of injustice."[22] Gerhard Lohfink writes:

The intention of the four sayings is clear. Jesus pressed his hearers: avoid just sanctions! Avoid retaliation! Do not answer force with counterforce! But when injustice is done to you, by no means remain in action-less passivity! Confront your adversary! Answer his coercion or brutality with overwhelming goodness! Perhaps in this way you can win him! . . . These are no extraordinary or seldomly seen cases, but the real everyday experience of Jesus' hearers and a whole scale of possibilities from inconvenience to direct violence. These last observations speak clearly against interpretations of our text as purely metaphorical. . . . It is put most clearly in each final clause: "Go two miles, give the coat, turn the other cheek"—therewith it turns the merely passive putting up with injustice into the highest active "Confront your adversary all the more." Indeed, directly "strive against your adversary," "strive to make him your brother." . . . Jesus speaks with prophetic-provocative incisiveness. But that does not at all change what he is driving at: redeeming real ways people relate and providing a model for illumining analogous cases. Jesus actually commands the turn away from violence, and he is persuaded that everyone who receives his word can live without counterviolence and retaliation.[23]

Jesus himself was struck and slapped, and his garments were taken from him (Matt. 26:67; 27:35). So this is an action imitating Christ in his Passion.[24] Similarly, the Roman soldiers *forced* Simon of Cyrene to carry Jesus' cross; it is the same word as here, "If anyone *forces* you to go one mile." This should tell us clearly that the call to follow Jesus' way of peacemaking is also a call to take up his cross. It will involve some sacrifice. But it is not sacrifice for the sake of sacrifice, or for the sake of purity and withdrawal from the world. It is sacrifice for the sake of deliverance from the alienating processes that destroy us. It is sacrifice of our dependence on the vicious cycles that have us in their grip, and it is participation in the redemption that is God's grace.

Although Paul did not use the same words, the climax of his teaching on peacemaking in Romans 12 makes the same point: He urges us not to avenge ourselves but to take a transforming initiative, "an alternative course of action, [which] Paul takes from the book of Proverbs where it stipulates that 'If your enemy is hungry, give bread to eat; and if your enemy is thirsty, give water to drink' (25:21)."[25] Klassen gives several examples of such transforming initiatives in Jewish history, including especially Elisha's teaching the king of Israel to feed rather than slaughter a large Syrian army, which stopped the vicious cycle of war. "It is important that we recognize the significance of eating and drinking with an enemy . . . as a means of breaking down enmities."[26]

Analogous to this biblical strategy of transforming initiatives, the strategy of "independent initiatives" has been spreading among church and peacemaking groups and thence to governments. It has played a major role in our turning from a vicious arms spiral to hope-inspiring mutual reductions. In his exposition of the Sermon on the Mount, Tübingen New Testament scholar Peter Stuhlmacher commends the Dutch church's advocacy of independent initiatives as the direction most consistent with Jesus' peacemaking in our context.[27]

The civil rights movement followed a strategy called "direct action." People did not wait passively, and certainly did not merely renounce rights, but took the initiative. A small group of blacks and whites would enter a segregated restaurant together and sit down to be served. Thus they would desegregate the restaurant directly until they were arrested. Then they turned the other cheek by serving time in jail rather than paying bail. In Durham, North Carolina, we filled the jail and the streets surrounding the jail. This and nonviolent picketing and boycotting confronted the restaurant owners and community leaders with the injustice of segregation and enabled them to share a bit of the pain, though nonviolently. It had powerful public moral appeal. It led to a dramatic repentance on Sunday afternoon after church by a shotgun-wielding restaurant owner, who then led the successful effort to desegregate all public accommodations.

Transforming initiatives or renouncing rights? Is Jesus' point that we should renounce our rights and comply, or that we should take transforming initiatives?[28] How can we decide between these two readings? Here are seven reasons for preferring a transforming-initiatives interpretation:

1. The larger context of fourteen transforming initiatives argues for emphasizing not only renunciation but also surprising initiatives.

2. Each of the four teachings explicitly advocates an initiative, and none explicitly states a renunciation. Of course, a renunciation is implied, but what is explicitly stated is the initiative: Turn the cheek, offer the cloak, go the second mile, give and lend.

3. Each of the four initiatives involves a surprise to the other person (if you lend, expect no repayment, as Luke

states). The surprise is not in renouncing what was co-erced but in doing something uncoerced and unexpected.

4. Each is designed to break down the over/under rela-tionship of oppression and hostility[29] and initiates a rela-tion of equality that can lead to talking and reconciliation.

5. Each has a twofold structure: not only one cheek but also the second cheek; not only one mile but also the sec-ond mile; not only the shirt but also the coat; not only the one demand that we give but also a second initiative, lend; not only the Pharisees' righteousness but also the righteousness that exceeds theirs. The emphasis clearly falls not on the first item—the renunciation—but on the surprising initiative.

6. Each refers to an Old Testament context of deliver-ance. Turning the cheek refers to Isaiah 50:6, a context not only of renunciation but also of God's action to de-liver. Giving the coat refers to Exodus 22:26, Deuteron-omy 24:10ff., and Amos 2:8, which state a firm law of justice, starkly revealing the injustice of the creditor and calling for repentance. Going the second mile probably refers to Amos 3:3, which along with Matthew 5:24–25 suggests walking together, talking, and making an agree-ment. Giving and lending relates to Exodus 22:25, Leviti-cus 25:36, and Deuteronomy 15:7–11, concerning God's compassion, delivering the poor from injustice.

7. Jesus confronts the authorities for their neglecting justice for the poor and excluding the outcasts. He goes to Jerusalem, not merely renouncing rights but also taking dramatic initiatives, riding in prophetic fulfillment to confront the authorities in Jerusalem and the money-changers in the Temple. Paul travels to Jerusalem to con-front his opponents and, when arrested, rather than renouncing his rights, asserts them (Acts 22:25ff.).

Much more is happening here than simply renouncing rights. It is a strategy of transforming initiatives. This is an essential part of an adequate paradigm of peacemaking.

Invest in "Delivering Justice"

"Give to the one who begs" calls us to do justice to the poor. In the time of Jesus, Paul, and Matthew, the poor had gotten poorer, while some rich had gotten much richer. The poor were in bondage to their poverty, and the rich to their wealth. Almsgiving was the welfare system then, so Jesus was calling for justice for the poor and a turning by all from the worship of money. Similarly, in Romans 12:13 and 15:25ff. Paul was urging his readers to support his collection from the Gentile churches for the poor in Jerusalem.

In Matthew's time, after the war against Rome in 70 A.D., there was a long economic depression. "Only an extraordinary effort at philanthropy on the part of the more fortunate ones could avail to preserve the nation." Judaism, which had always emphasized justice for the poor and oppressed, fashioned stronger regulations for almsgiving and justice for the poor.[30]

Perhaps no dimension of peacemaking is more strongly emphasized in the Sermon on the Mount than justice. Besides the emphases on giving to the poor, triads 11 and 12 in the Sermon on the Mount, both of which are also in Luke, emphasize *the reign of God and righteousness* in the context of economic justice. Matthew 6:19ff. asks us not to hoard wealth but to store our treasures in heaven (the reign of God). Matthew 6:33 places God's reign and God's righteousness in parallel, asking us to seek first God's reign and God's righteousness rather than trying to serve both God and money. Again, in Matthew 19:21 Jesus tells the rich young ruler to sell his possessions and give to the poor, and he will have treasure in heaven. The Lord's Prayer teaches us to pray for God's reign to come and God's will to be done on earth as in heaven, and to pray for the bread that we need—and for forgiveness of debts, which in the biblical language includes economic debts of the poor, a jubilee theme.

As we saw in the last chapter, *God's reign* (or kingdom) means the deliverance promised and anticipated in the Old Testament, with peace, justice, good news to the poor, forgiveness, and personal knowledge of God as Redeemer.

Righteousness is also part of the promised deliverance of the reign of God. It is often in parallel with justice, signaling that righteousness and justice have almost identical meanings.

In popular English-speaking piety, "righteousness" is badly misunderstood to mean something like self-righteousness, an individual possession. That position is miles from the biblical meaning. Jesus and Paul often criticized self-righteousness. We need to turn from the English "righteousness" to the Hebrew word, *tsedaqah,* which really means "community-restoring justice."

Elizabeth Achtemeier writes that in the Old Testament, the righteous person "preserved the peace and wholeness of the community, because he or she fulfilled the demands of communal living." Thus it "is sometimes correlated with 'mercy.' "[31] For this reason righteousness sometimes stands parallel with *shalom,* peace, and, more frequently, justice. Its meaning is very close to social justice; when God brings justice, it delivers us from alienation and oppression into a community with *shalom* (Isa. 32:16–17).

Community-restoring justice needs legal embodiment: The prophets frequently appeal for righteousness in the gate (law court) and the marketplace (economic institutions). It means restoring rights to the oppressed or deprived—"not an impartial decision between two parties, . . . but protecting, restoring, helping righteousness, which helps those who have had their right taken from them in the communal relationship to regain it. Righteousness is the fulfillment of the communal demands, and righteous judgments are those which restore community."[32]

The norm for righteousness is the character of Yahweh[33] revealed in the Exodus. The picture behind the word is Yahweh delivering those oppressed by the Pharaoh's tyranny into a new community with liberty and justice.

> Thus Israel constantly appeals to Yahweh's righteousness for deliverance from trouble (Pss. 31:1; 143:11); from enemies (Pss. 5:8; 143:1); from the wicked (Pss. 36; 71:2); for vindication of her cause before her foes (Ps. 35:24). Yahweh is righteous insofar as he heeds these pleas. His righteousness consists in his intervention for his people, in his deliverance of Zion. . . . So her people should call on their God in the day of trouble (Ps. 50:15). For Yahweh maintains the cause of the afflicted and needy (Ps. 140:12). . . .
>
> In short, Yahweh's righteous judgments are saving judgments (Ps. 36:6), and Deutero-Isaiah can therefore speak of Yahweh as a "righteous God and a Savior." . . .
>
> Yahweh's righteousness is never solely an act of condemnation or punishment. There is no verse in the Old Testament in which Yahweh's righteousness means vengeance on the sinner.[34]

When the Old Testament speaks of God's punishment, it uses other words: wrath, vengeance, judgment.

The Old Testament often speaks of the righteous as those who are oppressed and deprived of their rights. "Their hope is the Lord, for he it is who restores their right (Pss. 116:6; 146:8). His judgments are always favorable (Ps. 146:6–7) for the oppressed and the hungry, the prisoner and the blind, the widow and the fatherless, the alien and the poor (Amos 2:6)."[35]

Thus in Genesis 38, Tamar is seen as the model of righteousness. She delivered her deceased husbands from childlessness, as was her community-restoring obligation in that culture. Her father-in-law, Judah, repeatedly did not see, did not notice, and did not act to deliver his deceased sons from their childlessness. Finally she disguised herself as a prostitute, and he wanted her—not recognizing who she was. She made him give her his signet, cord, and staff as pledges that he would pay her later. When it became clear that she was pregnant, he was about to have her burned to death for adultery, until she played her trump cards (his credit cards), and he finally saw that she, not he, was righteous, because she had acted to deliver. And she delivered twins, one for each deceased husband![36]

Furthermore, "Under prophetic influence, the Messiah was often spoken of as the Righteous and as righteousness. Righteousness can have the sense of mercy in Messianic and eschatological expositions." And in the rabbinic literature, it refers both to God's action and to human action, especially the human action of almsgiving.[37] We see this in Matthew.

Benno Przybylski studied the Dead Sea Scrolls and the Tannaitic literature, not the Old Testament, and concluded that righteousness in Matthew means human conduct that is honest, fair, adheres to the law of the Old Testament, and expresses equality and mercy in judgment. It is closely related to almsgiving and mercy toward the poor and proper conduct in the sight of God.[38] Michael Crosby argues that "more than any other gospel, Matthew used Second Isaiah. For Matthew, Jesus was the fulfillment of the justice which Second Isaiah preached . . . , the fulfillment of the Law and the prophets." Therefore, "The better way to understand Matthew's meaning of justice is in the context of the Hebrew scriptures." Jesus in Matthew announces jubilee and demands from his disciples "a general reordering of possessions and status on behalf of those without possessions and status, namely the poor (Matt. 11:2–6 and 19:21). . . . Unless his followers' justice (*dikaiosyne*) exceeds that of the scribes and Pharisees they will never be able to enter God's kingdom (5:20) . . . , and the reordering of life on behalf of the poor is the *sine qua non* for entrance into heaven."[39]

Injustice is a major cause of war, as the prophets say again and again, and just before Matthew and Luke wrote their Gospels, it was a major cause of the Jewish war against Roman oppression in 70 A.D., devastating Israel. Working for community-restoring justice is a crucial transforming initiative.

An idealistic reading would take Jesus to be urging us to have good intentions, high ideals—to seek the reign of God in our intentions. But Jesus is speaking far more realistically. He makes clear that our hearts follow our interests. If our treasures are invested in jewels and gas-guzzlers, our loyalties will be divided (6:19–21). And a heart divided causes an eye divided, distorting everything (6:22–23). The realistic solution is to change where our money is invested. We should sell the jewels and gas-guzzlers and invest in justice for the poor. Then our interests will be in the welfare of the poor. Laying up treasures in heaven (God's reign) means not merely "keep your money but have good intentions" but also "invest your money in God's reign and community-restoring justice." It is a question of conversion, of surrendering all to God, of personal loyalty to God, and of how we structure our economic incentives.[40]

So the early church did not merely talk about having good intentions but organized actual community practices by which the poor were fed and clothed and did not need to be anxious about food and clothing because the community was sharing. Community-restoring justice may mean selling all and giving it to the poor (Matt. 19:21—rich young ruler), giving a significant part (Luke 19—Zacchaeus), contributing to the needs of others (Romans 12), practicing jubilee,[41] or organizing community practices by which the poor are fed and clothed. How it translates into practice for us in the time of the turning we will discuss in chapter 7. What is clear is that it means a turning in actual economic interests and practices.

This is a realistic word to those of us concerned about preserving the creation from ecological destruction. Conservation requires more than words or good intentions; it requires a realistic change in economic incentives for consumers and polluters.

When Jesus speaks of God's reign, it is intriguing how often he points to the creation and the earth. He almost sounds like an ecologist at Earth Day. He says those with tamed spirits will "inherit the earth" (Matt. 5:5; see also 5:13–14). The heavens are God's throne, and the earth is God's footstool (5:34ff.). The revelation of God's reign is that God shines the sun and rains the rain on the just and the unjust alike (5:45). "Your Kingdom come. Your will be done, on earth as it is in heaven. Give us this day our daily bread" (6:10–11). God's love is revealed not only in giving good news to the poor but also in caring lovingly for sparrows, the lilies, the grass, and the hairs on our heads (6:25–33). God gives bread, fish, and good things for our sustenance (7:9ff.). God causes good trees to bear good fruit (7:16–19). God is seen in the rock on which our house is founded, and in the rain and the winds that come (7:24ff.).

God is deeply engaged in caring for the creation, and our participating in God's reign and justice means our participating in caring for justice for the creation.[42] Redemption, biblically understood, includes redemption of the earth (Isa. 66:22; repeatedly in Jeremiah; Rom. 8:18–23; Rev. 21:1).

What is proposed is not merely a vague ideal. It requires a change in the structuring of our economic loyalties. Jesus calls us to a turning in which our treasures are not invested in consumerism but in God's reign and community-restoring justice. Because this is a question of justice, in continuity with Old Testament expectations, what is called for does not merely involve apolitical individual values but is both a turning in our private life-styles and also a turning in the political, legal, and economic practices of our community. Israel understood clearly that God's covenant calls for personal faithfulness and for societal structures of justice. God is one God, not a half-God; over all of life, not half of life. Thus Jesus confronted the authorities responsible for administering justice, and he confronted the economic practices at the Temple. Isaiah spoke of swords being changed into plowshares; that is economic conversion, a fundamental conversion of technology. Achieving ecological justice will not be a matter of changing attitudes without changing economic incentives and investments. Surely this is a delivering word for our time.

Love Your Enemies; Affirm Their Valid Interests

First Jesus identifies the process of alienation: loving our neighbors and hating our enemies. The international relations scholar Robert Jervis has shown that misperception in international relations is often caused by too quickly discrediting information from opponents, overperceiving hostility against us as the motive of their action, and assuming their context of decisions is like ours. Richard Barnet has reached similar conclusions by different methods.[43]

Our polycentric world after the Cold War will have more complexity, more diverse centers of power, and more need for accurately perceiving others' interests. Martin Luther King, Jr., put it starkly: "Upheaval after upheaval has reminded us that humankind is travelling along a road called hate, in a journey that will bring us to destruction and damnation. Far from being the pious injunction of a utopian dreamer, the command to love one's enemy is an absolute necessity for our survival."[44]

Hating enemies is a common human experience, not an Old Testament teaching. Nowhere does the Old Testament or the Talmud teach us to hate our enemies.[45] Many

Christians have blamed it on the Pharisees, but Jesus suggests we check out the log in our own eye. Blaming others for what we do ourselves is part of the process of alienation.

Jesus points to the process of deliverance: Love your enemies. "The unanimous opinion of scholars that this word does in fact go back to Jesus himself, the evidence that the early church took it with utmost seriousness, [and] the strikingly unique way in which this teaching cuts against the grain of popular morality in his day as in ours [indicate that the] church cannot ignore Jesus' teaching of the love of enemies if it wishes to be true to itself."[46]

Matthew "deliberately places in the emphatic concluding position Jesus' call to love one's enemies. All the other antitheses lead up to it as the climax."[47] "Love your enemies" is Jesus' innovation, and its echo can be heard in many places throughout the New Testament.[48]

New Testament research shows enemy love is not merely a feeling or sentiment. If it were only that, it probably would not be a major contribution to realistic peacemaking. Love means action, deeds, initiatives. "The numerous treatments of the Greek verb *agapao* (love) have repeatedly underscored the dynamic character of the term in contrast to a mere feeling or emotion."[49]

Lapide says it strongly:

> Because Jesus was neither a visionary nor a utopian, but a worldly-wise observer of human nature, he did not demand super-human selflessness or sentiments that would be overdemanding for almost any human heart, but practical demonstrations of love such as visiting the sick, giving alms in secret, supporting the needy, consoling the sorrowful, sharing bread with the hungry, and all the thousand and one effective good deeds that create trust, demolish enmity, and promote love. . . .
>
> Love of one's enemies, as Jesus understood it, means far more than covering things up with a smile by tolerating ene-

mies or holding them at a distance with politeness; it entails an honest effort, a campaigning and struggling with them, so that they change, give up their hate, and become reconciled. In short—a theopolitics of little loving steps aimed at making the enemy cease to be an enemy.[50]

Lapide tells of the rabbinic debate over what you should do if both your brother's donkey and your enemy's donkey have fallen in the ditch:

The answer, which Jesus surely knew, went: "First help your hater's donkey, for in doing that you not only save an animal but also touch the heart of your opponent and gain a friend. Only then go and help your brother's donkey." . . . It is just this practical method of disarming, which has nothing to do with extremism or superhuman quality, that Jesus proposes as a biblical realpolitik designed to deflate conflicts with either a foreign ruler or a local tyrant, to turn adversaries into good neighbors at least and real friends if possible. But a disarming love has two facets to it: change those around you and change yourself![51]

Love also means we seek to *understand and affirm our enemy's valid interests*. Where the Sermon on the Mount says, "Love your enemies," Romans 12:15 says, "Rejoice with those who rejoice, weep with those who weep."[52] This means we affirm their valid interests. It does not mean, however, that we affirm all the enemy does; Jesus and Paul both confronted their enemies directly when they did wrong.

Affirming adversaries' valid interests is a key step in conflict resolution. The adversary may make unacceptable demands and put forth impossible positions. Roger Fisher and other experts in conflict resolution strongly emphasize that the key is to listen for the basic interests that lie behind the demands and affirm those interests that can be affirmed.

When Dwight Eisenhower was president, Austria was divided just as Germany has been for forty-five years. The eastern third was occupied by the Soviet Union. A Christian in Eisenhower's cabinet suggested, "Let's think what Soviet interests are in Austria. They don't want Austria to join NATO [North Atlantic Treaty Organization] or to build a powerful offensive capability aimed at the Soviet Union. Suppose we propose that if they withdraw from the eastern half of Austria, we'll guarantee Austria won't threaten the Soviet Union militarily."[53]

Secretary of State John Foster Dulles ridiculed the proposal: "The Soviets want power; they'll never voluntarily back off an inch of territory."

The debate bounced back and forth until Eisenhower spoke: "Suppose Foster is right, what then? We'll be where we are now, no worse off. On the other hand, if they accept the offer, what then? Austria will be free. Foster, aren't you speaking in Texas next week? Could you float the idea as a trial balloon?"

So Dulles went to Texas as Jonah went to Ninevah, with a message he did not want to deliver.

The Soviet Union showed interest. Negotiations followed. They backed out. Austria was free. The Turning came to Austria thirty-some years earlier than it did for East Germany.

This transforming initiative would not have been taken if someone had not asked imaginatively about affirming our adversary's valid interests. For the people of Austria, love as seeking to understand and affirm valid interests is not a mere sentiment.

Christian Wolf points to the delivering power of love, calling it "de-enemizing love." Martin Luther King, Jr., spoke of the "double victory" of getting rid of an enemy and acquiring a friend. When we observe the destruction caused by enmity and resort to violence, love is hardly unreasonable; it begins to look like an intelligent thing to do.

But how is enemy-love in a world of violence possible?

Wolf answers: (1) When we are children of our Father in heaven, we have experience of enemy-love from God. "God's love is boundless. God's sun and rain are given to all without condition. Because God is no longer our enemy, we need no longer be enemies of our enemies." (2) "When we take the reality of the reign of God seriously, this reality states that love is in the process of coming and hate is on the way out; that the future belongs to peace and not to violence, . . . and the peacemaker will participate in God's peaceful reign."[54]

Thus like the other initiatives, love for the enemy points us toward participation in God's delivering love.[55] "The sanction for loving the enemy is simply to participate in the nature of God, to retaliate as God does, . . . or to participate in God's benevolent nature (Luke 6:35)."[56]

Pray for Your Enemies, and Persevere in Prayer

Matthew 5:44 says, "Pray for those who persecute you." Luke 6:28 says, "Bless those who curse you, pray for those who abuse you." Romans 12:12 and 14 say, "Persevere in prayer" and "bless those who persecute you." In the New Testament, blessing someone and praying for him or her means the same thing. Similarly, when Matthew 5:47 speaks of "greeting" enemies, it implies praying that God bless them with peace.[57] Thus prayer is a key step in peacemaking. In the short space of these three chapters in Matthew, Jesus speaks of prayer four times (5:44; 6:5–7; 6:9–15; and 7:7–11).

What kind of prayer is this? First, it is prayer for our enemies. The content of the prayer comes in part from the meaning of Jesus' command to love our enemies, described above. John Stott says it well:

> "This is the supreme command," wrote Bonhoeffer. "Through the medium of prayer we go to our enemy, stand by his side, and plead for him to God." Moreover, if inter-

cessory prayer is an expression of what love we have, it is a
means to increase our love as well. It is impossible to pray
for someone without . . . discovering that our love [for that
person] grows and matures. We must not, therefore, wait
before praying for an enemy until we feel some love . . . in
our heart. . . . [Jesus prayed,] "Father, forgive them; for
they know not what they do." If the cruel torture of crucifix-
ion could not silence our Lord's prayer for his enemies,
what pain, pride, prejudice or sloth could justify the silenc-
ing of ours?[58]

The New Call to Peacemaking distributes a poster with a
quote from Jim Wallis: "Fervent prayer for our enemies is
a great obstacle to war and the feelings that lead to it."

When we pray for our enemies in the presence of God
who is known in Christ as grace, mercy, deliverance, and
love, the appropriate prayer includes forgiveness. In the
Lord's Prayer and the explanation following it, Jesus emphasizes forgiveness as strongly as possible: We receive
God's forgiveness only if we forgive others their sins
against us (Matt. 6:12–15). The best explanation of this is
the parable of the unforgiving servant in Matthew 18:23–
25. Stendahl offers an intriguing insight: Matthew 6:14–
15; 18:15–35; Mark 11:20–25; and Luke 17:3–6 all say
that the power of our prayer depends on our forgiving.[59]

Davies and Allison point out that Jesus asks us to use
few words in praying, and his own prayers are terse; But
Jesus spent long hours praying in secret. That must mean
that the purpose of prayer "is not to exercise the tongue"
and is not only what we say to God, but is "worship, and
it serves to cleanse the mind, purify the heart, and align
one's will with God's will (cf. 6:10); it recalls to the suppli-
cant who God is and what God's purposes are."[60]

This suggests a reversal in emphasis in our usual praying. It suggests that we not spend most of our time composing words for God to hear but that we spend time
listening quietly in God's presence. Listening prayer is a

discipline practiced by many Christian peacemaking groups and by Buddhist, Hindu, Jewish, and other peacemakers in the contemplative tradition. Thomas Merton, Dorothy Day, Glenn Hinson, Edward Thornton, and the Quakers are examples.

When one is quiet before God, anxieties about hostilities between us and our enemies are likely to surface. We let them be examined in the presence of the God of forgiveness. New images of the valid interests of the adversary come forth. Anxieties about the priorities in our overcommitted lives also come forth. We let them be examined in God's presence, and they may be reprioritized. In the presence of one whose nature is revealed in the Sermon on the Mount, the priority of peacemaking is advanced, and other dimensions of life are simplified. Our own idolatries, images of the enemy, idiosyncratic hostilities, investing our interests in selfish concerns rather than the reign of God—all are examined in God's presence. New insights may come. Confession may come. Forgiveness may come. A new sense of God's presence may come.

When we pray "Our Father," we pray that God's name be hallowed, God's reign come and God's will be done on earth—the coming of God's reign, with peace, justice, and forgiveness. If we pray these words and then listen, usually we receive a painful awareness of the clash between God's reign and our world's destructive processes. We ask God about that conflict. Our praying becomes more real. We receive a more intense awareness of our calling to participate in the coming of God's reign. Thus as Davies and Allison say, the eschatological and the ethical go hand in hand; the New Testament is clearly expressing the faith that if we pray in forgiveness of our enemies, our praying can speed the coming of God's reign.[61] Those who participate actively in something like the eight steps of peacemaking can be given a surprising sense of partnership in God's transforming action.

To many realists, prayer may seem to be only turning inward, insignificant in the real, political world. Admittedly there is a kind of inward-directed piety that falsely splits the inner life from the life of peace, justice, and care for the creation, turning people away from action that participates in God's lordship as it is described biblically.

But those who have practiced truly listening prayer, such as Frances of Assisi, Thomas Merton, Dorothy Day, and the Quakers, have made distinctive contributions to peacemaking. This has also been the experience of several church peacemaker groups I know.[62] The literature on addictions of various sorts almost unanimously describes the problem as grounded in an inner spiritual emptiness and prescribes something like meditative prayer as an essential step for recovery. One glance at the size of the nuclear arsenals, the enormity of military spending, the irrationality of ethnic clashes, hypernationalism, and the paranoid inability of adversary nations to affirm one another's valid interests should convince us that the problem is both physical addiction to the interests and structures of the national security state and spiritual addiction to hating our enemies. Recovery requires both a change in the physical processes and inward spiritual change. The Sermon on the Mount prescribes prayer that participates in that health-giving kind of turning.

Don't Judge But Repent and Forgive

The Lord's Prayer focuses directly on the forgiveness we need, and the forgiveness needed by those we have something against. In Matthew 7:1–5, Jesus says "Do not judge. . . . for with the judgment you make you will be judged. . . . First take the log out of your own eye." The log in our eye, of course, is our own sin. So the transforming initiative is to work on our own repenting, and on our own forgiving. Paul echoes this in Romans 12:17, 19 and 14:1, 4, 10, 13.

What does it mean not to judge? It "cannot refer to simple ethical judgments, . . . Jesus himself, after all, delivered himself of numerous polemical utterances. One can, however, enjoin mercy, humility, and tolerance." It means don't condemn. Don't play God.[63]

Stuhlmacher writes, "Christians who as individuals or as community are ready to admit their offenses and to contribute their part to healing what has become broken through their guilt, work as peacemakers in the sense of the seventh beatitude, wherever they are found." He says the decision of the synod of the Protestant church in the Rheinland in 1980 to seek a renewal of relations between Christians and Jews begins with a confession of guilt for the Holocaust, the slandering, persecution, and murder of Jews in the Third Reich, and seeks to make repentance for the wrenching alienation that has come into being through the fateful guilt of the church toward Israel. That decision opened doors toward Israel that had seemed shut forever.[64]

On the first Sunday evening in August one year, our church showed the color film of the bombing of Hiroshima and Nagasaki, *Prophecy*. After the film, discussion groups dealt with the feelings that had been aroused. John, a U.S. Air Force veteran raised in Oklahoma, came to the discussion on the defensive about what the Air Force had done. Chigako, wife of a doctoral student from Japan, was the first to speak in John's group. But instead of accusing, *she apologized* for Japanese militarism and the Japanese role in starting World War II. She asked forgiveness. John was dumbfounded. His defenses had been breached and undermined. Before long he was confessing. Within a few weeks he was a member of our peacemaker group, probing the Scriptures for an understanding of the meaning of peacemaking. Within a year he had become the group's moderator. Chigako's not judging, as John had expected, but repenting and confessing was the surprising initiative of peacemaking.

The seventh step thus relates us back to the first step, "acknowledge realistically our alienation and God's grace." It is a crucial step in peacemaking. Like all the steps, it is rooted in the heart of the gospel. Each step conforms to the shape of God's grace. No step is arbitrary, either from the perspective of the gospel or from the perspective of effective peacemaking.

Our paradigm now lacks just one essential ingredient—the community context.

Do Peacemaking in a Church or a Group of Disciples

The context for both Jesus' and Paul's teachings is not merely isolated individuals and their ideals. It is the practice of the community of disciples and the people of Israel whom Jesus is addressing. Paul is addressing the household churches in Rome. He begins his twelfth chapter by appealing to the church as the body of Christ to practice mutual respect and love for one another. The fourteenth and fifteenth chapters are appeals to the churches in Rome to make peace as the gospel dictates.

The kind of gracious deliverance to which these chapters are pointing is not merely a small thing, easily carried off by an individual in a moment. It is a lifetime process, and it requires group support. Getting the log out of our eye and becoming part of the delivering process instead of the mechanism of bondage requires help. We are too powerless to do it alone. If we are to be peacemakers and justicemakers, we have to do it together. We need one another. We do not have enough information by ourselves. We do not have the self-discipline to do it alone. If we are to persevere with wisdom and strength, we need mutual support, mutual wisdom, mutual encouragement, and mutual responsibility. We need to pray together and work together. So Jesus called the disciples. So he calls us to peacemaking in groups: "We, who are many, are one body in Christ, and individually we are members one of another." And, "Love one another with mutual affection" (Rom. 12:5, 10).

My own experience is that I felt lonely and powerless until we began to organize peacemaker groups among the churches and my own congregation then began to concern itself for peacemaking. Now we share a sense of community support, empowerment, and hope.

Our group practices what Elizabeth O'Connor calls "the journey inward/journey outward": We share in a prayer discipline with mutual encouragement, we study and share information so that we are much more critical in our understanding of the context for peacemaking, and we share action projects in which we are linked together with peacemaker networks. The networks enable our actions to be timely, pertinent, and coordinated with others.

Our hope is not that we will always successfully persuade the government to do the peacemaking we believe should be done. Nor do we hope that the government will be without sin, or that we will be error free. Our hope is that together we can participate in God's gracious gift of peacemaking. We hope this will happen in our individual relations, our community projects, and our witness in our church, workplaces, and community as well as in our influence on Washington and the world. Our hope is that our church will be the body of Christ, truly following the one who took a dramatic transforming initiative toward us while we were yet enemies.

Questions for Thought

1. The argument is that each of the steps of peacemaking is rooted in the essential core of the gospel of Jesus Christ. Look through the eight steps in table 2.1 and ask whether they fit your understanding of the gospel.

2. Does the claim that each of these steps is a *practical* step of peacemaking fit your way of interpreting these teachings, or does it have a strange ring to it? How have you thought of "practicality" and Jesus' teachings?

3. Does the author minimize the realistic awareness of the world's sinfulness, or the realistic awareness of our need to take up our cross and be willing to sacrifice for the gospel?

4. You might try choosing one step per day as the theme of a morning or nighttime meditation on its meaning for your life.

4

The Seven Steps
of Just Peacemaking

The early Christians, until the time of Constantine, almost all understood that Christians were to be peacemakers and not to participate in warmaking.[1] They were pacifists. "Pacifist" means "peacemaker," active in making peace. It comes from the Latin *pax,* "peace," and *facere,* "to make." It is a direct translation of Matthew 5:9, "Blessed are the peacemakers," which in Greek is *eireno-poioi,* "peace-makers." "Pacifist" does not signify a passive but an *active maker* of peace.

In the fourth century, when Christendom was forming and the military leader Constantine had converted to the Christian faith and become emperor, Saint Ambrose and Saint Augustine developed a rival ethic, "just war theory." Just war theory argues that Christians should *not* fight in unjust wars but *should* fight in just ones. It offers seven principles for testing whether a war is just or unjust. (For more on pacifism and just war theory, see chapter 10.)

Ever since then, there has been a debate between pacifism and just war theory: Should Christians give clear witness to Christ by remaining nonviolent, or should they fight for justice for their neighbor when they can do so by just means? It is still an important debate today. But unfortunately, the debate has focused Christian ethics only on the negative side of the issue: Are Christians prohibited from making war? It has turned attention away from the positive mandate of active peacemaking: What should we do to make peace?

David Hollenbach, a Jesuit and professor of moral theology at Weston School of Theology, has written an especially wise and insightful book, *Nuclear Ethics.* It argues that pacifism and just war theory converge when they face the question of nuclear war. Nuclear war is unjust, and Christians should not participate in it. He argues further that ethics should not abstract from but pay close attention to the concrete conditions of likely use of nuclear weapons, the concrete realities of the weapons themselves and their political and military uses. He urges us to focus attention not only on nuclear weapons in general but also on specific policies that can do something about the threat that we all agree is morally horrendous. Sweeping judgments about deterrence are less helpful than influencing specific defense postures, weapons systems, and doctrines. We should apply two criteria to any new policy proposal: (1) It must make nuclear war less likely than the policies presently in effect, rather than more likely, and (2) it must increase rather than decrease the possibility of arms reduction.[2] Analogous arguments could be made about conventional, non-nuclear weapons.

Hollenbach is here shifting attention from the debate about the general question of whether we may fight to the more positive side of the original Christian concern for peacemaking. We need ethical discussion of the rightness and obligatoriness of key steps in Christian peacemaking. What steps make war less likely and arms reduction more likely? What ethical arguments have validity for and against these steps?

The social context in which pacifism and just war theory opposed each other was empire or monarchy. Christians had little voice in the decision to make war; their part was to do or refuse to do what the emperor decided. In our present social context we have responsibility for decisions to make peace and prevent war. Therefore, our questions are changing. What actions, what decisions, qualify as peacemaking?

The nature of war has also changed. Nuclear holocaust is not accurately named by the old word, "war." Our central question is not whether to participate in it but how to prevent it.

Many thoughtful persons are calling for the development of a just peacemaking theory. The East German churches concluded in their remarkable process of dialogue that we need a just peacemaking theory, and it should be built in dialogue with persons of other faiths and of no faith.[3]

Similarly, the U.S. Catholic bishops say in their pastoral letter, *The Challenge of Peace:*

> We are called to be a church at the service of peace, precisely because peace is one manifestation of God's word and work in our midst. Recognition of the Church's responsibility to join with others in the work of peace is a major force behind the call today to develop a theology of peace. Much of the history of Catholic theology on war and peace has focused on limiting the resort to force in human affairs; this task is still necessary, . . . but it is not a sufficient response to Vatican II's challenge "to undertake a completely fresh reappraisal of war."
>
> A fresh reappraisal which includes a developed theology of peace will require contributions from several sectors of the Church's life: biblical studies, systematic and moral theology, ecclesiology, and the experience and insights of members of the Church who have struggled in various ways to make and keep the peace in this often violent age.[4]

Official statements of the United Church of Christ, the United Methodist Church, and the Presbyterian Church

(U.S.A.) have made similar calls for a theology of just peace. The leading Christian pacifist, John Howard Yoder, writes:

> So while we discuss whether "nonviolence" or "nonresistance" is the right word for describing our reasons for not killing, a Southern Christian Leadership Council had to rise up in the 1960s to tell us the meaning of the cross for race relations. . . .
>
> Jesus showed us something about ending wars that most of our contemporaries haven't learned yet. . . . The only way to end the war is to make peace, and for that someone has to die. Someone has to back down. Someone has to be humiliated. Someone has to come up with an alternative, a vision of a new order for which one is ready to sacrifice one's future, one's popularity and even one's life.[5]

Not only Yoder but also noted Christian ethicists Alan Geyer, Edward Leroy Long, and Ronald Stone argue similarly for developing a just peacemaking theory.[6]

In sketching what the ingredients of a just peacemaking theory might be, I want to draw especially from documents of West German church-related peacemaking strategy, and from the East German Ecumenical Gathering for Peace, Justice, and the Preservation of Creation. They have brought together political scientists, church leaders both professional and lay, and activists in peace, environmental, women's, and third-world groups to develop constructive, suggestive, and persuasive peacemaking strategies. They have lived along the Wall between East and West, have had their minds focused on the problems of war by that Wall, have seen the authoritarian oppression of Communism, and have learned from one another, East and West, about realistic steps toward solution and realistic limitations and hindrances. They have lived especially aware of the threat of war, in the aftermath of World War II. More than most other nations, they have confessed their own responsibility for World War II and have thought deeply about war's causes and its remedies. They have lived in a country more densely armed with nuclear weapons than any other, where a World War III would destroy them thoroughly. They pioneered in developing a steady peacemaking strategy toward the East and tested it in the real world until it succeeded in breaking down the barriers—along with a little help from Solidarity, Hungary, economics, events, Gorbachev, and God.

Furthermore, the Turning in East Germany clearly symbolizes that the world has turned. The Cold War is over. The bipolar order imposed on the world has ceased. The world will now be multipolar. Ethnic nationalism, economic dissatisfaction, and religious tensions will have greater room to express their discontent and will need a new and more just order in which to work out their grievances. The causes of war and the conditions of peace after the Turning will be different. Just peacemaking theory must be developed in a new context. The West and East German ethicists I will cite already saw that change happening and worked to bring it about. Their suggestions are especially insightful. In keeping with their intention to work together with people of different faiths and no faith, they base each point on a reasoned analysis of essential elements in the process of peacemaking, rather than on explicit reference to Scripture. Similarly, my purpose in this chapter is to seek a theory of just peacemaking that can function effectively in inclusive public ethical discussion with people of varieties of faiths, based on reason and experience.

For centuries just war theory has functioned this way. I am seeking an analogous just peacemaking theory for public discourse. In public discourse, in a pluralistic society, we need *both* (1) an *explicitly Christian ethic* with a strong scriptural base and (2) a *public ethic* that appeals to reason, experience, and need and that cannot place the same emphasis on Scripture and prayer that an explicitly

Christian ethic can. (See chapter 6 for further development of a trilingual method based on Scripture, reason, and experience.)

Therefore, what follows will not be identical with the scriptural model identified in the preceding chapters. It is a "public ethic." It is based on the work of the political scientists and ethicists in Germany whom I cite. It lacks the emphasis on prayer, although prayer is crucial for Christian peacemaking and is implicit throughout, especially in loving enemies (praying for them) and in acknowledging the vicious cycles in which we are caught and our need of grace in the peacemaking processes. Nevertheless, the "middle axioms" of the public ethic are very similar to the biblical steps. The biblical steps of peacemaking, after all, do make sense; they are not mere arbitrary commands. They are intended to be inclusive. There are seven steps or axioms in just peacemaking, just as there are seven criteria in just war theory. They guide our peacemaking and measure the justice of the government's claim to be seeking peace.

1. Affirm Common Security

The first step is to *affirm our common security partnership with our adversaries and build an order of peace and justice that affirms their and our valid interests.* The core meaning is that our security is inextricably interwoven with the security of our adversaries; whether we like it or not, we have a security partnership. Rational policy must offer adversaries ways to affirm their valid interest in guarding their own security.

West German Chancellor Helmut Schmidt announced the concept in his address before the United Nations Special Session for Disarmament on May 25, 1978: "What we need is partnership. It must arise from the awareness that no nation alone can assure its security and peace. . . . In the interest of peace we need today a comprehensive political security partnership. Only in this way can we set in motion an effective process of limiting and reducing armaments."[7]

The fundamental reality of the nuclear age is that our security depends on the cooperation of our adversaries. We cannot defend ourselves against nuclear destruction by our own military might; even if we launch all our military forces, the other side can still destroy us. And the reality of the post–Cold War age is that economic, technical, political, cultural, and ethnic forces are becoming more important and our security and military forces less. These forces transcend our borders. Furthermore, in a multipolar world no longer dominated by the two superpowers, our security will depend on cooperation between many nations.[8]

Schritte zur Abrüstung (Steps Toward Disarmament), an influential group of political scientists and Christian ethicists, put it this way:

> The just security interests that we have ourselves, we want to acknowledge for our adversaries. We can increase our security only when we consider their security; we can reduce our fear, only when we take their fear seriously. . . . The command to love our enemy does not ask us to deny that we have real enemies . . . , or that they really threaten us. It demands only one thing: to conduct our resistance against the enemy with the goal of reconciliation and with the means that serve this goal. The command of enemy love is therefore a rational command.[9]

We must *recognize and respect national borders,* thus affirming others' valid security interests. Border changes can be made only through collective discussions and agreements.[10] During the nuclear age, borders have gained importance as firebreaks against war. Nations have joined in concerted opposition to military intervention across borders.

Security partnership also suggests the concept of *defensive deterrence* or a *defense-oriented military*. The purpose of the German military is not to threaten someone else's security but to defend Germany's security. Therefore the budget should not buy weapons for attacking other nations but weapons for destroying forces that would attack Germany. Germany should reject offensive war strategies like Air-Land Battle and terminate the Follow-On Forces Attack concept, both of which prepare massive attacks against the East.[11]

President Gorbachev eventually adopted this concept of a defensive military, withdrawing half the Soviet tanks, as well as all river-crossing and attack-supporting equipment, and a number of troops from Central Europe. This decreased the threat of attack, enabling the West to decrease its forces and begin assisting the Soviet economy.

Common security also means *building an order of peace* to replace the superpower-based order of the Cold War. Without the order imposed by the United States and the Soviet Union, a vacuum could allow ethnic nationalism, as in Yugoslavia, Azerbaijan, or the Middle East, to explode into war. We will need a "transition to new political forms of securing the peace," and in fact the transition is already occurring. Democracy was a transition from the assumption in monarchy that power had to be in the hands of one powerful figure to the understanding that all are safer if power is shared, with built-in mandatory consultation and checks and balances. We may be undergoing an analogous transition to an understanding of shared power among nations in our situation of security partnership.

The East German churches concluded that

> signs of this transition are unmistakable. People, states and alliance systems are beginning to learn that . . . security is no more to be achieved against adversaries, but only to be won with them. The first steps on this course are already under way through the dismantling of the medium-range

weapons, through the agreement of the Stockholm Conference for Security and Cooperation in Europe (CSCE) on confidence-building measures in the military realm and through the Vienna negotiations on conventional weapons in Europe, as well as through unilateral disarmament initiatives of the member states of the Warsaw Pact.[12]

They also agreed that we need a new, global, international system of security and cooperation, supported by the United Nations. The European region can serve as a model and field test, for example, for global control and supervision of economic and ecological cooperation. Some key components of a system of common security are collective European institutions to preserve borders; conflict regulation and arbitration on political, economic, and military matters; and broad economic cooperation and mutual interconnection between the states of East and West Europe. These elements will be aided by the greatest possible openness and communication of people between all parts of Europe; permanent and extensive dialogue about life-styles, social policy, cultural development, and economic and political structures, especially in view of the future of the two-thirds world;[13] common research and close cooperation in ecological data recording and analysis; ecologically meaningful economic and political decisions; conservation measures; and building an economy oriented toward ecological sustainability. Additional important factors are the increasingly far-reaching dynamics of disarmament, so that nonviolent social defense as a means of securing the peace becomes possible; developing direct contacts between parliaments and their committees; developing partner-city relationships; broad international grass roots contact between peace, ecology, and two-thirds–world groups and movements; cooperative structures for economic cooperation and for dealing with human rights questions; travel and encounter possibilities;

youth exchanges; cultural exchange; scientific exchange;
peace education; and teacher exchange.[14]

There is widespread German agreement that the new order of peace must be based on the politics of inclusion
rather than exclusion. Eastern Europe, and the Soviet republics, must be included. When a nation feels excluded,
isolated, and encircled, as Germany did after World War I
and Israel does now, it can cause internal instability and
external warmaking. A common security order that includes the Soviet republics eventually will be based on a
vastly expanded NATO or on a strengthened Conference
for Security and Cooperation in Europe, which includes
the United States, Canada, the Soviet Union, and thirty-
one other European nations. The United States must overcome the inertia of its enemy image of the Soviet Union.

2. Take Independent Initiatives

The second step is to *take independent initiatives.* This
strategy was developed by social psychologist Charles E.
Osgood in his book, *An Alternative to War or Surrender.*[15]
His proposal was picked up by the Catholic Pax Christi
movement in Holland and Germany, by the Dutch peace
movement, and by the German strategy group Schritte
zur Abrüstung, by the U.S. Nuclear Weapons Freeze Campaign, and by the U.S. Catholic bishops' pastoral letter
The Challenge of Peace.

Here is a summary of the argument as it is stated by
Schritte zur Abrüstung:[16] We find ourselves polarized. On
one side there is a politics of peace through strength, and
on the other a unilateral and unconditional renunciation
of all weapons. But the insights and fears of the large majority of our people do not allow unilateral disarmament.
Nor does it deal with the adversary's buildup, which is,
after all, half the problem. On the other hand, a policy of
continuing buildup, even in the name of balance or parity,

does not work for our security either. When a policy of parity is adopted, the two sides understand the balance differently, and each keeps building up to match a worst-case understanding of the other side's planned buildup. This costs one trillion dollars per year and cannot be stopped. It is driven by forces beyond rational calculation of security, such as technological invention of new weapons and economic interests of the military-industrial complex. It leads to overkill, to faster and more accurate weapons, and to weapons designed not only for deterrence but also for actual war fighting.

Therefore, both sides feel increasingly threatened, build up all the more, and increase their expectation of the likelihood of war. The distrust increases the danger of accidental war. It makes arms control slow and difficult and prevents it from achieving hopeful results. Arms control negotiations are still important for getting the adversaries to talk to one another, but they have shown themselves to be little more than a process of controlling the quantities of the ongoing buildup and legitimating each side's qualitatively new, quicker, more accurate, and more destabilizing generations of weapons.

Therefore, we need a new strategy of independent initiatives, directed toward transforming the reaction of the adversary. It takes independent initiatives as measures to make our defensive intent and our desire for detente credible. But it retains a sufficient deterrent to make aggression too great a risk to be considered.

Schritte zur Abrüstung proposed three specific initiatives that the German government could take: First, reject the escalation of medium-range nuclear weapons in Germany (Pershing II and ground-launched cruise missiles). These missiles were not necessary to deter attack against Germany; they only threatened offensive attack against Eastern Europe and the Soviet Union. They exacerbated tensions and stimulated a counterbuildup by the Soviet

Union, thus decreasing our security. Germany and NATO had plenty of other deterrents in submarines and on the ground. Second, concentrate German military spending on weapons and forces designed to devastate a military force that would try to invade Germany, but not designed for offensive attacks against other nations. Third, stop selling military weapons to third-world countries, which escalates their arms race and impoverishes them. This latter proposal now looks especially prescient in view of present German embarrassment that about one hundred German companies have aided the buildup of chemical/ biological and nuclear weapons, as well as missiles, in nations such as Libya and Iraq.

In 1989 the East German churches suggested that to break the logjam, more "calculated one-sided initiatives" were needed, such as withdrawing conventional offensive capacities from a central European corridor, a comprehensive nuclear test ban, and a chemical-weapons–free zone in Europe as a concrete step and a field test on the way toward worldwide abolition of these weapons. Locally, citizens with limited power can take initiatives that fit their location.[17]

The initiatives should be independent of the slow process of negotiations about exact reciprocation. An example is the U.S. Congress's initiatives to delete funds from the budget for antisatellite missile testing and Star Wars developments that would violate the Antiballistic Missile (ABM) Treaty as long as the Soviet Union refrains as well. For several years now, both sides have reciprocated with these restraints, independent of new treaty negotiations or agreement by the White House. Similarly, President Gorbachev halted underground testing of nuclear bombs for nineteen months, inviting U.S. reciprocation that never came. But it did influence the American people and Congress.

On September 27, 1991, President Bush took up the

theme, stating that negotiations take too long and that we need a sweeping initiative. He pointed out that the START talks took ten years, which meant ten more years of costly and dangerous nuclear buildup. His initiative responded to Congress's initiatives the week before. Congress had canceled the mobile MX missile and the Short-Range Attack Missile. The European governments, responding to the peacemaking work of their people, were already saying they wanted the short-range nuclear weapons removed. President Bush added to these an initiative on tactical or shorter-range nuclear missiles on ships and attack submarines and a relaxing of the alert readiness of bombers. President Gorbachev reciprocated equally and added an initiative stopping nuclear testing in response to the pressure of the peace movement in Kazakhstan, which had shut down the test range at Semi-Palatinsk.

At this writing, President Bush has not yet agreed to stop nuclear testing. Nuclear testing is the "camel's nose under the tent" for all new types of nuclear bombs or missiles. When new types are no longer tested, we will not produce them because we won't know their reliability. This can save $20 billion a year, stop the development of more dangerous types, and help stop the proliferation of nuclear weapons to other countries. I hope for a reciprocating initiative by the Congress or the president.

The point of independent initiatives is to build mutual credibility, decrease the sense of insecurity, and provide incentives so our adversary can begin to consider rational alternatives. "In a nutshell, this is a strategy of unilateral, calculated steps of disarmament, in order to create the basis for promising bilateral negotiations." But they ask, "Who begins? The love of the enemy demands not that the other take the first step, . . . but it requires me, I who hear it, to make a beginning. Exactly this one-sidedness makes it rational. For that is the only way to break through the cycle of retaliation."[18]

Hans-Richard Reuter relates the strategy of independent initiatives directly to Jesus' teaching in the Sermon
on the Mount: "The nonviolence that Jesus speaks of is a
provocative working on the adversary; it hopes to change
the adversary's behavior by a surprise-effect, a breakthrough in the vicious cycle of retaliation. To this end
it takes independent initiatives, unilateral first steps as
confidence-building measures, inviting reciprocation. De-
tailed political implications of such a strategy are worked
out in peace research."[19]

3. Talk with Your Enemy

The third step can be described briefly because it is so
clearly essential and is becoming increasingly well known.
It is to *talk: Seek negotiations, using methods of conflict
resolution.* Nations will not solve their problems if they do
not talk. Failure to solve problems that can cause millions
of persons to be destroyed does not fulfill the mandate
governments are given. So one requirement of just peacemaking theory is that governments talk with their adversaries, in a manner designed to resolve conflict.
Sometimes governments negotiate for show, seeking to
anesthetize the people who want peace but offering terms
designed to be rejected by their adversaries. This is not
the talk and the listening of conflict resolution.

There is now extensive research on conflict resolution
methods. It has powerful applications to families,
churches, and interpersonal conflict as well as to international peacemaking.[20] The East Germans point out that
"peace research has won broad acceptance; its results are
being used in practical policy."[21]

They also emphasize that the requirement for governments to seek negotiations entails strengthening the
United Nations.[22] And they emphasize the need for regional organizations, such as the CSCE. We could add the

Organization of American States and other regional organizations.

4. Seek Human Rights and Justice

The fourth step is *seek human rights and justice for all, especially the powerless, without double standards.* The lack of human rights is itself the absence of peace, holistically understood as *shalom.* Relative deprivation of human rights is the major cause of violent rebellion.[23] After the dissolution of the Soviet bloc, ethnic nationalism and economic decay will be likely causes of war. A major antidote is to push governments to respect the human rights of all groups, in the comprehensive sense of civil rights, economic rights, and participation rights.[24]

The churches in East Germany were acutely conscious of the need for human rights, comprehensively understood. Throughout their document they emphasized the economic rights of two-thirds–world peoples. A basic principle for their whole document was "a preferential option for the poor."[25] At public rallies and church services throughout East Germany, I was impressed by the frequency with which speakers urged the newly emerging East German society to give strong assistance to the peoples of the two-thirds world. This consciousness had pervaded the people.

A major section of the document focuses on the rights of foreigners in East Germany, naming specific injustices they experience and calling for concrete remedies. It is honest, confessional, and practical.[26]

Their own nonviolent revolution, the Turning, focused on their demands for civil rights in East Germany. The section entitled "More Justice in the GDR" spells that out concretely.[27] (See chapter 1 for a summary of its demands.)

In their theological grounding for the document, they

emphasize that *shalom* is the fruit of justice (Isa. 32:17). That means we need to see peace between East and West bound up with justice between North and South. "Military expenditures in East and West are therefore already irresponsible, because they devour the bread of the poor. . . . Under the criterion of justice in the North-South conflict we have to test whether and how the economy and economic policy of our land participate in the mechanisms which cause the injustice of the world economy, what in our land will be done against these mechanisms, and which *concrete steps* to greater justice can be taken."[28]

5. Acknowledge Vicious Cycles: Participate in Peacemaking Process

Closely related is the need for *realistic acknowledgment of the vicious cycles we are caught up in, and our need to participate in a realistic peacemaking process.* So, for example, the East German document says war would destroy the basis for human civilization, and would destroy life in Central Europe.

> Nevertheless humankind will not abstain from the threat and use of violence. This reality must also be taken into account in the evaluation of the legitimate security interests of people and governments. Therefore, limited military capabilities in Europe will still exist for the foreseeable future. Our present security systems and the means for maintaining them, however, are the expression of an absolute perversion of security. In the military sphere this perverting form has taken shape in the principle of deterrence through weapons of mass destruction, which is based on the incalculable risk of a self-contradictory threat with assured mutual destruction. Its consequences stand clearly before our eyes:

The document then outlines the consequences, here summarized:

1. The effort to achieve first-strike capability and nuclear war–fighting capabilities
2. The continuous and immense military buildup
3. The impoverishment of the greater part of the world and the growing incapacity to solve life-threatening ecological problems
4. The increasing resort to automatic means of military response, from prewarning to launch, which renders increasingly probable the outbreak of a nuclear war through technical or human error
5. The shrinking of possibilities for political action.[29]

The most dangerous time for recovering alcoholics is when they feel the problem is licked, and they are on top of the world. Then they may be tempted to take just a little drink; they have shown they can handle it. The most dangerous time for us may be when we feel we have our "nucleaholism" licked. Some significant reductions in nuclear weapons are happening. We may be tempted to relax our efforts just when we can win some real victories over the nucleaholism.

Hans Bethe, Kurt Gottfried, and Robert S. McNamara have diagnosed perceptively how the Turning in the Soviet Union has changed the nature of the threat of nuclear weapons.[30] I believe their proposal should set the standard for our policy:

The crumbling of Soviet power means the threat that the U.S. nuclear weapons buildup was intended to answer is now diminished. The Soviet Union does not have the ability or incentive to attack Europe or the United States. Three other threats are now more important:

1. The danger that nuclear weapons might spread to other countries
2. The danger that control over Soviet nuclear weapons might spread to irresponsible groups in a disintegrating Soviet Union

3. The danger that computer errors and false radar
   warnings might trigger a nuclear launch by military
   who fear their missiles could be destroyed in a Pearl
   Harbor–like surprise attack (called by the strategists
   a "first strike").

To counter these threats, we increase our safety if we
and the Soviets reduce our nuclear warheads from their
present total of approximately forty thousand warheads
to something on the order of two thousand. To do so
would, at one stroke, force the United States and the
U.S.S.R. to reduce greatly their capability to destroy the
other side's missiles in a surprise attack and strengthen
the global effort to halt the spread of nuclear weapons. It
would also greatly reduce the number of bombs that could
fall into the hands of mavericks. And it would save billions of dollars, freeing us to invest in people skills in the
United States; in the economic underpinnings of new democracies in Eastern Europe, the Soviet Union and Latin
America; and in reducing our deficit as well as our radio-
active pollution.
   Our political rapprochement has not stopped either
side from continuing to develop more accurate and
quicker missiles that threaten to destroy the other side's
missiles. These technological developments continue despite the fact that they are out of step with political reality
and make life ever more precarious. Furthermore, they
cost tens of billions of dollars each year, and they create a
thirst for the nuclear testing and uranium production
processes that will cause cancer and leukemia for tens of
thousands of years.
   "The [United States] must take the initiative. . . . A
combination of submarine-, air-, and land-based delivery
systems with constraints on multiple warheads would
render futile a 'counterforce' attack designed to eliminate
the other side's nuclear weapons. . . . There should be

verifiable means of ensuring that undesirable kinds of weapons 'modernization' not take place. To that end, antisatellite weapons should be banned and ceilings imposed on missile flight tests."[31] We should enforce the ABM treaty. We need a comprehensive test ban treaty. We need to cease the production of fissile materials, which are costing billions and will spread cancer for thousands of years to come.

In sum, these changes will save us many billions of dollars, and will increase our security from the real nuclear threat that is still very much with us, after the reductions that have happened.

6. End Judgmental Propaganda, Make Amends

Instead of judgmental propaganda, we can acknowledge to others that we have caused hurt and want to take actions to do better.

An especially significant feature of German writings on peacemaking is the awareness that repressed guilt distorts perceptions, is projected in virulent enemy images, sets up barriers of defensiveness and self-righteousness, and thus powerfully interferes with peacemaking. Unacknowledged guilt is not merely a moral sin but also, objectively seen, a powerful barrier to reconciliation. Therefore, honest acknowledgment is not a morally heroic option but an essential step for peacemaking.

The Workers Community of the United Church of Westphalen and Lippe confesses: "This guilt-burdened history obstructs and strains our relationship with those toward whom Germany has become guilty." It stands in the way of relations with former Western allies, and especially with the Soviet Union, "who became the greatest victim of German war rage, but up until today has remained the number one enemy." In defending what their country did to its former allies, Germans focus attention on the evil actions of the other nations, thus creating an enemy image that serves their own unacknowledged spiritual and psychological needs. "The guilt of Germany toward the Soviet Union, up until this very day, largely is repressed or denied. The guilt hardly is recognized, hardly talked about—not even to mention the 20 million victims and their descendants. This has grave political consequences for today. . . . This repression and justification syndrome largely explains the emotionally driving power" of Germans' strong, irrational anticommunism, their denunciation of the peace movement as soft on communism, their bias against disarmament negotiations, their justification of thousands of weapons designed to wreak the hideous moral evil of mass destruction against hundreds of millions of human persons, and their ideological attempts to use the churches for the crusade against communism.[32]

The East German churches ground their whole document in a call to repentance. This enables them to speak honestly of present realities that need changing, and to examine alternatives realistically and rationally. They speak of their allowing uncounted numbers of the poor in the two-thirds world to be buried in economic poverty and powerlessness. They confess racism, especially anti-semitic racism. They confess having justified war in the name of the gospel and just war theory. They insist that repentance must be social and historical as well as individual and must lead to changing hearts and changing structures and policies. They urge politicians and congregations to be open to learning repentance from grass roots movements—environmental, peace, women's and two-thirds world. Repentance does not lead nostalgically into the past but prophetically into the future. "Christians and churches have to introduce first and foremost this life-giving, liberating and future-opening character of the message of repentance into the present crisis of survival."[33] A West German book begins with a quote from Ba'al Shem Tov: "Repression holds up the process of redemption; to remember brings it closer."[34]

I have thought oftentimes that Germany is a healthier nation because of its work on remembering and repenting. But reading this material has impressed me that their approach needs to be a rational requirement for all nations. I think of my own denomination's inability to vote a resolution confessing guilt for past justification of slavery and segregation and thus get free of authoritarianism; my own nation's justification of its enormous buildup of weapons of mass destruction and the need to create a self-justifying, self-distorting, and self-imprisoning image of the enemy; the danger arising from my country's repressed guilt over Vietnam; the Carter administration's inability to speak of past U.S. error in relation to Iran and thus get the hostages free; and the destructive effect of repressing all this on our domestic politics and foreign policy. I sense the powerful and universal applicability of the truth that Germans have learned in their own experience of hell.

7. Work with Citizens' Groups for the Truth

The final step is to *participate in groups with accurate information and a voice in policy-making.* The East Germans repeatedly emphasize the liabilities of a society where governmental decisions are made in secret, information is kept from the people, and meetings to discuss issues and press for solutions are illegal. The right of participation in decisions that affect us is essential. So is the need for accurate information rather than secrecy.

> We live in a socialist land. . . . Central planning and leading, and the bureaucracy associated with it, conflicts with citizens' political participation, responsibility, and initiative. . . . The reality of our domestic politics is character-

ized by tension between state officials and population, by
pressure for conformity and the politics of exclusion on one
side, external adaptation and internal refusal on the other
side. . . . We feel our entanglement in the powers of sin and
death and live with divided conscience in a contradictory
existence.[35]

Governments often get stuck in self-justifying ideology, self-perpetuating bureaucracies, and self-interested
military-industrial complexes. They are unable to move
toward peacemaking if the people do not give them a
shove. This is true for all societies, but especially so in
East Germany, with its closed and authoritarian politics.
Lest we look self-righteously at them, not aware of the
beam in our own eyes, listen to the wise and experienced
testimony of Sidney Drell, arms control expert at Stanford University. He points out that the blocking forces
within the government need public dialogue and pressure
to get them unstuck:

> The atmospheric test ban treaty and the ABM debate that
> culminated in SALT I are two major successes in American
> nuclear weapons policy. Further, the MX program has been
> restructured and sharply cut back. . . . It is notable that
> these results were achieved with vigorous and constructive
> public participation and support.
>   By contrast, the development of the H-bomb and of
> MIRVs [were] . . . failures of our nuclear weapons policy.
> . . . I find it significant that these technical escalations were
> undertaken without public involvement or debate, and also
> without a serious effort at negotiating them away. Another
> serious setback . . . was the Senate's failure to ratify the
> SALT II treaty because of a similar lack of an involved pub-
> lic constituency.[36]

Most people feel powerless to influence their government to do peacemaking unless they are members of a
group. Alone, they lack the necessary information, connection to an effective national strategy, and mutual en-

couragement. To be helpful, groups must concentrate on empowering each member to have a participative role in the group's decisions and actions.

Conclusion

These seven principles are based on the experience and reasoning of political scientists, activists, and church leaders in Germany. But they are not unique to Germany, nor are they the exclusive property of Christians. They follow from the nature of peacemaking and the nature of human government. They are based on widespread experience, common sense, and reason.

As just war theory is an ethic of reason binding on governments, and not an ethic based only on a particular faith, so just peacemaking theory is an ethic of reason binding on governments, and not merely special pleading. Should we not conclude that governments are obligated to take these steps? Further, governments that do not take the essential steps of peacemaking in an effort to prevent war's destruction are violating their purpose and their contract with the people: to preserve our life, liberty, and pursuit of happiness.

Opposing war and building the conditions for peace are eminently reasonable. War threatens life, liberty, and the pursuit of happiness. It kills people, enchains liberty, and causes bitter misery. In the age of nuclear and chemical/biological weapons, as well as immensely more destructive conventional weapons and an annual cost of one trillion dollars for the maintenance and "improvement" of the world's arsenal, the enmity of war against life, against liberty, and against happiness has increased a thousand-fold. It is the task of governments to take effective action to build the conditions for peace.

The principles of just peacemaking theory are logically entailed in seeking to survive morally and physically in a world threatened by mass destruction. They are essential and obligatory ingredients of a government's mandate. Any government that does not fulfill these obligations does not fulfill its mandate and should be asked by the people and the churches to "turn" or to resign.

The seven steps of just peacemaking theory are not presented in the writings of the East and West German strategists as "just peacemaking theory" or as seven distinct steps. Nevertheless, the concepts are clearly there. Nor have they based these concepts on a "transforming initiatives" interpretation of the Sermon on the Mount and Romans. Nevertheless, it is intriguing how analogous these reason-based requirements of just peacemaking theory are to the transforming initiatives that we saw in our biblical study (chapters 2 and 3). In a striking way, this suggests a clear conclusion: The Sermon on the Mount is not irrelevant to the basic obligation of governments to guard and foster the lives of those fragile human beings entrusted to their care by the Creator of us all.[37] In fact, it points us to the mandate under which all of us live and have hope.

Questions for Thought

1. Are these steps inherently obligatory or merely pragmatic?

2. How are they related to a specifically Christian understanding of peacemaking?

3. Does common security suggest we pay increased attention to international organizations and their gradual strengthening by regular use to solve problems? This is called "functionalism" in international relations theory.

4. How should we understand the role of military pressure and deterrence in relation to independent initiatives and common security?

5. How can the extensive work in ethics about justice and human rights become a more crucial ingredient in the ethics of peacemaking?

6. Is there a "public ethics" analogy to the emphasis of Christian ethics on making ethics more deeply grace-based?

7. Can something like confession of sin, repentance, forgiveness, and invitation into community be translated into national politics? If so, should this be done in incremental steps? Or is this so unrealistic that it should be excluded from just peacemaking theory?

8. Should we place increased emphasis on the theme of voluntary associations, groups, and democratic participation emphasized by James Luther Adams, Walter Muelder, and their students, as well as by liberation theologians and political theorists of pluralism, consent, and democracy?

5

How Just Peacemaking
Got Rid of
the Missiles in Europe

Recall 1981.* The United States and the Soviet Union were engaged in a buildup of dangerous medium-range nuclear missiles in Europe. Afghanistan was being invaded and oppressed. The Strategic Arms Limitation (SALT) II Treaty was not being submitted for ratification. President Reagan was opposing the Nuclear Weapons Freeze Campaign and attacking the Soviet Union as the evil empire. The Soviet Union was blaming the United States for the nuclear buildup. Prospects for arms control were bleaker than they had been in years. We felt powerless, defeated, despairing. European distrust of the United States was growing visibly, focused especially by the rejection of SALT II, the buildup of medium-range Euromis-

*This is a revised version of the George and Jean Edwards Lecture and the Shalom Education Fund's John T. Conner Lecture delivered at the Louisville Presbyterian Theological Seminary on October 19, 1988, during the dedication process of the new Presbyterian Church (U.S.A.) headquarters in Louisville. I want to express my gratitude for the warm response of good people. And I want to salute the lives of great faithfulness and insight of John T. and Cathryn Connor; and Jean and George Edwards, friends for many years.

siles, new Cold War rhetoric, and a statement made by President Reagan that nuclear war in Europe was fightable. The long friendship built up by cooperation and sacrifice in World War II and the Marshall Plan was painfully crumbling.

No one expected that by the end of the 1980s we would be getting rid of all U.S. and Soviet medium-range and near–medium-range weapons on the earth. Or that we could now be turning toward dramatically improved relations with the Soviet Union and hard-won freedom and human rights in Eastern Europe. Or that President Reagan, who had been speaking so judgmentally of the Soviet Union, would return from Moscow saying we should do all we can to assist President Gorbachev and his reforms. Or that his successors would have the opportunity of teaming up with the Soviet Union to strengthen the United Nations and solve crucial regional conflicts.

The big first step in that dramatic turning of relations was the agreement to get rid of all medium-range and shorter-range nuclear missiles worldwide. Recall the historic implications of this accomplishment: reductions of over two thousand missiles; global riddance of the most destabilizing missiles in the arsenals; encouragement for the people who worked to get rid of these dangerous weapons; wide openness to intrusive verification of arms control agreements; improved relations between the United States and the Soviet Union; subsequent human rights progress in Eastern Europe and the Soviet Union; saving of billions of dollars that would have been spent in further medium-range missile buildups; prospects of strategic reductions of 50 percent; improved prospects for reducing conventional weapons in Europe; and a clear demonstration that the people, working together, can sometimes move their governments into peacemaking.

How was the INF Treaty achieved? It is a fascinating story, and we have much to learn from it—especially about the relevance of the concrete steps in peacemaking as transforming initiatives.

I should be clear that I tell the story as an engaged ethicist, a participant-observer, and not as a detached armchair theorist.[1] Throughout, however, I have sought to think analytically, critically, and ethically. My participation enables me to tell parts of the story not otherwise known. It helped turn me from a sense of the powerlessness of the people to a sense of participation and empowerment. I hope the story can give a similar sense of hope to the reader.

The Origin of the Zero Solution and Its Adoption by NATO

The proposal that solved the complex problem of the Euromissiles was the zero solution—the dramatic, bilateral, verifiable reduction of U.S. and Soviet medium-range missiles to zero. Where did this proposal come from, and how did the NATO governments come to adopt it?

Ironically, the U.S. government has claimed that the zero solution was its idea. But the authoritative account by the German scholar Lothar Rühl points out that the idea came from Germany, not from the United States, and Germany had to push strenuously to persuade the U.S. government to adopt it. "The German government of the Social Democrat and Liberal Coalition had fought for this proposal in Washington with intense energy."[2]

The authoritative book in English is Strobe Talbott's *Deadly Gambits,* based on insider interviews with members of the Reagan administration. Talbott[3] points out that the zero solution was originally proposed by Helmut Schmidt's Social Democratic Party, not by the Reagan administration. When Secretary of State Haig went to West Germany in September 1981, he was "not in the least predisposed to embrace the zero option—a European idea," and in Bonn he called its discussion "ludicrous." The zero solution was proposed in Germany because of pressure from the peace movement in Europe "as a means of dampening internal strife within the party and gaining West German public support. It caught on quickly elsewhere on the continent, but not in Washington."[4]

It was not proposed but *opposed* by Washington, reports Talbott. "In early and mid-1981, while the new Administration was wrestling with various options in Washington, hundreds of thousands of West Europeans were taking to the streets in a movement protesting the spread of nuclear weapons." Washington thought of the zero solution as a peace movement proposal and opposed it. National Security Advisor Richard Allen, in a speech to a Conservative Political Action Committee conference, said only "pacifist elements in Europe believe we can bargain the reduction of a deployed Soviet weapons system for a promise not to deploy our own offsetting system."[5]

Great pressure from the people against the Euromissiles was building in Europe. Rejecting these missiles was the first initiative advocated by Schritte zur Abrüstung. The people's strong opposition to the missiles threatened Chancellor Helmut Schmidt's Social Democratic Party with an internal split and a loss of votes. Therefore, he floated the idea of a "mutual zero solution" in his party's congress in early 1981.[6] At this stage his zero solution was merely a trial balloon; no official governmental action was taken. It was taken as an effort to put the onus on the Soviet Union, and to answer the peace movement in his own party and among the German voters.

In the United States, the conference at which Randall Forsberg first proposed the Nuclear Weapons Freeze Campaign took place in Louisville in 1979. The conference discussed the implications of NATO's upcoming decision to prepare Pershing II and cruise missiles for deployment in Europe. Several of us at the conference were well aware of the alienating processes and vicious cycles of the nuclear weapons buildup, and we saw these missiles as flagrantly pernicious. We had researched the nature of the Euromissiles in academic and foreign policy journals and concluded they would be dangerously destabilizing. Housed in a half-dozen storage sheds above ground, their location well known to the Soviet Union and well within range of Soviet missiles, the U.S. missiles would be a tempting sitting-duck target for a sudden Pearl Harbor–like attack in a time of crisis. For just this reason, it had been U.S. policy for twenty years not to locate such missiles above ground in Europe but to conceal them in submarines under the sea.

Furthermore, the Pershing II missiles were a close-in and highly accurate threat to the Soviet command and control center near Moscow. If Soviet radar or computers gave a false warning that the U.S. Euromissiles were being launched, their decision-makers would have less than eight minutes to use their missiles or lose them. But false warnings happen almost every month. Moreover, the cruise missiles were so small they could severely complicate verification, thus devastating hopes for arms control. They would be the most destabilizing missiles in our nuclear arsenal. They were the most likely trigger for a nuclear war that nobody wanted.[7]

Several considerations led the Freeze Strategy Committee to push for zero new U.S. deployments and to oppose the Soviet medium-range missiles as well:

1. The essence of the proposed freeze was a mutual halt in the nuclear buildup and then reductions by both the United States and the Soviet Union. A freeze did not mean a smaller buildup—say, half as many missiles as NATO planned—but a halt where we were, at zero.

2. The European peace movement was demanding zero deployments. We could hardly do otherwise.

3. The missiles had to be stopped at zero because it would take only a handful to be dangerously destabilizing.

4. We analyzed interests of the U.S. government. The Soviet Union had built up 200 (eventually 360) new SS-20 missiles, but the U.S. buildup had not yet begun. In order for a freeze to be in the interest of the U.S. government, the Soviet Union would have to do more than freeze; they would have to be pressured to reduce drastically, toward zero at least.

5. We analyzed Soviet interests. We concluded they would give up much more to achieve a zero solution than to achieve merely a halfway reduction in U.S. missiles:

- They knew that even a handful of Pershing II and cruise missiles could destroy the Soviet command-and-control center near Moscow.
- They knew these missiles' dangerous, destabilizing nature, and how many false warnings had occurred in their radar and computer systems. No halfway limits would allay this danger.
- World War II had made them fear war against their heartland, especially with nuclear weapons launched from German soil. The German assault on Stalingrad is still a bitter memory.
- They insisted that when they pulled their missiles out from Cuba in the Cuban missile crisis, and the United States then pulled out our Thor and Jupiter missiles from Europe, we had tacitly agreed not to put any missiles in Europe that could reach their homeland.

Because of these powerful Soviet interests, none of which could be met by a halfway solution, we had a realistic chance to achieve almost infinitely better Soviet reductions if the United States would offer *zero* deployments in return. This analysis turned out to be more accurate than we knew. The Soviet Union was unwilling to give up much for the halfway reductions the U.S. government proposed, but they were willing to give up all their medium-range missiles to achieve zero U.S. missiles.[8]

This approach dramatically confirms the principle *"Affirm your enemy's valid interests."*

In the years 1981 to 1982, while on sabbatical leave in Germany, I was the Freeze Campaign's International Task Force representative to the European peace movement. In late August 1981, I attended the annual meeting of the Christian Council on Approaches to Defense and Disarmament, a select group of scholars and officials interested in Christian ethics and international relations.

General Wolf Graf von Baudissin was there. He had served as commander of the NATO Defense College and deputy chief of staff in SHAPE (Supreme Headquarters of the Allied Powers in Europe) and was the founder and leader of the Institute for Peace Research and Security Policy in Hamburg. He had friends and contacts in the West German government. I knew him, respected him, and had read articles he had published criticizing the Euromissiles.

Sensing it was a propitious moment, I asked if we could set a time to talk. He agreed. But who was I to be suggesting a transforming initiative by the West German government? One peacemaking step is to pray, and here was a time to pray intensely.

When we met, I asked General von Baudissin what he thought of the Pershing II and ground-launched cruise missiles. "The best outcome," he said,

> would be dramatic Soviet reductions so these missiles would not have to be deployed. Second best would be a United States buildup in submarines under the ocean, invulnerable to Soviet attack. The worst option was the present plan to place the Pershing missiles above ground, vulnerable, and only on German soil. All allies, not only Germans, must share a high level of vulnerability. That would make any intention to start a war clearly unreasonable and provide more strategic stability.

I suggested the U.S. and Soviet governments were stuck on a deployment track. They were deadlocked and could not produce a feasible negotiating proposal.[9] If Germany relied on urging the superpowers to develop a remedy, it would get no action. "Could the German government take an initiative, develop a feasible solution itself, and then propose it to the other governments?"

"It would be difficult for Germany to take such an initiative itself," he mused, "because Germany should not take the lead on nuclear weapons."

"Could Germany join with another NATO member in taking an initiative?"

"Yes," he replied, "perhaps with the Dutch."

I urged earnestly that if Germany did develop its own initiative, it should set the level at zero Pershing IIs and ground-launched cruise missiles and should specify how far the Soviet Union should reduce to justify zero new Western missiles.

General von Baudissin has told me subsequently that he is not aware of anyone's suggesting such an initiative for a zero solution prior to our conversation. He took the idea back to his research institute for discussion. The experts there liked it. He then took it up with a Social Democratic leader in the federal government in Bonn. He also favored it and proposed it to the government. They debated it and decided for it.[10]

During this time of discussion, on October 10, 1981, the largest demonstration in modern German history filled Bonn, West Germany's capital, to overflowing. My sons and I were there, along with a quarter of a million other people. So many came that we could not get near enough to hear the loudspeakers until one hour into the rally. This was the first in a series of rallies in the capitals of Western Europe. Over a million people protested against the U.S. and Soviet medium-range missiles. It made a powerful impression. Polls showed most Europeans supported the rallies and opposed the missiles.[11] The governments were feeling the pressure from the people. David Cortright, former executive director of SANE and then SANE/Freeze, has recently written an excellent description of the extent of the pressure from the European peace movements, showing from the writings of U.S. and European governmental leaders how the peace movements were critical in achieving the zero solution.[12]

So on October 21, 1981, at the meeting of the NATO Defense Ministers in Gleneagle, Scotland, the German and Dutch ministers initiated the zero solution proposal: NATO would agree to zero U.S. deployments if the Soviet Union would reduce their medium-range missiles to zero. All twelve defense ministers favored the initiative except U.S. Defense Secretary Caspar Weinberger, who opposed it. The Dutch Defense Minister credited the people with "helping push the 'zero-level language' through this thirtieth meeting of the NATO Nuclear Planning Group."[13]

The Washington Post of November 20, 1981, reported that after the meeting Secretary Weinberger and his aide, Richard Perle, toured the European capitals, including Germany. Apparently they were told forcefully that if they did not switch their position and announce support for the zero solution, they could not count on Europe to deploy the INF missiles. The people's opposition was too strong. Returning to Washington, Weinberger and Perle persuaded President Reagan to favor the zero solution. As Strobe Talbott reports, Perle decided to favor it because "to judge from public-opinion polls, parliamentary debates, and demonstrations in the streets, . . . the United States was hellbent on loading the continent up with new missiles and starting a new arms race. Now the United States would be able to shift the onus back onto the Soviets."[14] Again, the people were the key.

And so, on November 18, 1981, President Reagan announced the United States would support the zero solution.

Where did the zero solution come from? It came from the people—from the peace movement in Germany and Holland, from Helmut Schmidt's effort to respond to that movement, from General von Baudissin, and from the U.S. Nuclear Weapons Freeze Campaign.

Why and how was it officially adopted by the U.S. government? Because pressure from the people was exerted through the European governments. Because of a strategy of initiatives, people organized in groups, pushing governments to talk, and affirming each side's valid security interests.

Why did the zero solution endure as U.S. policy? Powerful Reagan advisers pushed for *other* solutions: the "walk in the woods" proposal of partial reductions; settling for three hundred on each side; the "zero plus" proposal. But the zero solution had lasting power. Why? There were three reasons, according to Strobe Talbott:[15]

1. A halfway solution would never satisfy Europeans. Even a handful of these missiles would encounter powerful opposition.
2. President Reagan liked the zero solution because it was a simple concept the people could readily understand. Here Reagan and the Freeze agreed. Both wanted straightforward and dramatic proposals readily understandable by the people at the grass roots.
3. The administration believed the Soviet Union would never accept the zero solution. Therefore, it was the most effective way to anesthetize the peace movement, put the blame on the Soviet Union, and get the missiles deployed.

The Freeze Campaign also considered the Soviet Union unlikely to accept the zero solution and knew it was intended to weaken the peace movement. Therefore, most greeted it with lukewarm enthusiasm. However, some saw that it committed the United States *for the first time* to the possibility of zero Euromissiles and strengthened that possibility and expectation in people's minds. It put zero on the table for everyone to look at when other options failed. And it put that possibility before the Soviet Union, posing the question, "How far are you willing to reduce? You *could achieve zero* if you became more flexible."

We now had the United States officially favoring a zero solution. Could we do anything to entice the Soviet Union toward zero?

How the Soviet Union Came to Accept the Zero Solution

The full story of how the Soviet government came to propose the zero solution at the Reykjavik summit is, of course, unknown. But I can tell at least some parts of the story the media missed.

In 1983 the Strategy Committee of the Freeze Campaign realized the negotiations were deadlocking. The missiles were moving toward inevitable deployment. It was time for us to take our own independent initiative. So we wrote letters to Soviet leader Andropov and to President Reagan, composing them carefully to take their interests seriously. We wanted to move them off dead center.

We said there was too much distrust and inertia for mere verbal offers to succeed. Action was needed—independent initiatives. We urged the Soviet Union to take five specific steps. These initiatives might get Congress to hold up funding for U.S. deployments and give time for a negotiated solution, we suggested. Our proposal had strength because millions supported the Freeze—and because European peace movement leaders added their support, sending letters seconding our initiative.

On October 27, *Pravda* printed Andropov's answer to

"some people in the West [who] say that the Soviet Union already now could carry out unilateral" initiatives.[16] He expressed some discomfort with unilateral initiatives but said yes to all five initiatives we had recommended:

- He destroyed all SS-5 missiles without waiting for negotiations.
- He announced a schedule of step-by-step reductions if the United States halted.
- He would reduce to 140 missiles (later 120) as the end point of those reductions if the United States halted.
- He would "liquidate the missiles instead of redeploying them."
- He would deploy no more SS-20 missiles in the eastern Soviet Union.

This would be a reduction from the historic level of 750 megatons of explosive power to 53 megatons. It moved the Soviet Union a long way *toward* zero. And here is where some critics of the Freeze have missed a crucial point: The Freeze did not simply work to halt *U.S.* deployment of Euromissiles unilaterally. We pressed the Soviet Union to take its own initiatives, to move toward zero. As Strobe Talbott's account makes clear, Andropov's response was the best Soviet offer until Gorbachev's offer of zero at Reykjavik.

Our letter also recalled President Eisenhower's and President Kennedy's independent initiatives in halting U.S. nuclear weapons testing above ground, resulting in the successful Atmospheric Test Ban Treaty. We were seeking to persuade the Soviet Union, as well as the United States, to adopt the strategy of independent initiatives.

Later, Daniel Ellsberg of the Freeze Strategy Committee and others from the Center for Defense Information urged another Soviet initiative: Halt *underground* nuclear testing as Eisenhower and Kennedy had halted aboveground testing. The Soviets agreed, halting for nineteen months and asking for reciprocation, thus adopting the strategy of independent initiatives.

Meanwhile, the Freeze adopted a strategy of persuading Congress to take its own independent initiatives. Congress could cut off money for parts of the nuclear buildup, thus bringing them to a halt, as long as the Soviet Union also halted. Thus we could achieve a mutual freeze step by step.

Congress was closer to the people than the White House was, and we had a much better chance of success there. And the strategy was veto-proof: If Congress appropriated no money for nuclear testing, the president could not veto money into existence. He *could* veto the whole military spending bill, but even that drastic action would not create money for testing.

At first, members of Congress were reluctant to take the lead on foreign policy. But we pointed out that Congress has constitutional responsibility to appropriate money. Congress could take the initiative, halting money for key elements in the nuclear buildup, contingent on the Soviet Union's verifiable reciprocation.

Congress gradually adopted this strategy, with the House moving more strongly than the Senate. The House of Representatives voted to stop money for

1. Any MX missiles beyond the fifty in the pipeline
2. Any missile deployments exceeding SALT II Treaty limits
3. One third of the Star Wars program
4. Star Wars tests violating the ABM Treaty
5. Half of the chemical weapons program
6. Contra Aid for the war in Nicaragua
7. Any increase in the military budget
8. Flight testing of antisatellite missiles (apparently slamming shut this Pandora's box in space)
9. Underground nuclear testing.

The U.S. Senate was beginning to agree with some of the House's funding halts. Eventually they agreed to all but halting underground testing. And the Soviet Union was halting as well. The strategy of initiatives was beginning to achieve major parts of the freeze without waiting for slow, drawn-out negotiations.

As Elizabeth Drew reports in *The New Yorker*,[17] based on insider interviews, the congressional initiatives were putting pressure on the White House. By now, Mikhail Gorbachev had become the Soviet leader and was adopting the strategy of independent initiatives in dramatic fashion, withdrawing large numbers of tanks and troops from Eastern Europe and withdrawing completely from Afghanistan, decreasing the offensive threat but retaining strong defenses. His initiatives were winning worldwide praise.

President Reagan still had never held a summit meeting with a Soviet leader, and we were not negotiating about the Euromissiles. He was judging the Soviet Union as the focus of evil in the world.

Drew reports that a powerful group of administration officials were advising him not to meet with Soviet leaders and not to negotiate resolutions of alleged Soviet violations of SALT II. A meeting could hinder the momentum for a military buildup. But now other advisers were saying he was losing credibility in Congress. Congress was taking the initiative in its own hands and halting money for the buildup. This trend could expand, halting other weapons programs. He needed to reclaim some initiative. President Reagan compromised by holding a "get-acquainted" summit in Geneva in 1985, without prepared proposals to negotiate. He came away saying Gorbachev is sincere about arms control. His rhetoric began changing in response to the pressure of Congress and public opinion and the experience of talking personally with Gorbachev.

To make peace, you have to talk, but the United States

and the Soviet Union had not been talking. The Freeze
congressional strategy prodded the president to talk. And
now we were prodding for some results. Gorbachev had
said he would come to the United States for a second
summit *if* there was a prospect of achieving a significant
agreement. But the administration saw no prospect of
reaching an agreement, and Gorbachev was "holding off
setting a date for the meeting in the United States on the
ground that he did not want to (and probably could not
afford to) attend another one where there was no sub-
stantive progress on arms control. The 'smile-and-a-
handshake' Geneva summit, apparently, had not stood
Gorbachev in good stead with his Politburo colleagues."[18]

By now the Senate was coming closer to supporting the
House's initiatives. The joint House-Senate Conference
Committee had set the date for its meeting to iron out the
differences. So the administration scheduled another
summit meeting at Reykjavik for the very day after the
Conference Committee meeting, urging Congress, "Don't
tie our hands just before we negotiate with the Soviets."
The strategy worked, halfway. The Conference Committee did partly back off. But the strategy also worked in
reverse. The administration was now under pressure to
produce something significant from the summit meeting.
So it was a propitious time for Gorbachev to propose his
own surprising initiative. He picked up the exact words
from the German-Dutch zero solution and proposed that
the Soviet Union would reduce to zero if the United
States would.

Now the problem was, How do you take yes for an answer? Many in the administration "had qualms about entirely eliminating America's nuclear-missile deterrence in
Europe."[19] But there was pressure from the people not to
say no.

Another problem was that Gorbachev linked the zero
solution to a halt in space testing of Star Wars. The Soviet

Union would not demolish key parts of its deterrent if the United States continued to develop weapons to destroy the remaining deterrent. But President Reagan was committed to Star Wars. So Reykjavik ended in temporary failure. Once again, the Freeze and Congress came to the rescue. With the encouragement of the people, Congress was placing crucial limits on Star Wars. One limit was to reduce the funding. More important was the agreement of both houses of Congress to refuse any money for Star Wars tests violating the traditional interpretation of the ABM Treaty. The Soviet Union then announced that because Star Wars was being handled for the time being in Congress, they would accept the zero solution without requiring administration agreement on Star Wars. Thus we got the solution of zero medium-range missiles worldwide with extensive inspection and verification, and greatly increased hopes for other dramatic agreements.

Now Germany had to decide whether to support the zero solution. Its government was no longer Helmut Schmidt's Social Democrats but Helmut Kohl's Christian Democrats, in coalition with Genscher's Free Democrats. Kohl was waffling. His defense minister, Woerner, opposed the zero solution. But the people were for it. Each November 30,000 churches and other groups in Germany, East and West, had sponsored the Friedensdekade or "Ten Days of Peace," with forums and prayers about the Euromissiles and peacemaking. When *Der Spiegel* polled the German people, they found that an astounding 92 percent favored the zero solution. In the state elections in Hamburg and Rhineland-Pfalz the parties favoring the zero solution gained dramatically, while the conservative party of Helmut Kohl lost dramatically. Kohl saw the political handwriting on the wall and said the zero solution was a great idea. Again, the people were crucial.

What interests led Gorbachev to propose the zero solution? First, the Soviet Union desperately needed trade and economic stimulus. That depended on good relations with Western Europe, whose main stumbling block was the conflict over the Euromissiles.[20]

Second, he wanted improved relations and trade with Asia, which had now become aroused about SS-20s targeted at them. It was while he was in Indonesia that Gorbachev first announced his support for the global zero solution.

Third, he wanted to stop the U.S. buildup of Pershing and cruise missiles.

Fourth, he needed a quick foreign policy success for domestic political support. Economic improvements would take years to show results. A dramatic treaty, an improvement in relations, and a successful summit would provide a big boost.

Finally, he expected that the United States would say yes. As Elizabeth Drew has pointed out, Soviet leaders do not like to climb out on a limb that will be sawed off. They do not like to make dramatic summit offers when the likely answer will be no. Because the peace movement had persuaded NATO to adopt the zero solution in 1981 and had worked to persuade Congress to take nine initiatives cutting off funding and pressuring Reagan, Gorbachev now had far better reason to expect he would have an answering partner in the United States—either the president or the people and the Congress.

The Soviet Union was learning the strategy of independent initiatives, beginning as early as Brezhnev and Andropov but bursting into bloom with Gorbachev. In June 1987 Schritte zur Abrüstung could list nine independent initiatives the Soviet Union had taken recently. They expressed surprise: They thought Western governments would learn the strategy more quickly, but the Soviet Union was now doing it dramatically![21] The Soviet initiative of accepting the zero solution was part of a new strategy, a flurry of independent initiatives.

If all the United States had to do to persuade the Soviet Union to accept the zero solution was to demonstrate we would succeed in building up Pershing and cruise missiles, then all the conditions were met in late 1983. The missiles were in fact being installed. But the Soviet Union was not picking up the zero solution. Other factors were necessary: a new leader, Gorbachev, emphasizing economic needs and opening toward the West; learning and adopting the new strategy of independent initiatives; new pressure from people and the Congress finally pushing the president toward summit meetings, a change in rhetoric, and reaching agreements; and congressional limitations on Star Wars funding. Those conditions were met in 1987. Gorbachev proposed the zero solution in 1987, not 1983. The buildup was not a sufficient cause; the people and Congress and independent initiatives were necessary before Gorbachev would accept the zero solution.

One of the incentives for the Soviet Union to accept the zero solution was to stop the U.S. buildup, as the peace-through-strength argument urges. However, this response hardly proves the Freeze wrong; it confirms the Freeze's consistent theme: A freeze is in both sides' national interest because it is the only way to stop the other side's buildup. The Freeze was designed to affirm each side's valid interest in stopping the other side's buildup.

The Freeze knew the usual history of such "bargaining chip" pressure: New missiles develop their own political, economic, and ideological constituencies and almost never get cashed in for the bargain of a mutual reduction; instead they stimulate the other side's buildup. Thus on the one hand, the Freeze opposed the momentum of the new U.S. weapons systems, hoping to make a halt at zero politically possible for the West. On the other hand, the Freeze worked to achieve Soviet reductions by creating a realistic hope of stopping the U.S. missiles at zero if they would reduce enough. The strategy had to be complex be-

cause the reality was complex. The goal was to make the
alternative to a buildup possible—a mutual reduction to
zero. Nothing more would do.

This history shows the causal interplay was more complex than some assume. In the actual interaction, with its
complexity, the people had more of the power and took
more initiative than is usually perceived.

The media usually report only what finally happens and
ignore the efforts of the people in advance of the achievement. The government usually has an interest in down-
playing the role of the people, both to decrease the
pressure and criticism it feels from the people and to try
to take full credit itself. The president's advisers give the
president credit, not themselves or others, if they expect
to have the president's ear in the future. Thus the official
account disempowers the people and places all the power
in the hands of the president and the special interests.
That is not by accident. Such an attribution serves their
interests, but it does not serve the empowerment of the
people. Nor does it serve the purpose of accurate understanding or of peacemaking. Governments get stuck in
their own ideological rivalries and elite power interests.
They need a push from the people to get their peacemaking engine started. The facts of causal connection are
more complex than "the president decided, so it happened."

It is too simple to say that the problem was how to get
the Soviet Union to the bargaining table. The problem
was bilateral: *Two sides* had to come to the table with feasible proposals. It is naive to assume that the U.S. government is always naturally putting forth helpful proposals,
and the only obstacle is the blocking forces in the Soviet
Union, Iraq, or whatever adversary comes along. U.S.
negotiators, too, have often been blocked by forces in our
government.

The Freeze Campaign knew it was difficult to pressure

the Soviet government directly; our primary influence would be in the United States. Nor could the people of the Soviet Union prod their government as directly as we can ours. The first task was to get NATO and the U.S. government to take an initiative for a mutual, bilateral halt at zero. That would then pressure the Soviet Union to move toward zero, or there would be no deal. It had to be mutual. Thus through our government we could pressure the Soviet government—along with the pressures of their economy, their interest in better relations, their interest in stopping our buildup, and their interest in a more stable nuclear balance less likely to get out of control and kill us all.

But the U.S. buildup is not enough to explain the success of the INF Treaty. Nor is the buildup enough to guide us toward greater strategic reductions, a comprehensive test ban, and a cost-saving conventional balance. Buildups are nothing new; they are the same old story. Until the zero solution, the nuclear arms race has been just one dangerous buildup after another. Historically, buildups have not led to reductions but to counter-buildups. That is how we got to thirty thousand nuclear weapons on each side, costing us fifty billion dollars per year: one buildup after another.

In political science, if you always see buildups being followed by counter-buildups, and then suddenly you notice a buildup followed by a *reduction,* you do not just say, "*This time* a buildup caused a reduction." You ask, "*What was new* that led to a different outcome this time?"

Three things were new: the strategy of independent initiatives, the pressure of the people, and Gorbachev's perception of the needs and opportunities of his situation.

One cannot help but notice more than a little irony. The Reagan administration, which worked to undermine the Freeze Campaign, was led to its greatest foreign policy success by the very Freeze Campaign it had opposed. And

the Freeze Campaign, which had been so maligned by
President Reagan, was given its greatest success because
President Reagan agreed that the solution should be simple and readily communicated to the people. Both were
thinking the key is the grass roots, the people. God works
in mysterious ways, God's wonders to perform. Thanks be
to God. Thanks also to the people.

Let us give some credit to the Reagan and Gorbachev
administrations for their eventual role in this drama, in
spite of their initial intentions. They each were led, perhaps grudgingly, to take some surprising initiatives. Let us
at the same time tell the truth: Both governments spent
many billions of dollars and rubles for missiles destined
for destruction, money unjustly lifted from the pockets of
millions of people who needed education, food, homes,
transportation, and health care.

As we seek to give some credit to the eventual role both
governments played, let us ask both governments to be
magnanimous enough to give some credit to the people
for their initiating role and their steady prodding. Subsequent administrations and new Congresses will need that
prodding in the new era into which we are turning, when
economic and ecological needs will be more important,
and cutting military costs will be all the more essential.

Questions for Thought

The following is a correlation between the INF story
and the steps of peacemaking. Look it over to see how
many of the correlations you noticed. Are there factors
that you think should be added to any of the steps, or any
that should be dropped?

1. *Affirm valid interests and security partnership:* After
analyzing the interests of the United States and Soviet
Union, the Freeze campaign predicted each would give a
great deal to achieve zero Euromissiles.

2. *Take independent initiatives; don't wait for negotiations:* The following initiatives were taken:

- General von Baudissin and the German-Dutch initiative
- Andropov's learning to take independent initiatives
- The example of Eisenhower's and Kennedy's initiatives
- Effectiveness of the congressional freeze strategy
- The congressional initiative, the key to stopping Star Wars space testing.

3. *Talk: Seek negotiations, using methods of conflict resolution:* The initiative strategies adopted by Congress and Gorbachev pressed a reluctant president to agree finally to summit meetings.

4. *Seek human rights and justice for all, especially the powerless:* The cost of building missiles destined only for destruction was theft from the needy.

5. *Realistically acknowledge vicious cycles and the need to participate in the peacemaking process:* Those who saw the threat of the Euromissiles and committed themselves to stopping them were scholars and activists who clearly acknowledged the alienating, vicious cycle of the arms race. They also rightly perceived that the superpower negotiations were deadlocking and independent initiatives were needed. They acknowledged that *both* governments were stuck in processes of alienation, and the solution must affirm both sides' interests bilaterally. This took some grace. They sought to avoid the self-righteousness of (let us confess our sins) hawks and doves.

6. *Less judgmentalism, more acknowledgment that we have caused hurt and want to do better:* The Nuclear Weapons Freeze Campaign and the European peace movement were aware that the causes of buildup were mutual, involving errors by the Soviet Union in its SS-20 buildup and by the West in its Euromissile buildup. That helped us envision mutually affirming initiatives. This was part of the spirit of the teaching and praying about

peacemaking that went on each November in thirty thousand churches in Germany. Most Freeze founders and leaders are persons of faith and know we all need forgiveness. President Reagan first judged the Soviet Union as the source of evil in the world, then proclaimed that Gorbachev was serious about arms control, and later said we should do what we can to support him. Many need to confess the self-righteousness of our judging him.

7. *Work with groups and churches:* In Europe peacemaking groups and churches stimulated the German-Dutch proposal of the zero solution and then pushed the United States to accept it. In the United States they pushed for congressional initiatives. In Germany they prodded Helmut Kohl to support the zero solution.

6

The Christian Origin
of Human Rights

An essential peacemaking step is the struggle for justice: Injustice is a major cause of war; justice is an essential ingredient of peace. In the latter half of the twentieth century, justice has become concrete in the almost universal struggle for human rights. The people press for human rights and push their governments to do likewise.[1]

A dramatic, worldwide convergence of opinion on *human rights* has blossomed forth. The United Nations' Universal Declaration of Human Rights was signed by almost every nation. Third-world peoples have increasingly cast their struggle for justice in the language of human rights. Martin Luther King, Jr., and the civil rights movement in the United States injected great energy into the struggle, and their nonviolent methods and demands for human rights have spread worldwide. Since *Pacem in Terris* and the Second Vatican Council, the Roman Catholic Church has emphasized human rights as its norm for social ethics and has devoted much energy to the struggle for human rights East and West, North and South. Protestants of various kinds, and my own denomination, the Baptists, once pioneers in human rights, have been influenced by Martin Luther King, Jr., and Jimmy Carter to recover their tradition. More recently the central demand of the remarkable revolutions in East Germany, Czechoslovakia, Poland, and other Eastern European nations was for human rights, as promised in the Helsinki Accords. There is now a growing awareness that respect for the human rights of all persons is essential if tensions between ethnic nationalities in the Soviet Union and elsewhere are not to erupt repeatedly in violence. The same is true of the Middle East.

But three errors weaken Christian support for human rights. First, our definition of human rights is too narrow. In the United States, we emphasize the freedoms of speech and press, religious liberty, and freedom from torture or arbitrary imprisonment but de-emphasize economic rights to health care, housing, food, and jobs.

Second, many become confused when they try to relate Christian ethics to public ethics as part of a pluralistic society. They have difficulty explaining how human rights are grounded both in Christian faith and in a public ethic for all people regardless of their faith.

Third, few know the history of the concept of human rights. Many think the idea came from the rationalism of the Enlightenment, and thus human rights are seen as a product only of rationalistic and individualistic reasoning.[2] For example, in eighteenth-century Germany people first heard of human rights not from the Puritan Revolution in England but from the slogans of the French Revolution. Therefore, human rights were labeled secular and unchristian, especially by privileged groups that opposed democratic change.[3]

With this viewpoint, it seems surprising and even ironic that the nonviolent human rights revolutions of 1989 in Eastern Europe were led by groups in churches. The churches' determined struggle to defend their right to religious liberty provided essential space and courage for human rights groups to meet and organize, against their governments' objections. Church members provided many of the supporters for Poland's solidarity movement and East Germany's "revolution of the candles." If we knew the history of the origin of human rights, we would not be surprised to see human rights spring from religious conviction.

In fact, the concept and the term "human rights" originated *more than a half-century prior to the Enlightenment* and the French Revolution, among the free churches at the time of the Puritan Revolution, as an affirmation of the religious liberty of all persons. The concept was based not only in natural reason but also in Christian struggle for liberty, justice, and peace for all. Knowing the story enables Christians to identify with nonchristians in the struggle for human rights. Awareness of the story makes it clear that human rights should not be defined narrowly, including only those rights our society emphasizes. Furthermore, this heritage *suggests clear and extensive biblical and experiential grounding for human rights,* some of which is being used in present-day Christian ethics, but some of which we can learn from in new ways. To recover this lost part of our heritage will strengthen us in our current struggle.

The background of this story lies in the time of the English Revolution. From 1629 to 1640 King Charles I refused to let Parliament even meet. He had been restoring some kingly privileges and alienating many Christians by favoring some churches over others. There was fierce rivalry between Anglican, Presbyterian, Roman Catholic, and free churches. There were mounting tensions over taxes, government-controlled trade monopolies, a bad economy, the establishment of religion, censorship of the press, the authority of king versus Parliament, and the authority of common law versus monarchy. When Parliament finally did meet, it used its power to provide or deny funds (just as in the Nuclear Weapons Freeze Campaign congressional strategy of the 1980s), to deprive the king of funds unless he agreed to limits on his power. King Charles refused.

In October 1641 a rebellion broke out in Ireland. Massacres and atrocities and seizing of Protestant property in the name of King Charles exacerbated all the polarization in England. In November and December Parliament demanded the king submit the names of his cabinet advisers for Parliament's approval, and relinquish control of the army to Parliament. In the first week of January 1642 the king tried unsuccessfully to arrest five leaders of Parliament, and on August 22 he began war against Parliament. The New Model Army, led by Oliver Cromwell and Lord Fairfax and comprised of soldiers who were religious enthusiasts as well as skilled fighters, defended Parliament. Parliament was mostly Presbyterian, but the army was mostly Independent (Baptist, Congregationalist, and others). By June 1645 the people's army had won the decisive victory, although the war dragged on another year.

After the war came an economic depression. In June 1647 war broke out again briefly between the army and supporters of Parliament over army pay, the extent of reform, and religious liberty. In the meantime, the Leveller Movement had developed, seeking to persuade the people and the army to support genuine democracy. A short civil war broke out from spring through fall 1648, as the king made new alliances and rose up to fight again. Finally Parliament had Charles beheaded January 30, 1649. But "the Long Parliament" neither adopted the democracy demanded by the Levellers nor even allowed a vote on its own reelection, staying in office for twelve years, 1640 to 1653. Finally in 1653, after some confusion, Cromwell was installed as Lord Protector.[4] All this rapid change was both the cause and the result of a plethora of new ideas about politics, religion, economics, and science.[5] The times stimulated some of the most far-reaching political thought of human history.

Richard Overton, Pioneer of Human Rights

The story of Richard Overton's development of the concept of human rights is surprisingly unknown. You can find one sentence written sixty years ago by the great scholar of Puritan literature, William Haller: "The task of turning the statement of the law of nature into a ringing declaration of the rights of man fell to Richard Overton."[6] If you read Richard Tuck's philosophically technical history of human rights very carefully, you learn it was the Levellers who first argued for human rights as belonging to all human persons, and Richard Overton offered "undoubtedly the best statements of the Leveller case."[7] Yet his story is all but lost. Few seem to know how he came to develop the concept or his grounding in the biblical sources. Therefore, I want to trace the development of his thought step by step so we can track the origin of his concept of human rights with clarity and accuracy.

Our first historical record of Richard Overton places him in the midst of a small group of Puritans who left the Church of England in 1607 to form two congregations, one led by John Robinson and the other by John Smyth. Faced with severe persecution, they fled to Holland in 1608. In 1620 part of the Robinson group came to North America on the Mayflower, the Pilgrim founders of what is now the United States. The Smyth group remained in Holland, living on property owned by the Waterlander Mennonites. Convinced that the Bible teaches believer's baptism, they became Baptists. In 1615 Overton applied for membership and was baptized into Smyth's General Baptist group just after it had been accepted for merger with the Waterlander Mennonite congregation.[8]

Overton thus had interdenominational experience. He also had international experience. Not only had he lived in Holland, which he saw as a model for toleration, but he

wrote Latin and German,[9] and probably had experienced
the Thirty Years' War in Germany—a war fought between
Protestant and Catholic princes over which religion
would dominate. Overton argued passionately against
such wars and for peacemaking.

To be accepted for baptism in 1615, he wrote a statement of his faith, in Latin.[10] It is orthodox and trinitarian,
with a few special Mennonite and Baptist emphases. Four
themes in this statement foreshadow his reasons for giving voice to human rights:

1. *All humankind is created in the image of God, and
Christ died for all*—"the people of all and every nation in
the whole universe."[11] The General Baptists got their
name from their insistence that Christ died for *all humankind generally,* rejecting the Particular Baptist teaching
that Christ died only for particular predestined persons.

2. *Christ is the norm* for the church, as witnessed to by
the New Testament, and not the traditions of the hierarchy. "His church ought to be governed by no other in
heaven, earth, or hell, but by himself." The sole lordship
of Christ was a favorite Baptist and Mennonite theme.

3. For an advocate of tolerance and peace, Overton had
a *fairly antagonistic spirit toward hierarchical traditions:*
"All human traditions and opinions are to be pursued
with cordial hatred . . . and avoided." Having been converted from the Anglican church "by the Word and Holy
Spirit of God, I give up all its errors, and renounce its
maternity, and with the whole soul and mind, desire to
enter by baptism into the true church."

4. The Baptist confession of 1612 was the first in history
to affirm the Mennonite advocacy of *freedom of conscience and separation of church and state.*[12] It opposes
persecution. It advocates *love for enemies, peace, and nonviolence,* by rulers as well as church members. It commits
the church to *serve the needs of the poor:* In necessities, all
things are to be in common (Acts 4:32). The 1612 confes-

sion says there should be both male and female deacons, whose task is to minister to the poor and the sick.

For the next twenty-seven years, Overton's thoughts are lost to history. But by 1642 he is back in London, writing and printing booklets. His first two are satires in the name of the people against ecclesiastical hierarchy and their various symbols of authority and schemes of greed.[13] He attacks any hierarchy that denies religious liberty and other rights and persecutes the faithful while feeding its own greed for money and luxury. He asks us

> To see such millions frying in the fire
> while this stern tyrant gnashed his teeth with ire,
> the skins of saints, their tongues, their eyes and ears
> were at sale with floods of brinish tears.[14]

His implicit themes in these satires are the sole authority of Christ versus ecclesiastical hierarchy, peace and religious liberty versus religious persecution and religious wars,[15] and believer's baptism versus infant baptism.

In January 1644 Overton published "Man's Mortality," an extended argument against the hierarchy's traditional teaching of the immortality of the soul. His title page summarizes the argument: " 'Tis proved, both theologically and philosophically, that whole man (as a rational creature) is a compound wholly mortal, contrary to that common distinction of soul and body: and that the present going of the soul into heaven or hell is a mere fiction: and that at the resurrection is the beginning of our immortality, and then condemnation, and salvation, and not before." Overton supported his case by extensive biblical study, by reasoned philosophical argument, and by the science of anatomy.

Because he used reason and science, as well as Bible, to attack tradition, some have called him a skeptic, a secular thinker. For example, William Godwin, "who had a violent prejudice against" Overton,[16] and W. K. Jordan and

William Haller, writing over a half-century ago,[17] assumed that to attack the traditional teaching of the immortality of the soul is to attack all revealed religion and to supplant it with secular reason. This assumption may have diverted people from noticing his biblically based arguments for human rights.

So we need to be clear that when Overton attacked the notion of an immortal soul trapped in a perishable body, he was attacking a traditional Platonic idea, not a biblical one. His biblical scholarship was impressively accurate. Christian theologians now agree with him: The biblical teaching is not the immortality of the soul but the resurrection of the body. Resurrection is not a natural human possession but God's gift of redemption. The self is not a soul trapped in a body but a psychosomatic unity. In other words, what Overton was arguing is now understood as biblical orthodoxy.

Does Overton's use of reason against tradition make him a skeptic, a secular thinker? I think not. Calvin praised reason as well as biblical study, and so did Erasmus and many Anabaptists, as well as Augustine and Aquinas—all people of faith. Overton's reasoned conclusions do not contradict his biblical study but rather support it. The New Science Movement of the 1640s and 1650s in England advocated personal experience and empirical research over authoritarian tradition, the unity of theological and philosophical truth, and democratic reform and justice for the poor, as Overton did, and in all these it paralleled and was influenced by the Puritan reform movement.[18] My own reading agrees with H. N. Brailsford's careful assessment that Overton's teaching "that the soul perishes at death and comes to life again only with the body in the miracle of the resurrection had been for more than a century the tenet of the Anabaptists. . . . He was no 'unbeliever,' yet he had strong rationalist tendencies."[19]

For Anabaptists, baptism into the death and resurrection of Christ was their way of stating their faith. They were often put to death for it. They died identifying with Christ in his death and hoping in his resurrection. For Overton to emphasize death and resurrection was no mere rational skepticism; he was working out the meaning of his original baptism into Christ's death and resurrection, and God's equalitarian offer of grace to all persons, versus hierarchical traditions.[20]

The Arraignment of Mr. Persecution

Overton wrote with striking humor, satire, and imagination, and the consensus is that he was the best writer among the Levellers—the original movement to establish democracy. His wit and style come to a colorful climax in his masterpiece, *The Arraignment of Mr. Persecution,* which deserves to be a classic. Its arguments develop the themes we saw at the time of his baptism in Holland in 1615. He personifies the practice of religious persecution as "Mr. Persecution" and puts him on trial

- For being an arch traitor against Christ and his commands
- For causing division and strife in nations
- For setting son against father and friend against friend in wars that embroil them in each other's blood
- For consuming nations' wealth and destroying their cities in war
- For depriving Congregationalists and Baptists, who had hazarded their lives for the democratic revolution, of their just liberty.[21]

At the preliminary inquest, ten persons bring charges. The first is Mr. Sovereignty of Christ, who says Mr. Persecution is an "arch-traitor" to the rule of Jesus Christ over the consciences of humankind (p. 4). Christ is "sole Head

and King forever over human consciences." He charges
"the kings of the earth to let the tares and the wheat grow
together in the field of the world until the harvest day of
judgment" (Matt. 13:25). Christ's command that we toler-
ate both wheat and tares was a central theme in Baptist
arguments for religious liberty and human rights.[22]

Eight of the ten accusers charge that Mr. Persecution is
guilty and should be banished because he causes wars, in-
surrections, bloodshed, and hatred, and destroys peace,
"contrary to the peace of our Sovereign Lord the King"
(pp. 4–6). "Thou art guilty of . . . yea almost all of the
blood of the whole earth from the blood of righteous Abel
unto the blood of these present times, contrary to the
peace of our Sovereign Lord the King" (p. 6). The first
witness in the trial says:

> What was the main cause so many nations have been rent
> and divided in themselves, and one against another, and in
> their divisions devoured one another of late days? What
> occasioned the revolt of the German princes from the
> House of Austria, of the Netherlanders from the king of
> Spain, the bloody misery in France: And amongst our-
> selves, what occasioned the driving of the Scots, the rebel-
> lion in Ireland, and those bloody divisions in England, but
> this devilish spirit of binding the conscience? One would
> compel the other to their faith, and force them from their
> own. (pp. 12–13)

We have not sufficiently noticed how the original cham-
pions of religious liberty like Richard Overton and Roger
Williams were motivated by peacemaking, and how they
grounded it in Christ's death on the cross for all, "who
came not to destroy, but to save men's lives; and therefore
would have all *taught* in all nations, that all might be *persuaded* to the obedience of the truth, that all might be
saved: Therefore to kill the unbeliever, as Turk [Muslim],
Pagan, Jew etc. is to slay such as Christ would have to live
to repent" (pp. 10–11).

God's-Vengeance affirms Overton's early faith that *God's love is for all humankind:* "Are we not all the Creatures of one God? Redeemed by one Lord Jesus Christ? This should provoke us to love and peace one towards another." If some have "more light of the gospel" than others, we should not trample the ignorant under our feet but with patience persuade one another, hoping "God will turn their hearts" (p. 12).

The second witness is Christian, who echoes a central teaching learned by Baptists from Menno Simons.[23] Those baptized must be first taught, brought to faith and repentance, and made disciples, before they are baptized. Christ commanded the Apostles in the Great Commission that the way to approach unbelievers is to "go teach all nations, etc. (Matt. 28:19); where teaching, not violent compulsion, is constituted and once for ever ordained the means and only way for conversion to the faith of Jesus in all nations. Now compulsion and persuasion all know are directly opposite" (pp. 14–15).

The apostles did not use force but gave themselves over to scourgings, imprisonments, stonings, and the like. "And the worst that they did, or were commanded to do, to such as would not receive the gospel, was but to shake off the dust from their feet (Matt. 10:14; Luke 10:11; Acts 13:51)" (p. 15).

Moreover, Christ commands us to judge not (Matt. 7:1–2). Judgment is to be left to Christ at the last day (Isa. 11:4; John 12:47–84; 1 Cor. 4:5), and to judge others now is to usurp Christ's authority (p. 16).

The evidence against Mr. Persecution is overwhelming, and the jury's verdict is unanimous: "Guilty, my Lord." Offered a chance to reply, Mr. Persecution is too "terrified in myself at the apprehension of death" to speak. A clergyman comes to his defense, but Mr. Justice Reason reveals the greed that motivates the established-church clergy: They fill their bellies with the state-collected tithe and are exempted from the tax and the draft, while common people, poor and hungry, are both taxed and drafted.

Economic justice for the poor is essential to Overton's argument for human rights:

> Poor men that have not bread to still the cry of their children, must either pay or go in person to the wars, while those devouring Church-lubbers live at ease, feed on dainties, neither pay nor go themselves but preach out our very hearts. . . . Let the sick, the lame and maimed soldiers, and those that have lost their limbs, and beg in the streets, let women that have lost their husbands, let parents that have lost their children, let children that have lost their parents, and let all that have or suffer oppression and misery, in and for the public cause consider this, and be no longer ridden and jaded by clergy masters. (pp. 36–37)

At the conclusion of the trial, Justice Reason makes what is probably the first assertion in history of the concept of human rights, here in 1645, decades before the Enlightenment. He says Mr. Persecution threatens *"the general and equal rights and liberties of the common people . . . their native and just liberties in general"* (pp. 43–44).

The distinctive characteristics of human rights are that they belong to all persons as persons, not only to Englishmen or persons of one particular faith. And they override the authority of a government that violates them. The rights Overton is advocating clearly belong to all because all persons are created in the image of God and all are the objects of God's love shown in Christ's sacrificial death on the cross. His New Testament arguments are deeply Christian, but they establish the right of Protestants, Catholics, Jews, Muslims, and atheists—all humankind. His argument for justice for the poor is based on the unfairness of their misery, which is true of all poor and oppressed persons. All these arguments are biblical, and they are universal. They are grounded in Scripture and in experience, and they are universal in application.

The Theme Springs Forth

Once the concept of human rights had flowed from Overton's printing press, its implications led to a flood of publications.

On May 31, 1645, he published *A Sacred Decretal*, defending Roger Williams' *Bloody Tenet of Persecution*, William Walwyn's *The Compassionate Samaritan*, and his own *Arraignment of Mr. Persecution*. He criticizes the divine-rights claims of the established hierarchy and defends the rights of the people. "If the people once understand *their own rights*, and that the exaction of tithes is mere theft and robbery; . . . then the Parliament will regain their powers, and the people *their native liberties*." He urges the people "that they may clearly see their own *privileges, rights and liberties . . . the equal liberties of all* the common people, one as well as another" (pp. 9 and 12–13; italics not in original).

Martin's Echo (June 27, 1645) and *The Ordinance for Tithes Dismounted* (December 29, 1645) argue against the tithe or church tax. Our norm should be New Testament teaching. The New Testament practice was *voluntary* collection the First Day *for the general needs of the poor* (1 Corinthians 16; 2 Corinthians 9). During the Middle Ages this shifted, in ignorance, to a collection for rich priests and abbots, who then claimed it by divine right. They were taking money that should have gone to the fatherless, the widow, and the stranger—the poor in the land. They "rob the poor of *their right*."[24] Here we see that Overton is advocating the separation of church and state and opposing the system of governmental taxation to support the church. We thus see that his advocacy of human rights is not narrowly limited to religious or political liberties but includes a passion for economic justice for the poor—grounded both in the Bible and in the separation of church and state.

Now events (and publishing) moved rapidly. Overton's *The Last Warning to All the Inhabitants of London* (March 20, 1646) caused an explosion of authoritarian anger on the part of the government, which threw his bookseller in jail. Next the Lords jailed John Lilburne, a chief leader of the Levellers. Overton protested this by publishing *A Remonstrance* on July 7 and *An Alarm to the House of Lords* on July 31. The Lords expressed their sense of freedom of the press by jailing Overton himself on August 11.[25]

In *A Remonstrance of Many Thousand Citizens,*[26] Overton informs Parliament: your authority comes from the people. The people give you that authority only so you will "deliver us from all kind of bondage, and to preserve the Commonwealth in peace and happiness." This is only a temporary trust by the people, so you must submit to regular elections. "You were chosen to work our deliverance, and to estate us in natural and just liberty agreeable to reason and common equity." Overton is making a social contract argument based on natural reason: People cannot reasonably give authority to a government to place themselves in bondage, and to destroy their peace, happiness, and well-being.

He also argues for the right not to be imprisoned without showing cause (p. 11). He speaks of the rights of the poor and hungry, attacking imprisonment for debt and stating, "You suffer poor Christians, for whom Christ died, to kneel before you in the streets, aged, sick, and crippled, begging" (pp. 15–16). He argues for the right of freedom of the press (p. 12 *et passim*). He also argues forcefully against the draft "to serve in your war. . . . If any tyranny or cruelty exceed this, it must be worse than that of a Turkish galley-slave."

In *An Alarm to the House of Lords* (July 31, 1646), Overton combines the New Testament theme that we are not to lord it over one another (Mark 10:35ff.) with an argument for political democracy as in the New Testament—by common election and consent (p. 3). "We are resolved upon our natural rights and freedoms, and to be enslaved to none, how magnificent soever, with rotten titles of honor" (p. 6).

In *A Defiance Against All Arbitrary Usurpations* (September 9, 1646), the page-long title finally reaches a climax in the words, "upon the Rights, Properties and Freedoms of the people in general." In the context of arguing against religious persecution, twice he argues for "natural rights and natural immunities . . . wherewith God by nature hath made them free" (p. 2). He also translates the Golden Rule of the New Testament into a principle of natural reason and fairness: "Do as you would be done unto" (p. 5). Authorities should not persecute persons of other faiths since they would not want to be persecuted for their faith. He describes his own arrest for his printing, and his dedication to the rights even of his persecutors (pp. 7ff.).

Overton makes clear that his advocacy of human rights is not simply grounded on his selfish concerns but on "the trust which God has reposed in me for the good of others. . . . I was not born for myself alone, but for my neighbor as well as myself." When Patrick Henry uttered the declaration a century later that made him famous in all U.S. history courses—"Give me liberty or give me death"—he may have borrowed the line from Richard Overton, who deserves to be equally famous. Overton wrote: "Let me have justice, or let me perish." Overton said more: "I'll not sell my birth-right for a mess of pottage, for justice is my natural right, my heirdom, my inheritance by lineal descent from the loins of Adam, and so to all the sons of men as their proper right without respect of persons" (pp. 5–6).

In *An Arrow Against all Tyrants* (October 12, 1646), Overton says all are equally born to natural rights "delivered of God by the hand of nature" (p. 1). He argues that

everyone has an individual selfhood by nature, because
without this we could not be ourselves. God delivers all of
us equally into this world with a selfhood that is naturally
free. "For by nature we are the sons of Adam, and from
him have legitimately derived a natural property, right
and freedom." These are given to us by God, and rulers
may not take them away. We may consent to give power
to rulers for our own "better being, weal or safety," but we
would not consent to giving rulers unlimited authority
over what is ours by right. He argues from natural reason,
consent theory, and social contract, as well as from God's
gift to Adam, Christian love, and biblical justice (Lev.
19:15; Matt. 7:12; 1 Corinthians 13) (pp. 3–6, 11–12,
14, 16).

In *The Commoners Complaint* (February 10, 1647),
Overton published the story of his own and his wife's arrest in the struggle for human rights, for printing without
the approval of government censors. He was dragged to
jail clutching his copy of the Magna Charta.

After he was jailed, he kept writing more booklets,
which his wife courageously printed until she was discovered and arrested. Her conscience would not allow her to
cooperate in her unjust arrest, so she committed nonviolent passive resistance, refusing to walk to jail and going
limp. The marshall threatened to drag her by the axle of a
cart. She replied "he might do as it seemed good unto him
for she was resolved on her course." The marshall "strut-
ted in fury, as if he would have forthwith levied whole
armies and droves of porters and car-men, to advance the
poor little harmless innocent woman and her tender
babe" to Bridewell Prison. He ordered his deputies to
drag her, but they were so impressed with how she was
"constant to her just resolutions" that they refused.
"Then forth again goes this their Lordship; furious cham-
pion with his prerogative commission of Array, to raise
up new Forces to encounter this weak woman, and her

tender babe on her breast." But his new set of carriers also "hearing what this beleaguered woman was, wisely refused to lay any hands on her, and departed in peace." He then mustered up his hangmen deputies, "caused his men to break open the door, and entering her chamber, struts towards her like a Crow in a gutter, and with his valiant looks like a man of mettle tries violently" to snatch her baby from her arms, "but she forcibly defended it, and kept it in despite of his manhood." Finally they dragged her to court headlong upon the stones in all the dirt and mire of the streets, "with the poor infant still crying and mourning in her arms, whose life they spared not to hazard by that inhumane barbarous usage, and all the way as they went, . . . calling her strumpet and wild whore, thereby to possess the people, that she was no woman of honest and godly conversation, whom they so barbarously abused" (pp. 16–20).

In prison the Overtons shared the hunger and poverty of their fellow inmates. No provision was made to feed them. Their biblical compassion for the poor and oppressed was intensified by experience; human rights must include basic economic needs.

In *An Appeal . . . to the Free People* Overton makes his full statement of "our natural human rights and freedoms."[27] His title page consists primarily of two quotes from 2 Chronicles 10:16 and 11:4, describing how the people of Israel withdrew their allegiance from the oppressive king Rehoboam, and God blessed their rebellion. Overton again presents a trilingual argument, speaking the languages of reason, experience, and Scripture:

1. *Reason:* All God's communications are reasonable and just, and right reason is the fountain of all justice and mercy (p. 158). Reason tells us that all people have a natural right to defend themselves from all oppression, violence and cruelty (p. 160). If the government "act not for the weal and safety of" the people who betrusted them

their power, "they depart from their just power," and the people have the right to oppose, change, or rebel against the government.

2. *Experience:* He tells the dramatic story of how the government oppresses people, arresting them for exercising their right to speech and press and their right to petition Parliament. And he retells the story of their arbitrary way of arresting him, his wife, and others who have merely petitioned Parliament for redress.

3. *Scripture:* Romans 13 limits government to praising those who do well and punishing those who do evil. (Here is biblical grounding for the essential human rights principle of limited government.) Luke 20:25 limits government to outward action, insofar as it is under God's deputation; government has no business in religious matters. Revelation 2:23; Jeremiah 17:10; and Psalm 139:23 tell us that only God knows the heart, and the government does not. Ephesians 6:10–18 tells us that the only weapons to be used for spiritual matters are spiritual weapons, not force. Luke 12:48 tells us that to whom much is given, of them shall much be required, including action to oppose tyranny. Matthew 7:12 tells us we must do unto others as we would have others do unto us, which means we must treat all persons equally before the law as we would have ourselves be treated. Luke 10:30–37, the parable of the compassionate Samaritan, tells us now is the time to rescue the body politic from the thieves that have fallen upon it, and bind up its wounds and defend its miserable people; "for greater love and mercy cannot be amongst us than to take compassion over the helpless and destitute" (pp. 178–183). And finally, the army should be warned that at the resurrection they will be judged according to their deeds (p. 187).

To his *Appeal* Overton attached a Bill of Rights entitled *Certain Articles for the Good of the Commonwealth.* It is remarkably comprehensive in so short a space, and so early in the development of the concept of human rights. He includes the *three major categories of rights* that are well known in our century: (1) *freedoms of religious and civil liberty and freedoms from arbitrary treatment* by the forces of the law: the right to speedy trial; the right of prisoners not to be starved, tortured, or extorted; the right not to be arbitrarily arrested nor forced to incriminate oneself; the right to understand the law (in one's own language); equality before the law; and freedom from coercion in religion, from governmental establishment of religion, and from taxation for religion; (2) *basic needs and economic rights:* the right not to be imprisoned for debt; the right to trade internationally (not restricted by governmentally granted monopolies); the right to a free education for everyone; the right to housing and care for poor orphans, the widowed, the aged, and the handicapped; and the right to land for the poor; and (3) *rights of participation* in choosing a government that is responsive to the people and the common good: the right to vote and participate in government regardless of one's beliefs and the right to petition Parliament.

The concept of human rights spread among Baptists and Congregationalists, Independents and Puritans, and thence to John Locke and others in the Enlightenment a half-century later.[28]

A Trilingual Basis for Human Rights

Three centuries later, a far more widely known "turning" toward a human rights ethic occurred. It was the turning of the Roman Catholic Church at the Second Vatican Council from a somewhat hierarchical understanding of natural law to a human rights understanding that communicates far more powerfully in our pluralistic global society.

David Hollenbach's explanation of this shift gives us an

uncanny sense of having seen the same drama once before. It shows Overton's contemporary relevance. Hollenbach says the key to Vatican II's development of human
rights was its strong affirmation of religious liberty.[29] Furthermore, the experience of pluralism was crucial. Just as
Overton developed his understanding of religious liberty
and human rights in response to the pluralism of England
in the seventeenth century, with its strife between Catholic, Anglican, Presbyterian, Congregationalist, Baptist,
and Quaker, so the Second Vatican Council developed its
human rights ethic in response to "the realities of the religious, cultural, social, economic, political, and ideological
pluralism of the contemporary world."[30] Both the United
Nations and Vatican II "gathered representatives from all
regions of the globe, persons with vastly different cultural
backgrounds, from countries with enormously different
levels of economic development and wealth, from societies with opposed political and ideological systems."[31]
Confronted by this diverse array of perspectives, they
needed an ethic that would communicate to people of plu-
ralities of perspectives and that would affirm the basic
needs of varieties of peoples.

Furthermore, like Overton, both the United Nations
and Vatican II were powerfully concerned to promote
world peace.[32] Overton saw that as long as people's different beliefs are persecuted, we will have wars of religion.
Religious liberty and human rights constituted a history-
transforming initiative for peace, practically eliminating
the rationale for religious wars. Vatican II saw that injustice is the major cause of war, and that recognizing the
human rights of diverse, pluralistic peoples is a major initiative for peace.

The ethic of human rights can be a universal ethic, not
because its *source* is a common philosophy believed by all
people but because its *intention and application* affirm the
rights of all persons. "In a world that is simultaneously

pluralistic and interdependent, human-rights norms have gained a central place because they attempt to articulate the immunities and entitlements that are due every person" as a person, irrespective of status, religion, gender, or class. "This quality of universality," affirming all people's rights, and the quality of human rights as moral claims with validity even when societies violate them are especially helpful for developing "a transnational ethic for a pluralist world order."[33] In other words, the universality of a human rights ethic does not result from a claim that it is grounded on an underlying natural law ethic on which all rational persons implicitly agree. In our pluralistic age, we cannot find a persuasive set of ethical assumptions common to us all. Rather there are many different faiths and ethics (and interests and loyalties) on which different people ground their support for human rights. The universality is not in the commonly agreed grounding but in the intent—to include all persons as having human rights that must be respected. Thus the valid interests of all are included, though we come from different faiths.

We may claim a universal dimension to our faith, even if not all persons agree. Thus Hollenbach can affirm, "The beliefs that all persons are created in the image of God, that they are redeemed by Jesus Christ, and that they are summoned by God to a destiny beyond history . . . both illuminate general human experience and are themselves illuminated by such experience. With this [understanding], the Catholic tradition does not hesitate to claim a universal validity for the way it seeks to ground human rights in the dignity of the person."[34]

This means we do not have to reduce our grounding for a human rights ethic to a thin rationalism; we can affirm the richness of different faiths as they each provide their own faith-narratives and depth-theologies for advocating human rights for all persons. "The Council did not abandon Catholic commitment to the truth of the Christian religion. Far from it. Rather it asserted that a Christian understanding of the human person, rooted both in the Christian tradition and the tradition of reason, demands that human dignity be respected through the civil guarantee of religious freedom."[35]

This is just what we have seen in Overton. The story of his creative discovery of the language of human rights comes out of Christian and specifically Mennonite and Baptist faith in dialogue with pluralistic political, class, and faith loyalties. Overton does not "give up" his biblically based ethic. He grounds his human rights ethic in biblical faith. At the same time he translates his biblically based ethic into a language persons of other faiths or unfaiths can speak and uses both languages to analyze our empirical social experience and social struggles for human rights. In our pluralistic world, our very selfhoods are multilingual: We belong to various communities, and translate our concerns into the language of those communities as we move from one community to another. This gives us multiple perspectives from which to see new insights and from which to see ways to correct the exclusivistic biases of our communities.[36]

I have tried to be similarly trilingual in developing the seven-step model of just peacemaking. The steps are grounded in Jesus' teachings and Paul's Letter to the Romans, and they are also grounded in a reasoned approach to the essentials of peacemaking and in historical experience of the struggle to make peace. Just as with human rights, the three languages do not translate into one another without remainder, but they each communicate sensibly, and they each correct the other.

Hollenbach offers an insightful essay on the impact of religious diversity on human rights in the Middle East.[37] He shows how Muslims, Jews, and Christians ground their understanding of human rights differently, and this affects what they emphasize in their definition of human rights. How can they come to agreement? The solution moves on two levels. All three need to emphasize human rights, seeking to speak a similar language. At the same time, all three need to develop grounds within their particular faiths for affirming one another's human rights. Such a development is what we saw in Richard Overton, and what the world has seen in the Second Vatican Council. It does not mean the abandonment of specifically Christian, Jewish, or Muslim faith as the grounding for human rights. Far from it. It means the grounding is trilingual: Each speaks the language of its own faith, as well as a language of human rights shared by other faiths, and the experiential language of the struggle for peace and justice.

> Each community must find a basis for respecting the distinctiveness of the other communities within the structure of its own belief. The task, then, is not the homogenization of the religious faiths but of their *development* in a new direction. . . . The language of universal human rights remains a different tongue from that of Judaism, Christianity, or Islam. But if believers can learn to speak their own language in a new way, they will also be able to speak the language of universal human rights more fluently. If they can reconceive the relation between their own faith communities and the other faith communities of the world, then universal civil community will become a concrete possibility rather than an abstract and formal ideal. And this new way of speaking their own tongue will develop when Jews, Christians, and Muslims learn to talk to one another as *believers.*[38]

Hollenbach emphasizes, as Overton did, that all three dimensions of human rights are necessary:[39] "Respect for freedom (emphasized by liberal democracies), the meeting of basic needs (emphasized by developing peoples), and participation in community and social relationships (emphasized by democratic socialism)." Ignoring one of the dimensions violates the human dignity on which human rights are grounded. And it alienates large groups of people struggling for the elements of justice they need or are committed to defend.[40]

Deepening our understanding of the grounding of human rights in faith is important but not enough. We need to deepen our sense of their grounding in real, historical struggle as well. We have seen how Overton was struggling at a time of religious persecution, censorship of the press, repression of the new development of democracy, and unfair taxation of those least able to pay. It was a time of revolution. The twentieth-century focus on human rights has been in part a reaction against the racist oppression of Adolf Hitler,[41] a struggle for independence and political and economic growth by third-world nations, a struggle for civil rights against racist and sexist discrimination, a struggle of diverse ethnic groups for liberation from being treated as second-class citizens, and a struggle of East European peoples for freedom from governments that denied their participation in decision-making that shaped their lives. The language of human rights is not merely ideals, nor merely a demand for "my rights," but a struggle of love and justice for fellow human beings who are oppressed.

Monika Hellwig puts it exactly:

> The idea of human rights is surely first shaped by the sense of violation. It has its origin in an existential scream of pain or deprivation. When we hear the scream, we know what it means not because we can explain it but because we can feel it. It is by the capacity for empathy that we know what it means. But we have to hear the scream first. It may be a scream of fear or a scream of rage. It may be the hoarse scream of those who have suffered all their lives or the shrill scream of those suddenly overtaken by acute suffering.[42]

Hellwig explains that communicating the meaning of the scream so it can move a community to action requires a tradition that interprets it, logic, and the effort of communication across different traditions—much as I have suggested concerning Overton.

Max Stackhouse suggests another dimension. Movements for human rights are not merely the product of individuals acting alone but of people in groups, voluntary associations, and congregations of believers.[43] Human rights are socially rooted.

Stackhouse also shows some roots of human rights in the free-church movement of seventeenth-century England.[44] A strong basis for human rights can arise from other faiths as well as in the experience of historical struggle for justice. Riffat Hassan has demonstrated this especially well for Islam.[45]

H. E. Tödt and Wolfgang Huber, from their Lutheran perspective, provide a wise caution, warning Christians against claiming a monopoly over the grounding for human rights. The historical development of human rights has been the work of many oppressed groups, jurists, philosophers, political leaders, and varieties of unsung heroes of many faiths and no official faith.[46] Christians have often violated human rights and have much to repent for. Overton would agree.

Ronald Stone, working in the realist tradition of Reinhold Niebuhr, reminds us that mere affirmation of human rights is not enough. Niebuhr emphasized that "institutional guarantees of a free judicial system with a veto over policies and rulers, and guarantees of freedom of expression," were necessary to protect human rights. "These institutional guarantees had to be buttressed by a sense of the broader community, intellectual competence of the electorate, and a balance of power in the economic realm."[47]

Similarly, Tödt and Huber emphasize that human rights must be embedded in law, including international law. Human rights are not merely a set of ideals but products of real social struggle in need of grounding in the laws and customs of societies, and of the legal status of agreements by the international community. This gives them additional leverage on nations that violate them. When we press nations to respect human rights, we are not merely imposing our peculiar morality on them. The international community is developing an interwoven set of agreements, precedents, and pressures that can turn a government around or topple it when it denies the rights of people.[48] Richard Overton struggled mightily to embed human rights in the laws of his nation, to call his government to repent, and even to topple it when it rejected his call. He did not succeed in toppling the government, but he did succeed in giving us a powerful heritage, for which we can give thanks.

Questions for Thought

1. Is it more important to you to ground human rights in religious faith or in a universal claim of reason? Which motivates you most strongly? Which is most available in our pluralistic age, when people think differently but live together in a shrinking world?

2. Is it important to show respect for how a Hindu, Muslim, Jew, or Christian would support human rights in his or her faith? Or simply to ask others to speak the language of a universal reason? Why?

3. Can you explain the significance of some of the biblical teachings that shaped Overton's discovery of human rights? Do these passages also persuade and motivate you? Why?

4. Can you explain Overton's argument from reason that each of us owns our own selfhood and would not give consent to a government that takes away our rights? Does this reasoning persuade and motivate you? Why?

5. Can you explain his argument for human rights based on historical experience when rights are suppressed or violated? Does this experiential reasoning persuade and motivate you? Why?

6. What are the three different dimensions of human rights? Which is most important for you? Which is important for most third-world persons? What would be wrong with focusing primarily on only two of the dimensions?

7. Perhaps each of us has our own story: Human rights began in our experience when we (or others), for example, picketed, boycotted, or marched for freedom against segregation and discrimination; or when we organized in churches and marched with candles against an authoritarian communist regime; or when we learned to grow a balanced diet and got a local health clinic and a school. What is your own story that gives you your strongest identification with the global struggle for human rights?

7

The Children's
Defense Fund Fights
for Human Rights

U.S. citizens can work for human rights around the world by urging their government to press other governments to improve their human rights practices, by sending appeals directly to the other governments as suggested by Amnesty International, or by combatting world hunger through Bread for the World and hunger relief programs. Such efforts have saved millions of lives and decreased the unimaginable torture of millions by governments and by malnutrition, starvation, and disease.

Pressing for human rights is an essential part of just peacemaking. Biblical faith repeatedly emphasizes compassionate justice and investing in the reign of God as essential ingredients of just peacemaking. Political science research shows that relative deprivation of human rights is a powerful cause of revolution and war.[1]

Ronald Stone has presented a thoughtful and balanced Christian realist case for pushing the government to pursue human rights in its foreign policy.[2] Peacemakers press governments to feed the hungry, free the press, refrain from torture and state terrorism, and risk free elections. Peacemakers take direct action through church hunger programs, both local and international. They join Bread for the World and Amnesty International, and they urge their government to press for rights throughout the world.

But Jesus calls us up short: Do we see clearly enough to press other governments? Or is there a serious injustice in our own national practice that distorts our perception of the corrections other nations need to make?

> The eye is the lamp of the body. So, if your eye is healthy, your whole body will be full of light; but if your eye is unhealthy, your whole body will be full of darkness. If then the light in you is darkness, how great is the darkness!
>
> No one can serve two masters, for a slave will either hate the one and love the other, or be devoted to the one and despise the other. You cannot serve God and wealth. (Matt. 6:22–24; see Luke 11:34–36; 16:13)
>
> Why do you see the speck in your neighbor's eye, but do not notice the log in your own eye? Or how can you say to your neighbor, "Let me take the speck out of your eye," while the log is in your own eye? You hypocrite, first take the log out of your own eye, and then you will see clearly to take the speck out of your neighbor's eye (Matt. 7:3–5; cf. Luke 6:41–42).

This teaching is a realistic diagnosis of the process of perception. Loyalties and interests do shape what we see. Distorting interests and divided loyalties do distort our vision. Healthy interests and faithful loyalties do clear up our vision.

What is the log in our own eye that distorts our perception of human rights internationally? What corrections can we make so that our perception is more on target?

The log is the defeatist belief that nothing works to overcome the cycle of poverty. This defeatist belief is causing us to waste our nation's children, and we project it on other nations as well.

The Children's Defense Fund (CDF), a research and advocacy group, has such a strong concern for the health and education of children that they do not assume things have to be as they are. They focus on what we can do, not as a stopgap but as an integrated strategy to prevent the stunting, wasting, and discouraging of our children and their futures. They research carefully what works and what does not work. They pay attention to data and good scientific research. They develop proposals that are unifying rather than polarizing. They have an outstanding reputation for caring for children and for research about programs that work. Marian Wright Edelman, the director of CDF, writes: "For God's sake and our children's future, let us seize the opportunities and avoid the dangers that we know are lurking. Let us focus on what unites us, on the overwhelming majority of poverty that we can do something about now."[3]

CDF helps us remove the ideological log in our eye that tells us nothing works, there is nothing we can do.

What Works

"What Works" has been a CDF theme for years. Effectiveness is crucial, because CDF is focused on defending children from destructive forces in our society, and because CDF intentionally confronts the fatalism that says nothing works. CDF employs extensive social science research to understand what actually causes teens to drop out of school, to get pregnant, to lack job skills, and to raise children who will cause a lifetime of problems for society and for themselves. CDF researches what actually works to prevent these problems and what is cost-effective.

CDF's *Children 1990* includes a chart titled "Investments to Make and Savings to Gain."[4] Here is a summary of some investments that work:

WIC, the Special Supplemental Food Program for Women, Infants and Children, provides nutritional help to the needy. It reduces infant mortality and underweight births, and it improves nutritional outcomes for children in the first six years of life. One dollar invested in the prenatal component of WIC saves as much as three dollars in short-term hospital costs, plus the long-term costs of retardation and poor health. As of 1989, WIC had funding to serve only 59 percent of those eligible.

Medicaid, including *Early and Periodic Screening, Diagnosis and Treatment* (EPSDT) for children, results in earlier prenatal care, increased birthweight, and decreased abnormalities among children. One dollar invested in comprehensive prenatal care saves $3.38; annual health care costs are 10 percent lower for children receiving EPSDT services. As of 1987, fewer than half of poor pregnant women and children in the United States were covered by Medicaid.

The *childhood immunization program* has effected dramatic declines in the incidence of rubella, mumps, polio, diphtheria, tetanus, and pertussis and the consequent impairments and institutionalization. One dollar invested in this program saves ten dollars in later medical costs. Yet immunization rates generally fell in the early 1980s. For the uses of some types of vaccine among some groups, the rates fell below 80 percent. By 1991 only about half of two-year-olds in the inner cities had been immunized, and nationally the rate was about 70 percent. Measles, once thought basically eradicated, made a comeback. "In 1990, there were more than 25,000 measles cases, 16 times the number in 1983."[5] Eighty-nine children died of measles, and about 270 suffered permanent brain damage. In 1991 the Citizens' Advisory Committee to the national vaccine program, the House of Representatives, and federal officials developed and funded a restoration of the program of inoculation. "To the amazement of the public health world," President Bush, apparently under the influence of the ideology that doubts we can do anything, decided on a year's study process rather than action.[6] (My own son, David, was severely handicapped by rubella—German measles—which was almost eradicated until we cut the funds for the vaccination program. He is legally blind, has had nine operations, and has other handicaps.)

Head Start gives disadvantaged children preschool training and a range of crucial services. Researchers widely agree that "children who attend Head Start score higher on achievement tests and are more likely to meet the basic requirements for school than control groups." They are "less likely to be placed in special education classes or to be held back in school." Years later, they "are more likely than their peers to be literate, employed, or enrolled in postsecondary education. They are less likely to be school dropouts, teen parents, dependent on welfare, or in trouble with the law. Both the business community and Congress have estimated that every dollar the nation invests in high-quality preschool programs saves about six dollars in the cost of special education, welfare, and crime later on."[7] Yet Head Start is funded to serve fewer than one of six eligible youngsters.

Quality child care enables low-income parents to work while their children begin preschool training. It costs the public a small fraction of what monthly welfare payments cost for a family without a working parent. In addition, employers report less absenteeism and greater productivity if there is adequate child care. Yet more than half the federal money (Title XX) for child care was deleted from 1977 to 1989.

Chapter I *Compensatory Education* gives extra educational help to disadvantaged children and is linked to achievement gains in reading and math for children enrolled in the program. Investing six hundred dollars for a child for one year of compensatory education can save four thousand in the cost of a repeated grade and make later school success and job success more likely. (A learning disability teacher, Vernice Kelley, saved my handicapped son from a complete disaster in early grades; now he is making all A's and B's in the University of Louisville.) In 1987 Chapter I served about half of the children who needed remedial education.

Adjusting the minimum wage for inflation so a full-time worker can at least support a small family at the poverty line increases incentives to work and provides an adequate economic base to meet children's basic needs. It reduces costs for income support programs and is an incentive for entry into work experience that can develop into better-paying jobs. During the first nine years of the 1980s there was no adjustment in the minimum wage while inflation ate up one third of its 1980 value. In 1991, after partial catch-up increases take effect, a full-time worker at minimum wage pay will still earn less than 90 percent of the poverty level for a family of three.

Youth employment and training and the Job Corps prepare disadvantaged young people for the world of work. One dollar invested in Job Corps yields $1.45 in benefits to society in the United States. Other youth employment and training programs have raised postprogram employment rates by nearly one fourth and annual earnings by more than $1,300 per participant. Currently only 3 percent of the 1.2 million teenagers officially counted as unemployed are served.

These data correct the assumption that we cannot do anything to achieve more effective training for youth so they can contribute to the health of our economy and be healthy themselves. They also correct the assumption that doing something effective about these people-destroying problems would cost so much that the United States would not be competitive in the world market. Taking these actions *saves* money.

If this is not clear enough from research in the United

States, it should be clear from comparisons with the political economies of Western Europe and Japan. They have more effective programs to meet these needs and hence lower infant mortality rates, lower dropout rates, a more skilled workforce, and faster-growing economies. It just makes sense to do things right, see that people are educated and healthy, and have job skills. The result is a healthier economy.

Let me back this up with some data: The United States ranks nineteenth in infant mortality, twenty-second in child mortality for children younger than five, twenty-ninth in low birth weight births, fifteenth in proportion of one-year-olds fully immunized against polio, nineteenth in number of school-age children per teacher, eighth among eight industrialized countries in childhood poverty, and twelfth in mathematical achievement of eighth-grade students. Some of these ratings put us behind Singapore, Hong Kong, Spain, Libya, Lebanon, Cuba, and Hungary, as well as Sweden, Norway, Canada, Japan, France, England, Wales, the Netherlands, Germany, and Ireland.[8]

The point of these comparisons is not just to feel sorry or ashamed for the United States. The point is that many less wealthy countries do find they can afford to do better for their children. Investing in skills for their youth has not slowed their economies; most of their economies are now growing faster than ours. The point is also to overcome the "can't do" assumption that the way things are is the way they have to be.

Compare Minnesota, where I used to live, with Kentucky, where I now live. Minnesota has taken measures to decrease teenage pregnancy and ranks first in the nation for its low teenage pregnancy rate. Kentucky ranks forty-ninth. Minnesota also ranks first for its low school dropout rate; Kentucky ranks last. It's not true that nothing works.

Causes and Cures of Teenage Pregnancy

Progressives and conservatives alike are alarmed at the astounding increases in unmarried teenagers giving birth to babies. So is CDF. CDF has diagnosed teenage pregnancy as a major cause of long-term poverty and a major focus for preventive action.

When unmarried teenagers have babies, it almost guarantees big increases in numbers of youth who drop out of school, lack skills, are unemployed, have unhealthy babies, and live in poverty. Their babies have problems that are debilitating for them and for our future society. The devastating consequences of this trend will be visited on the children of the children for generations to come. It hurts the whole society—all of us.

We need to understand accurately what forces are causing the rapid increase in the number of unmarried teens having babies.

> Black teens are having fewer rather than more babies: 172,000 births in 1970; 137,000 in 1983. The proportion of black women under twenty who have given birth has been falling steadily since the early 1970s and will probably reach the 1940s level before the end of the decade. However, the percentage of those births that were to unmarried teens soared 50 percent—from 36 percent in 1950 to 86 percent by 1981. . . . From 1947 to 1977 the marriage rate for pregnant black fifteen- to seventeen-year-olds dropped about 80 percent.[9]

The crux of the problem for black families is that young black women do not marry as often as they used to. *The same problem is rapidly developing among white teenagers.* Senator Daniel Patrick Moynihan saw the problem developing among African American teenagers in 1965, when he was a Harvard professor.[10] The data for white teenagers are now worse than they were at that time for African American teenagers. "In some respects the white family crisis has been growing while the black family crisis has stabilized or grown more slowly."[11]

CDF and scholars it cites have focused large amounts of research on the problem and have detected not a single cause, but multiple causes of teenage pregnancy. These include limited education, lack of skills, poverty, lack of hope and meaning-giving support, lack of contraceptive and sex education, and male joblessness. These factors work together to engender in teens a sense of limited life options and increased sexual activity, which then leads to school dropout, unwed parenthood or abortion, and welfare dependency. The babies who are born to teenage mothers are often underweight and often demonstrate low learning ability later in life.

Teen pregnancy is a major cause of, as well as consequence of, poverty. Three of four families headed by a mother under twenty-five are poor.[12]

Teen pregnancy causes long-term welfare dependency, "shamefully high American infant mortality rates," rates of sexually transmitted diseases twice or three times higher for teenagers than for people over twenty, and large numbers of abortions (teens account for 13 percent of the births but about 26 percent of the abortions; about half of pregnant teens get abortions); "teen pregnancy and parenthood are the major cause of school dropout by girls and a major cause of school dropout among males as well." They "add $1.3 billion to taxpayer costs annually." If we can learn how to prevent teen pregnancy, we can "save multiple generations of children from the ravages of child poverty and the instability it often breeds."[13]

"CDF believes that one of the best contraceptives is hope. Hope is a byproduct of high self-esteem that comes from doing well in school, or in a job, or . . . community or religious service."[14] Caring adult appreciation is also a factor. Expectation that a job will be there after school is also important.

One myth is that mothers have more babies to get higher welfare (AFDC) grants. But "in most states, when an additional child is added to an AFDC family the grant increase is so small that it cannot support the additional child. . . . For example, when a family went from two to three members in January 1986, the AFDC grant increased by $30 a month or less in Alabama, Kentucky, and Mississippi and by $60 monthly or less in 22 other states." Furthermore, AFDC families on the average are smaller than poor families generally. "Teen pregnancy rates are higher in states with the lowest welfare benefits and lowest in states with higher welfare benefits."[15] We know from longitudinal studies and transnational studies that nations' birthrates drop when basic needs are met: Poor nations have high birthrates, but when they successfully make the transition into industrialization or into meeting their people's basic needs, they achieve lowered birthrates. This is called "the demographic transition." Trying to reduce birthrates by cutting off aid and starving babies causes an explosion in birthrates. To stop the population explosion, it is necessary to meet people's basic needs, their basic human rights. Then they know the babies they have are likely to live, and they can expect fulfilling life options in other activities such as education, work, and creativity, so they do not need more and more babies. Family planning methods are important in facilitating this demographic transition. But family planning without meeting basic needs does not work to stop the population explosion. Surely this widely understood transnational truth has application to teenagers in the United States. Youth who are poor and lack basic academic skills are six times more likely to get pregnant regardless of race.[16]

"What has become of the fathers? They remain single. The pattern is quite clear."[17] The drop in marriage rates parallels the drop in employment prospects.[18] Conversely, "Young men with earnings above the three-person poverty line are three to four times more likely to be married than their peers without such adequate earnings."[19]

Causes of Economic and Family Stability

CDF asks, What can be done to achieve stable families and to prevent teenage pregnancy? Many things can be done to counter the causes that have been identified. CDF advocates church action, community action, action by leaders of all kinds, and action by business and government. It studies and describes many different local groups and organizations that are taking effective action. The best success comes when the focus is on "youth development rather than a youth problem, recognizing that the prevention of negative outcomes is easier when positive alternatives are presented." It gives a dozen examples.[20]

One such example, which fleshes out the statistics and detached, scientific studies, is Louisville's special high school for pregnant teenagers where my wife is a nurse and teacher. In addition to the usual high school classes, there are classes in nutrition, prenatal care, and child care. There is a clinic where the students receive regular medical care. The girls take turns helping in the daycare nursery, where their babies receive care to enable the mothers to stay in school, and where they receive instruction on childcare. Counselors help them plan their future and prepare for jobs. The school is trying to do what figure 7.1 suggests. My wife, a realist if there ever was one, says the students are not free of problems in spite of their and the school's efforts, but the school is making a significant difference for many students. A recent study by medical experts from the University of Louisville of the 2,293 students who have attended the school reports dramatic decreases in second pregnancies, dramatic improvements in the health of babies, and significant improvements in school attendance and decreases in dropout rates.[21]

Known repeat pregnancies during high school years are only 1 percent.

The oldest school-based clinic is in St. Paul, Minnesota. There first teen pregnancies have been reduced "from 80 per thousand to 29 per thousand, and repeat pregnancies to 1.4 percent, compared to 33 percent nationally." The school has also seen "an increase to 87 percent of pregnant students graduating, compared to 50 percent nationally."[22]

For job training, the most effective programs combine actual job experience with training and remedial education, along with adult counseling and modeling.[23] When youths' hope and self-esteem increase because they are actually doing a job, they are more motivated to learn skills and academic subjects; when they see that more learning can be useful to their job or to job advancement, they are doubly motivated to learn. For example, Jobs for Ohio's Graduates assigns about forty students to an on-site counselor who ensures that students get the education and job training they need, helps them get placed in a job and follows up for nine months. "Almost 90 percent of recent JOG graduates either obtained full-time employment, enrolled in college, or entered the military. More than 92 percent of the participants graduated from high school. . . . On the average they earned 30 percent more per week and averaged 26 more hours of work per week" than nonparticipants.[24]

The problem is there are not enough jobs. The unemployment rate hovers between 6 and 7 percent, is double that for youth, and triple again as high for African American youth as for white youth. To train youth for jobs and inculcate a work ethic in them when the jobs are not there is cruel. Youth unemployment rates are worse than they were in the Great Depression. During that Depression, my father-in-law found a job working for the Civilian Conservation Corps, funded by the government, that ena-

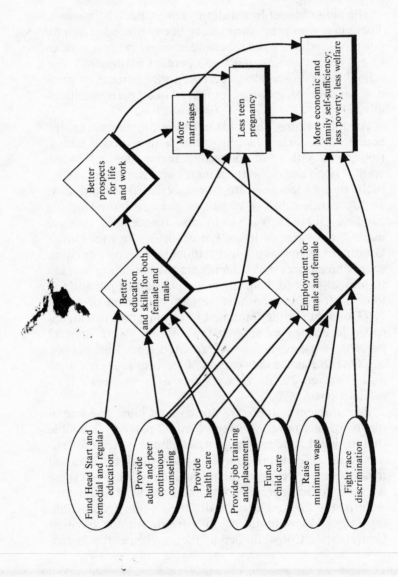

bled him to hold his family together. This is just what CDF advocates: "Thirteen states already operate [youth conservation and service corps programs] on a year-round basis, putting unemployed youths to work in valuable projects within state parks of their own communities. Corps members typically work in closely supervised teams, learning new job skills while also participating in remedial education programs to improve their basic academic skills."[25] Yet the federal government canceled most of its job training and job providing programs. Its major remaining program, the Job Training Partnership Act (JTPA), "prohibits using federal funds to create paid work opportunities for young people, even when unsubsidized jobs are not otherwise available."[26] Edelman points out what we all know: "An entire generation of poor and minority youth are being left out or shut out of the mainstream of American society right now."[27] With our population aging and birthrates declining, our future labor force will depend on the skills of minority youth. By the year 2000, according to the estimate of the Hudson Institute, "only 15 percent of all new labor force entrants will be white males born in the United States."[28] If we do not train our youth and help them find job experience and skills, not only they but we are in serious trouble.

Overcoming an Ideology of Despair

The ideological argument that there is nothing to be done was made by Charles Murray in his book, *Losing Ground.* He saw what CDF and Moynihan had seen: An increasing number of households had only one parent, and as a result the number of families and children living in poverty was increasing. But he blamed this on the War on Poverty. He argued that when federal expenditures for the poor were increasing, family instability and poverty were also increasing. The solution he advocated was that the government cancel its programs for the poor: Leave the poor to fend for themselves; they will do better on their own.[29] This argument fit the short-term interests of those who wanted to double military spending while cutting taxes for the wealthy. Federal programs for jobs, job training, vaccinations, education, drug clinics, housing, children's nutrition, college loans, and other efforts to help the poor create stable families and make it into the workforce were slashed severely.

There are several problems with Murray's argument:

1. During the period Murray focused on, AFDC was paid only to families with one parent; mothers had to remain unmarried or their husbands had to leave if they were to receive benefits. As Moynihan said, we had no family policy; we had an antifamily policy. Murray's ideological allies were unwilling to vote money to assist stable families with two parents present. (This problem is now partly corrected, but only partly.)[30]

2. During the period Murray focused on, welfare benefits, adjusted for inflation, did not increase; they decreased. The problems he pointed to could not have been caused by an increase in benefits. As programs have been cut, poverty has increased, and so has youth joblessness.

3. During this period, the minimum wage did not keep up with inflation, because Murray's ideological allies were unwilling to pass legislation to that effect. Furthermore, they were unwilling to vote that assistance to the working poor should not drop off completely as soon as they got a job but should gradually taper off as they earned more income, so that they would have an incentive to take what jobs they could find. Therefore, as Murray's own description of incentives shows, there was decreasing incentive to take minimum-wage jobs and lose benefits. CDF advocates that we should keep minimum wage current and assist the working poor with health insurance, child care, and income credit so they do better financially when they work.

4. Murray did not present arguments that the specific programs CDF advocates, such as Head Start, Job Training, and WIC, do not work. He made an aggregate argument that we are losing ground, which is correct, and then an aggregate argument that the government can do nothing, which is incorrect. He did not seek to refute CDF's more specific analyses.

5. Murray's argument looks suspiciously like ideological justification of the greed of interest groups who want the money for themselves. It does not look like detached social science.

6. When Murray's policies have been applied in other nations, their poor have experienced increased population growth and increased poverty. (See the explanation of "the demographic transition" above.)

7. Murray's policies were applied in the United States in the 1980s, and the result was disastrous for children and their human rights. The minimum wage was not adjusted for almost a decade during a period of high inflation, so it lost one third of its value. Even after partial correction to $4.25 in April 1991, it was still only 80 percent of its 1979 purchasing power.[31] The median value of AFDC payments for a family of four "fell by 30 percent between July 1970 and July 1988." Rents soared, and federal housing assistance was cut by more than three fourths, so that "in all but four states, the amount the federal government estimates is necessary to rent a modest two-bedroom apartment in the least expensive metropolitan area in the state is more than 75 percent of the entire state AFDC grant for a family of three."[32] No wonder there is an epidemic of children's homelessness. We have already noticed many other cuts in programs that have been shown to work and to save the economy money.

The result of these policies has been to cause greatly increased child poverty and teenage pregnancy, while quadrupling the national indebtedness that had accumulated during all previous administrations.

The 26 percent drop in median family income that young families with children experienced between 1973 and 1986 was virtually identical with the 27 percent drop in per capita income that occurred for the country as a whole from 1929, the last year before the Depression, to 1933, the worst year. Nearly three-fourths of the income decline for young families took place during the 1980s.[33]

Edelman points out that under the Gramm-Rudman-Hollings budget constraint bill, "The Defense Department and programs for children are supposed to suffer roughly equal percentage cuts . . . , although defense spending has more than doubled since 1980, while spending for children and families has shrunk dramatically." This is like "putting an overweight child and a malnourished child on the same diet."[34]

Conservatives emphasize cultural solutions like inculcating a work ethic, teaching sexual responsibility, encouraging family values, and providing economic incentives for working. Progressives emphasize governmental action like providing jobs, sex education in schools, and health insurance and income credits for families and raising the minimum wage. CDF says both are right. We need both cultural values and governmental action. The governmental policies should be in line with the cultural values. CDF seeks to advocate policies that can unite us rather than divide us, and that can build broad support in our society.

The remedy requires government and private sector steps to overcome discrimination and the lack of jobs, and it takes a concerted effort by families, community leaders, and agencies to resurrect strong work and family values.[35]

In spite of all the obstacles thrown in its path, CDF and other groups with whom it works, such as Bread for the

World, have had significant success. In 1990 WIC funding was increased significantly. Furthermore,

> Congress passed the nation's first comprehensive child care legislation, approved a landmark bill that for the first time authorizes Head Start to expand in rapid steps to serve all eligible children, approved a ten-year Medicaid expansion to phase in coverage of all poor children, passed legislation that will improve the lives of disabled children and other disabled Americans, provided significantly increased tax credits for low-income families with children, and moved forward in the areas of housing, help for vulnerable families, and youth service.[36]

The *CDF* report of the following year continued to record a sense of achievement:

> All of us who care about children should take enormous satisfaction in the gains we won for children in 1990. Congress enacted more than $30 billion in new budget authority and entitlements in key child and family support programs.
> Because of the combined efforts of so many across America, hundreds of thousands of additional children from low-income families will have the opportunity to benefit from decent child care and Head Start programs. Low-income working families will have more money in their budget thanks to an expanded earned income credit. A poor family with two children could receive a maximum tax credit of $2,015 in 1994 compared with $1,126 under the old law. And every year for the next 10 years, more poor children will be added to the rolls of those having access to health care through Medicaid.
> Working together, child advocates proved in 1990 that determination and commitment do pay off and that families' and children's interests *can* prevail.[37]

Now CDF has a specific legislative strategy to encourage Congress to fund the programs fully as promised, and to expand programs that make a difference, such as WIC and Job Corps. And CDF wants to build a local constituency of groups and individuals that cuts across race, class, age, and political party, and "to empower parents and grandparents, who are the most important protectors of children."[38]

Two kinds of despair are our enemies: teenagers' despair about their life prospects and society's despair about effective remedies. I hope the data from CDF and our own sense of human rights slay those dragons of despair. Hope is the most effective remedy.

Listen to Lee Atwater, the Republican Party chairman who masterminded some of the crucial political campaigns of the 1980s:

> Long before I was struck with cancer, I felt something stirring in American society. It was a sense among the people of the country—Republicans and Democrats alike—that something was missing from their lives, something crucial. I was trying to position the Republican Party to take advantage of it. But I wasn't exactly sure what "it" was. My illness helped me to see that what was missing in society is what was missing in me: a little heart, a lot of brotherhood.
>
> The '80s were about acquiring—acquiring wealth, power, prestige. But you can acquire all you want and still feel empty. . . . It took a deadly illness to put me eye to eye with that truth, but it is a truth that the country, caught up in its ruthless ambitions and moral decay, can learn on my dime. I don't know who will lead us through the '90s, but they must be made to speak to this spiritual vacuum at the heart of American society, this tumor of the soul.[39]

Unless we overcome our society's ideological despair that blocks us from doing what is right, effective, and wise, I fear our influence on human rights in the new era will be to spread an ideology that nations should not take the actions that follow from love for their own children. I fear we will project our own shortcomings on other nations. I fear we will confuse a free-market economy with a political ideology that says governments can do nothing effective for their society's children. It should be obvious that Europe's democracies have free-market economies that are growing more rapidly than ours, and they have medical insurance, housing, job training, family leave, and anti–teenage-pregnancy programs. A free market does not require a noncaring government. Nor does democracy. Democracy requires human rights for children.

Chapter 1 describes how people in East Germany were agreed that the authoritarian state-communism they had been experiencing was shipwrecked. They were discussing what sort of economic system they wanted to develop instead. They knew about the U.S. political economy because their media and the West German media had told them about it: millions of people homeless, millions of the unemployed without unemployment compensation, a lack of day care programs for children of workers, a lack of funding for Head Start for five-sixths of the eligible children, 37 million people without health insurance. The East German system, though much weaker economically than ours, was meeting all these needs. The West German system, economically more healthy than ours, was also meeting these needs, as were the systems in most of Europe. They found it difficult to believe, and, puzzled, asked me if it was true. I had to admit it. Their disbelief dramatized for me that these insensitivities in our political economy were not simply natural and inevitable. Plenty of other democracies, with political and economic freedom, market economies, and economic growth, like West Germany, France, Norway, Sweden, England, each somewhat different, meet many of these basic needs.

The East German government had given its people the impression there were basically two alternatives: their system, which had met basic needs but had fewer luxuries, and the U.S. laissez-faire capitalist system, which had luxuries for the wealthy but kept many people poor, without medical insurance, housing, or good education. They did not discuss the democratic alternatives of Western Europe that have both political and economic freedom, plenty of consumer goods, and cover the basic needs. Their propaganda tried to keep their people content by telling about the injustices of laissez-faire capitalism and not telling about the other alternatives. I thought their approach was a mirror-image of what we hear in the United States: There is authoritarian communism, which does not work, and there is our system, which has freedom, more luxuries, and problems for the poor. Neither they nor we talk much about how the Western European democracies work, with full democratic freedoms, a market economy, economic growth, and greater support for the basic medical, housing, job training, and education needs of all the citizens. That way people will not imagine the workable alternatives but will assume things have to be the way they are.

Questions for Thought

1. Talk with your pastor or a staff person concerned about children and families. Ask them what needs of children they have observed in your community.

2. Are there others in your congregation or community who are concerned about beginning a peacemaking, hunger, or child advocacy project?

Find an interested group already at work or a few people in your congregation to work with you. Be clear about the channels that you must use to gain approval and official sanction. Know the system for your congregation and work through it. No matter what your congregational profile or workstyle, don't do it alone!

3. CDF's *Welcome the Child: A Child Advocacy Guide for Churches* gives a set of suggestions to help you discover

- The interest and support for child advocacy in your congregation
- The resources available in your congregation to meet children's needs
- Children's needs not being met in your community
- How to match your congregation's resources to existing needs
- Ways other persons and congregations have been child and family advocates.

It also gives a set of suggestions for developing a "Study-Into-Action Program." The packet is available from the Children's Defense Fund, 122 C Street NW, Washington DC 20001, for $14.95 postpaid. It also includes sermon outlines, Bible studies, prayers, litanies, stories and songs for a Children's Day worship service, and a section on "Giving Voice to the Voiceless." The back pages list denominational public policy offices and national organizations and suggest lots of resources.

8

Twelve Steps
of Recovery
from Addiction

In this chapter I compare the eight steps of peacemaking as transforming initiatives and the twelve steps of Alcoholics Anonymous (AA), Al-Anon, and other twelve-step recovery groups that are proving so meaningful for many. I have several reasons for doing so.

One reason is that it will provide a quick review of the biblical grounding for the steps. Beyond that, twelve-step groups are one way millions of persons have experienced peacemaking in their lives and their relationships. They may be the most significant peacemaking movement in the United States. For many participants, the result is significant peacemaking with their families, coworkers, friends, God, and self. Anyone who knows dysfunctional families, shame-based families, or families with addictions knows the need for peacemaking. Peacemaking in one's family is the intense prayer of millions.

So far I have argued that *experiential verification* is one of the three languages for grounding an understanding of human rights and peacemaking. I have also argued that peacemaking should not be merely a general ideal but a process with *concrete steps*. One way to verify the eight concrete steps of peacemaking is to look briefly at the analogous experience of the twelve steps of Al-Anon.

I have also argued that participation in a group is one essential step of peacemaking. Participants and professionals widely agree that twelve-step groups are remarkably effective, and that recovery from addictions or codependency is unlikely without participation in a group. Might peacemaking groups learn from twelve-step groups? Just as twelve-step groups emphasize one step at a time, telling stories of their own experiences, could peacemaker groups occasionally focus on one peacemaking step, sharing experiences in their own journeys? We might grow both spiritually and in peacemaking skills.

A principle of twelve-step groups is that addictions have an external or physical dimension like drinking or eating and an internal or spiritual dimension like shame or the need to control. We cannot recover without changing the physical dimension, and we cannot recover without doing the inner work. Otherwise we get stuck in "stinkin' thinkin' " or become a "dry drunk." The same is true of peacemaking: We cannot recover without changing our physical investments in greed, in the military-industrial complex, and in consumption and production habits that cause ecological destruction. Further, we cannot recover without doing the inner spiritual work to correct our own assumptions, fears, and loves. Doing so requires a group that works on the inward and outward journey simultaneously.

There is another important reason to compare the steps of just peacemaking with the steps of recovery groups. Such a comparison explains the kind of reasoning behind the steps and why these particular steps are needed. Some expect that the reasoning behind just peacemaking will be the same as the Aristotelian means-ends reasoning in just war theory: an efficient cause, a clear goal or intention, a choice of right means, an assessment of the cost and benefits of the means, an assessment of the probability that the means will achieve the goal, and so on. In the theory of international relations this is called a utility-maximizing model of reasoning, or a rational actor model.

Biblical realism does not assume a rational actor model. Realistically, our perception of means and ends is distorted by our interests and investments, and our reasoning processes are distorted by our loyalties and idolatries. Not that human reason sees no truth or knows no right; we do have "natural knowledge" of right and wrong, justice and injustice, gratitude and ingratitude (Rom. 2:14–15; Acts 17:22–31). However, our knowledge gets distorted by our loyalties to whatever powers we serve, and by our bondages, addictions, or alienating processes.[1]

Similarly, theorists of international relations are suggesting significant deficiencies in the utility-maximizing model.[2] It does not accurately portray how we in fact decide. It causes us to overlook

- The importance of perception and misperception of the context
- The cognitive processing and cognitive-dissonance–reducing of exploratory action, perceiving feedback, and adjusting
- The organizational procedures and processes that shape decisions
- The loyalties and interests that shape perceptions, choices and actions
- The defense mechanisms that shield awareness of our own complicities in alienating processes
- The impact of historical experiences of threat, authority, social change, and information integrity.

Therefore, the logic of just peacemaking assumes a perception/misperception model of reasoning, or an alienation/deliverance model. Its steps are steps of error correction, repentance and new direction, conversion and transformation, delivery and recovery.

Explicating the research into cognitive processing in international relations would take more space and reader patience than I can presume, and some readers might even see it as esoteric and removed from experience. There is, however, an experiential base close at hand that can make the point readily. The logic of just peacemaking resembles, in interesting ways, the twelve-step process of recovery. The twelve-step model does not assume a utility-maximizing model of reasoning but works at correcting the distortions in our perceiving and reasoning. Therefore, I want to look briefly at the wisdom in Al-Anon groups (which are designed for families and codependents of alcoholics). All of us to some extent are codependents of the "nucleaholism," militarism, racism, sexism, classism, and overconsumptionism that pervade our world. All of us could use a process of continuous correction of our errors in perception and decision.

Acknowledge Our Need of Grace

The first initiative is to acknowledge that recovery is based on grace. We admit our own powerlessness to save ourselves.

From time to time in Al-Anon meetings, you can hear someone say, "Lots of times my children would rather be with my spouse, the alcoholic, than with me, because I've been self-righteous and judgmental while my spouse was laid-back. Sometimes the children say they were hurt by me more than by him. I learned I was *opinionated, stubborn, and self-righteous.* Through the program I'm now becoming less judgmental."

Similarly, so many of us have such an implicitly judgmental interpretation of the Sermon on the Mount that we can hardly hear the good news of deliverance.

Is the Sermon on the Mount about impossibly high ideals, as some believe? Is it meant only for relations among good, peaceful, righteous Christians? Is it only for angels, or only for the inner self? Consider three telling points: First, the Sermon on the Mount, in its own words, tells us it is for people who are stuck in the vicious cycles of anger and killing, lust and adultery, accusing one another, judging one another, hate, hypocrisy, lying, poverty, divorce, anxiety about possessions, serving money (mammon) and hoarding treasures that moths can eat and thieves can steal. That does not sound like angels to me but a lot more like us. The first step in peacemaking is *to name the vicious cycle that we are caught in and to confess our feeling of powerlessness in its wake.* We are not flawless peacemakers; we are sinners ourselves. Second, the Sermon on the Mount is *good news* about *happiness* or blessedness because *God is delivering us* from these vicious cycles. The Beatitudes are basically a meditation on Isaiah 61, the passage Jesus read in his first home-church sermon in Luke 4. Isaiah 61 says blessed are the poor, those who mourn shall be comforted, the people shall inherit the land, the Lord will make righteousness, and praise will spring up. It is about the deliverance the Lord is bringing, not about our striving toward ideals. Third, the Sermon on the Mount is based on God's *already delivering:* giving rain and sunshine to the unjust as well as the just, caring for the sparrows and the lilies of the field and for us, coming in Jesus and speaking with authority. It is based on God's *presently active grace,* not on our mighty striving toward high ideals.

Similarly, Paul emphasizes *grace* and *peace;* peacemaking is based on grace, not on our own self-righteousness. When Paul says that Jews *and* Gentiles *alike* are all under sin (see Rom. 3:9), he is undercutting the boasting and judging going on between Jews and Gentiles so they can make peace. When he says, "All have sinned and fall short of the glory of God, they are now justified by [God's] grace as a gift, through the redemption that is in Christ Jesus" (Rom. 3:23), Paul is saying none of us is righteous. None of us can refuse to dialogue with another because we are more righteous than the other.

Peacemaking is based on grace—on God's transforming initiative toward us while we were yet enemies—not on self-righteousness, boasting or judging. Peacemaking is based on grace not just as a doctrine to be believed but as a way of life to be experienced and lived daily. It is based on our confessing that we are not righteous but that we ourselves are in captivity and can be saved only by God's initiative.

Too often grace has been understood as a static state—either being untouched by sin or forgiven—and not as the dynamic relationship that it means biblically. Instead, as Patrick McCormick writes, grace is a dynamic process: "To say that I am a recovering sinner [pictures] the dynamic and life-giving character of grace. . . . Here grace is a verb, a verb that breathes and works and prays and hopes and grows and changes."[3]

The first step of Al-Anon is "We admitted we were powerless over alcohol—that our lives had become unmanageable." The book *Al-Anon's Twelve Steps* says,

> Many of us came to Al-Anon to learn the secret of compelling a well-loved someone to stop the damaging and degrading overuse of alcohol. . . . By taking Step One we acknowledged that we had no power to make another person stop drinking; that threats, pleas and the determined use of our will were equally futile. Our schemes and threats had succeeded only in our being physically and emotionally exhausted. . . . We . . . had to realize the futility of trying to control. When we found ourselves continuing to direct, we reminded ourselves that we had no power, no right to exercise power, over anyone but ourselves.[4]

Al-Anon emphasizes the trap of codependency. An addict's spouse feels trapped and learns to adapt. An addict's child is trapped and does not learn normal family relationships. Both get shaped and warped by the addiction. They experience depression from the loss of a healthy relationship or from not having had that relationship from the start. They practice denial. They lose the ability to express a full range of feelings (like anger, hope, or affection) because they are taught to suppress these feelings to avoid fights, disappointment, and rejection. They may develop a martyr complex, fantasies of future success, lack of trust, blaming and projecting, and judgmentalism based on hidden shame and self-blame.[5] So the problem is not just the disease the *addict* has. The problem is the disease the *family members* have as well. We are all in bondage. No one is righteous, not one. We have to begin by acknowledging that we are not in control of our own relationships or our own selfhood.

One key to the twelve-step group process is honesty in acknowledging one's own complicity and seeing through distorting defense mechanisms. I have been impressed with the honesty of persons in groups in which I have participated, and in that spirit of honesty I should confess that I am a workaholic. (I am the son of a hard-working crusader and may also be the husband of a romance novel addict.) My colleague, Wayne Oates, invented the term "workaholic" and wrote the book describing the disease.[6] I have learned much from him.

Many people laugh about workaholism. But it deprives people of love, joy, and peace. It contributes to the onset of heart attacks, cancer, and other diseases. It alienates parents from their children, spouses, and friends. It can deprive children of the nurturance and intimacy they need for themselves, and of the example of nurturance and intimacy between adults that they need to experience, so "they grow up without the tools to establish joyful, healthy relationships."[7] Ironically, it can tie you into knots so that you live in fear of not getting your most important work accomplished; you become blocked, you contract "procrastinatoritis," and you end up not getting the work done. Then the shame gets worse.

The second step of Al-Anon is "We came to believe that a Power greater than ourselves could restore us to sanity."

"The words 'came to believe' meant a gradual awakening to the reality of a Higher Power in our lives. . . . We made our first timid moves toward establishing a working relationship with 'a Power greater than ourselves.' . . . Those of us who were brought up in a religious faith may have naturally used prayer to ask God for what we wanted."[8] Now the emphasis in prayer is on listening to God's direction, waiting on God, giving our lives over into God's hands, and not trying to control.

Al-Anon's third step is "We made a decision to turn our will and our lives over to the care of God as we understood Him."

The Al-Anon book asks, "What did we have to lose by making this decision? Only our stubborn determination to have things our way; only the despair that came from repeated disappointments."[9]

And the Alcoholics Anonymous Book says,

> The great fact is just this, and nothing less: That we have had deep and effective spiritual experiences which have revolutionized our whole attitude toward life, toward our fellows and toward God's universe. The central fact of our lives today is the absolute certainty that our Creator has entered into our hearts and lives in a way which is indeed miraculous. [God] has commenced to accomplish those things for us which we could never do by ourselves.[10]

Talk with One Another

The second transforming initiative is to go talk to one another and seek to be reconciled.

Jesus says, "If you . . . remember that your brother or

sister has something against you, leave your gift there before the altar and go; first be reconciled to your brother or sister, and then come and offer your gift" (Matt. 5:23–24). In Romans 12:18 Paul asks us to seek to live peaceably with all. And in chapter 15 he addresses household churches that are not on speaking terms with one another, urging them to "welcome one another as Christ has welcomed you" (see 15:7). To welcome one another means to talk with one another, to engage in dialogue, to seek to make peace with one another.

Families in which there is addiction are notorious for covering up their feelings, covering up the truth, and developing distorted perceptions of one another. The rule in Al-Anon is "check it out." That means you cannot rely on assumptions. You have got to talk. You have got to ask. You have got to find out what the other person is feeling.

This axiom seems such an elementary rule of peacemaking. It is so obvious. Nevertheless, many millions of persons are suffering needless grief because people think they are above talking with someone who has offended them or who is not righteous enough. We are not righteous enough, yet God has come in Jesus of Nazareth to seek peace between us when we have not deserved it.

Jesus tells us that nursing anger leads us to destruction (Matt. 5:22). So what is the solution? Never to be angry? No. That would be impossible. Instead, he suggests we take a transforming initiative: Go, talk it out and seek peace. Stuck in anger, we feel powerless and helpless, because we are in bondage to the vicious cycle of anger. When you go to talk, you may gain a friend; if not, at least you can sleep better and pray better because you are not languishing, powerless, in captivity to the clutches of anger.

Janet Woititz describes the bondage to anger: "Anger, in one form or another, is always present in the alcoholic home. The tension is thick enough to cut with a knife." You live with anxieties about what your spouse will do next. "All these uncertainties lead to anger with people you are not really angry at. You become rigid and distrustful. Rage consumes you without a satisfying outlet. Anyone who walks into your house can feel the angry vibrations. There is no escape from it. Who ever thought you would turn into such a self-righteous witch?"[11]

Robert Subby and John Friel as well as Sarah Frances Hines point out that "when you can't talk about your feelings, you are forced to *project your feelings away from yourself,* blaming someone else, and the message early on in the alcoholic family is to develop this kind of maladaptive behavior just to survive emotionally."[12]

The first rule in an addictive family is that it is not okay to talk about problems. Then that means we have to cover up problems. This leads to a deep sense of shame. "And, of course, as you might expect, it is impossible to solve a problem if you don't know how to talk about it, or even acknowledge that you have one. This perhaps is the most frustrating, saddening outcome of the 'no talk' rule." As Sarah Frances Hines goes on to say, "It's not trauma that damages a child, but the inability to talk about the trauma."[13]

Here is a story that shows the transforming power of finally talking, even if it does not exactly model the perfect way to talk:

> I was the type who never got openly angry with the alcoholic. I was a silent martyr, ready to kill myself without raising my voice. Imagine how a man must feel living with such a saint . . . !
>
> One night I really let the alcoholic know how I felt. While he was driving home, I screamed and shouted for all the nights I hadn't had the courage to do so. I even grabbed the back of his neck and shook him a little. He almost lost control of the car. The squeals of the brakes brought me back to my senses, and I saw with horror that for the first time in my life I had used physical violence. I was so crushed with

shame that for a week I avoided my sponsor and my Al-Anon friends, until I decided to face it and speak openly about it at meetings.

The strange thing is that I started to feel better about myself because I was no longer pretending to be somebody I was not. It is true I had done something shameful, but now I was a real person, not the perfectionist nor the self-righteous martyr. The alcoholic did not appreciate the shaking but he did appreciate my being more of a real person.[14]

The Dilemma of the Alcoholic Marriage gives five rules for talking:[15]

1. Discuss, don't attack. "The sober alcoholic is overly sensitive to criticism; . . . His self-esteem is still fragile. He's so braced for rejection that he imagines it even when it isn't intended. Anything I might say that seems critical of him as a person would make him react emotionally and defensively."

2. Keep the voice low and pleasant.

3. Stick to the subject. "It seems I was always using the opportunity to list ten other things I'd been meaning to bring up. At last I sat myself down and said: 'One thing at a time is sufficient. If I confuse the issue, we'll end up fighting about his cousin Joe and my aunt Charlotte.' "

4. Listen to his or her complaints. "When it's my turn to be on the receiving end of a complaint I keep myself receptive to what he's saying, reminding myself that I want to be cool-headed, open-minded and reasonable." As Roger Fisher and William Ury put it, "Take turns; only one person get angry at a time."[16] Let the other person finish expressing the reason for her or his anger, and see that she or he feels heard, before you try to defend yourself or state your own feelings.

5. Don't make demands. Leave the door open for the other to participate in shaping solutions. "Believe me, it was hard work to overcome my feeling that 'my way is the only right way.' "

It should be clear that talking may include confronting. In *Confessions of a Workaholic,*[17] Wayne Oates tells how a son was able to confront his father successfully about his workaholism and probably save his life. But confronting does not mean nagging, which is self-righteous and judging. The five rules above help to tell the difference. Chapter 5 of the book *I'll Quit Tomorrow*[18] describes how to do a successful confrontation. Daniel Day Williams, Pat McCullough, my son Bill, and my wife Dot have confronted me thoughtfully about my particular variety of workaholism, and I am grateful to them.

Take Transforming Initiatives

The third initiative is to take transforming initiatives (deeds, not just words) instead of setting yourself violently against someone and seeking revenge.

Perhaps the most common reaction to the addict is to punish him or her. "I'm good; he's bad; he deserves to be punished." But punishment and retaliation help no one, prolong the addiction, and widen the rift in the marriage.[19]

Every one of Jesus' teachings in Matthew 5 is a positive transforming initiative and not merely a negative prohibition: Talk and seek peace, quickly make peace with your accuser, turn the other cheek, go the second mile, give to the one who begs, pray for your enemy. Many misread the "But I say" sayings as if Jesus' emphasis is on telling us *not* to be angry, *not* to look on someone lustfully, *not* to divorce, *not* to resist an evil person. How can we do that? Thinking ourselves righteous, we pretend we do not do any of those things. Consequently, we are harder to live with than an alcoholic is. That is hardly peaceful. Jesus does not emphasize these "don'ts" but practical transforming initiatives (see chapter 2).

One kind of transforming initiative to take toward an

addict is confrontation, as just discussed. Another is detachment—not turning your back on the person but detaching yourself from enabling the addiction, covering up for it, paying for it, or shielding the addict from its consequences. These points are discussed often in the literature.[20] Jesus' examples also point out another dimension—mercy and simple kindness. It is important to distinguish this from enabling and covering up.

One Al-Anon member tells of hitting bottom in her marriage after her husband had begun recovery through Alcoholics Anonymous. The marriage was falling apart. She speaks wisdom:

> I did it with a single word: *Courtesy.* People with normally good dispositions have no difficulty being courteous to strangers and friends. It is when our strong emotions are involved that we swing to the limits of the pendulum. . . . We are so deeply involved that we treat those closest to us as though they were part of us. . . . Keeping in mind the one word *courtesy* helped to remind me that my husband is other things besides a husband. . . . He is a person to be respected, to be considerate of, to treat always with courtesy. . . . I have learned that courtesy generates courtesy. It makes you more pleased with yourself. It makes others, particularly those near to you, reconsider their own attitudes.[21]

In other words, transforming initiatives transform you, and they often transform others as well.

Martin Luther King, Jr., taught us this. He saw that it was necessary to confront; we cannot wait another hundred years for people to be changed by gradualism without confrontation. At the same time, he taught courtesy and love toward the enemy. That way, after the confrontation, all of us could come out with dignity and with the possibility of making peace with one another. Martin Luther King, Jr., taught transforming initiatives.

The ninth step of Alcoholics Anonymous and Al-Anon is to make direct amends to people we have harmed wherever possible, except when to do so would injure them or others. That means to take transforming initiatives toward them.

In a group in which I participate, one member told how she apologized to her spouse for several ways in which she had hurt him. He answered, "What are you up to? *I'm* the alcoholic. What do you mean—*you* hurt *me*?" She explained she was in the program, and she was learning how indeed she had hurt him. He then became more open and talked some of how he had hurt her.

Others cautioned that you cannot do the ninth step expecting a warm reception. The other may turn out to be an empty well. You do not make amends because you expect a positive response, but because you need it for your own health. You need transforming.

Both are true. You *hope* for the other's transformation, but you get transformed in any case.

Seek Justice

Justice is peacemaking, because *shalom* includes justice and meeting the needs and rights of everyone. While injustice is a major cause of hostility and war, the effect of justice is peace (Isa. 32:17).

One wife of an active alcoholic tells how she learned that "when a wife pays for the consequences of her husband's drinking, she removes the dimension of justice from her married life. This creates an atmosphere which soon can extinguish any love that does exist." It is unjust to the husband, because he needs to experience the consequences if he is to have a chance to begin recovery. And it "is no less damaging to the wife, because she feels she is being taken unfair advantage of, that her marriage is all one-sided. This leads to self-pity, resentment, bitterness and hatred."[22]

The biblical emphasis on justice for the powerless

points to a larger issue of injustice. An article in *The Fundamentalist Journal* points out that in many cities there are six- to nine-month waiting lists for drug clinics because the government has severely cut the budget for drug clinics.[23] What is a drug addict going to do, after finally admitting the need for treatment, while waiting six or nine months to begin treatment? Another article reports an extensive study showing that every treatment method studied saves much more expense to society than the treatment cost. All were cost-effective. Yet we have severely cut funding for clinics. It is a grave injustice, to the addicts, to their families, and to our society, which pays the consequences. Even when President Bush announced his war on drugs, he did not restore the funding for clinics to even its level before the cuts. The restoration he proposed amounted to less than the cost of one Stealth bomber.

Love, Affirm Interests

The next initiative is to love your enemies. Paul says we should grieve with our enemies when they grieve and rejoice with them when they rejoice (Rom. 12:15). This does not mean that you do whatever your enemy says or desires. Jesus often confronted his enemies, and so did Paul. It does mean that our enemies have some valid interests, and we should rejoice when their valid interests succeed and grieve when they are defeated.

Love is important to peacemaking in families. Love asks, "What interests does the other have that I could affirm? What hurts does the other have that I need to hear and be sensitive to?"

The Al-Anon literature speaks of the importance of loving your spouse whom you resent and shows how engaging in the twelve steps can remove some of the barriers to love. We need to distinguish healthy love from enabling an addiction and overprotecting or dominating. You separate the addiction, which is a destructive kind of bondage, from the person, who very much needs unconditional delivering love. Especially interesting is Robin Norwood's bestseller *Women Who Love Too Much,*[24] whose title more accurately should be *Women Who Love Too Codependently and Too Compulsively.*

Christian love, as in the parable of the compassionate Samaritan (Luke 10:30ff.), means (1) compassionately entering into the situation of those in bondage, (2) doing deeds of deliverance, (3) confronting those who exclude, and (4) inviting into community with freedom to be an individual and justice for all. Each of those themes is crucial for peacemaking in the family.

Persevere in Prayer

I already explained something about Al-Anon's discovery of the importance of the discipline of listening prayer for peacemaking in families. What Al-Anon has discovered here has been important to many of us in Christian peacemaker groups as we have practiced listening prayer. We had been used to doing more praying as thanking God and confessing and making requests. But we had not practiced listening prayer enough. So we began. We practiced simply sitting silently in prayer without saying anything, just waiting. Our worries, our busy schedules, our concerns, or our anxieties about our relations with others would come before us in God's presence. They would be examined by God and by us. We would let whatever comes forth be offered to God and listen for God's gift of a word, or a picture, or a presence, or a call to us to allow a correction in our own lives. We were given a greater sense of God's presence in our lives, and of the gift of not having to try to control others but of letting go and letting God. Gradually we were changed. My own sons, my best critics, began saying that I had mellowed. We are closer now than we were.

The first three steps of Al-Anon are our confessing our powerlessness, believing that God can restore us to sanity, and turning our lives over to God's care. These are best done in prayer, along with the help of others. They are never finished; we return to them again and again.

The same is true of the fourth through seventh Al-Anon steps: make a moral inventory of ourselves, admit our wrongs to God and to another human being, become ready to have God remove these character defects, and humbly ask God to remove our shortcomings. Furthermore, the eighth step—make a list of all persons we have harmed and become willing to make amends to them—is a process of meditation and journaling. Melody Beattie describes this step especially well, including paying attention to the resistance and self-deception involved, and the need for meditative prayer and journaling.[25]

The eleventh step is explicit about prayer: "We sought through prayer and meditation to improve our conscious contact with God as we understood God, praying only for knowledge of God's will for us and the power to carry that out." The experience of many persons following these steps is that prayerful meditation deepens their praying and makes it much more vital. These steps define much of the content of truly peacemaking prayer.

The various books I have read agree that addictions have their roots not only in a chemical or material force but also in spiritual emptiness. Reading *Alcoholics Anonymous* (the "Big Book") is a spiritual experience. A friend of mine says this is *the* American contribution to spirituality. (I could think of a few others as well, but surely she has a point.)

The Big Book describes how we try to run our lives on self-will and try to run the whole show. We contract "controlitis." This causes conflict with others, with ourselves, and with God.

Driven by a hundred forms of fear, self-delusion, self-seeking, and self-pity, we step on the toes of our fellows and they retaliate. Sometimes they hurt us. . . . The alcoholic is an extreme example of self-will run riot, though he usually doesn't think so. Above everything, we alcoholics must be rid of this selfishness. We must, or it kills us! God makes that possible. . . . This is the how and why of it. First of all, we had to quit playing God. It didn't work. Next, we decided that thereafter in this drama of life, God was going to be our Director. He is the Principal; we are His agents. He is the Father, and we are His children.[26]

And then the book gives a prayer in which we offer ourselves to God, as in Romans 12:1, and ask God, "Relieve me of the bondage of self, that I may better do Thy will."

Many of us have found it helpful and interesting to keep a journal of insights that come as we meditate, as Al-Anon recommends.[27]

Prayer helps us understand our own anger, fear, hurt, and shame, which we have been ignoring. It gives us new understandings of the anger, fear, hurt, and shame that others are experiencing. It helps us let go and quit trying to control everything, including others and ourselves. It makes us much more peaceful.

Forgive and Repent Rather Than Judging Others

Jesus asks us to pray for forgiveness for our debts as we have forgiven our debtors and says if you forgive those who sin against you, God will forgive you (Matt. 6:12–15). Do not judge, or you too will be judged. Instead of trying to take the speck out of others' eyes, work on getting the log out of your own eye (7:1–5). Paul makes the same points in Romans 12:17–19, and 14:1, 4, 10, 13.

Self-righteousness is the hobgoblin of addictive personalities and codependents. William Sloane Coffin says some peacemakers hate war and its preparation more than they love peace and people. They become good haters and bad lovers.

A fundamental theme in Al-Anon focuses on the speck and the log: I have got to quit trying to straighten out the other person and realize that I have been warped myself and need my own straightening out. The most effective way to help the other is to start chopping away at the log in my own eye.

For example,

> If Joe marries Mary because he was attracted by her warm maternal quality, as many alcoholics do, he is likely to be the dependent one. . . . And while she is managing him, the children, the household and the finances, she's awash in self-pity because of the big load she has to carry.
>
> If Joe is drinking, her constant protective watchfulness makes it easy for him to sidestep getting help. . . . She hasn't learned, as she would in Al-Anon, that shielding him from the consequences of his drinking only prolongs its course.
>
> When he's drunk, her natural reaction is to reproach him for his behavior, and that's the very worst time to attempt to communicate with him. In fact it can't be done without triggering a family war.
>
> Until she learns what is wrong with her attitude and how to change *herself* so he will be forced to face his responsibilities, the situation isn't likely to improve.
>
> If Pete married Helen because she's shy, timid and submissive, he unconsciously chose a wife who would satisfy his need to dominate. If she turns out to be an alcoholic, he will have the complete dependent he wants, no matter how desperately he *thinks* he wants her sober.[28]

Until Pete works consistently on his own need to dominate rather than to live in mutual servanthood, he will be perpetuating both their addictions while blaming her.

Here is the testimony of the wife of a recovering alcoholic:

I was always trying to be a peacemaker, without knowing how. I realize now, since Al-Anon, that I was trying to do God's work without knowing what God wanted me to do. . . .
I was still "taking his inventory." I felt that if he were working his AA program, he would be more mature. . . .
I wanted everyone to be happy, but I just couldn't recognize that I was trying to manage everyone's life. . . . I was always asking God for help, but I didn't listen for the answers. . . .
When I finally did go to a meeting with an Al-Anon friend, I went with a self-righteous attitude. . . .
One Sunday my husband was in a bad mood. I kept quiet because I was apprehensive. Finally I got up courage to suggest that he call an AA friend to help bring him out of his depression. . . . Well, that was the straw that broke the camel's back! He turned on me and told me in no uncertain terms that I'd better find a program of my own and let him work his AA program by himself. The bottom fell out of my world. Hadn't I been a perfect little mouse to this man, hadn't I always tried to be careful what I said and did? I felt completely lost and helpless. I knew I must find an answer or I couldn't go on.
Two days later I went to my second Al-Anon meeting, this time . . . for myself, ready to listen and accept whatever would help me understand my problem rather than his. . . .
I found that the only inventory I could take was my own.[29]

Forgiveness is crucial to peacemaking. In a twelve-step group, one person said, "If you have this problem too, please laugh." And we did. This alerted me to one key part of the group process: We do laugh when someone tells a story in which we recognize ourselves—especially when the story makes fun of the teller's way of pretending to be righteous, or the teller's defense mechanisms that we recognize in ourselves as well. That shared laughter helps people feel accepted and supported. It is genuine, authentic, spontaneous, bodily acceptance. It is forgiveness. And it is healing.

One Sunday evening I was guest preacher in a church in suburban Chicago. During the invitation, a man came forward, confessed his alcoholism, gave himself to Christ, and asked for help in recovery. He was asking for forgiveness. A circle of people came around him and hugged him and cried with him. Biblical forgiveness does not just say "that's OK" from a distance. It runs up and embraces and welcomes into the community of fellow sinners.

I know a couple who could not do the peacemaking soon enough to stay married. They are now divorced. But they have worked it through enough to understand and have compassion for the other's interests. There has been a large amount of forgiveness. They are being responsible in the commitments to support one another, which is not always easy. They are working together to support their children and work through crises without much judging. She is confessing her own codependent anger and how it contributed to the problem. She now says, "I never gave him a chance. I didn't really listen to him." So now they are making peace with one another. I give God thanks for that. It could be so much worse—for them and for their children.

Work with a Group

These transforming initiatives are not in serial order, as if we were to finish one before going on to the next. They provide a process of growth in Christ and participation in the Spirit, in and with a group of fellow strugglers and its support, and we are to keep doing them again and again, strengthening our relationship with God, with others, and with self. The twelve steps of Al-Anon are similar; you keep coming back to them, seeing new implications and working them in new parts of your life. They are far more meaningful, and indeed more fun, if done in a group. The humor, shared insight, and mutual support are genuine peacemaking, even if it does not save the whole world.

Jesus and Paul are inviting us to be part of the support group of disciples, part of the church that is the body of Christ, the *koinonia,* the community. The church is community. The process of peacemaking can be a lonely and unsuccessful struggle without the support of a group. Surely we have learned that through Alcoholics Anonymous and Al-Anon. We need a support group.

After all, it is all based on grace. It is not self-help. The process begins by admitting we are powerless to save ourselves. We have to turn our lives over to the care of God. We need group support. We cannot do it alone. The help is there for us. Thank God!

Questions for Thought

1. If you began some journaling today or tomorrow, which step do you think would hook your interest first?

2. Why do you think the twelve steps and the eight steps are so similar?

3. Have you heard of the effectiveness of twelve-step groups? Do you think that experience carries over to the problems where peacemaking is needed? How so and how not?

4. If you are intrigued by the thought of participating in a peacemaker group, start asking friends, one at a time, if they might have an interest. You might share this book with them. Most people feel incompetent to work at peacemaking because they have thought they would be alone and would have to rely totally on their own skills and knowledge. In a group, skills and knowledge are shared, and they grow in the process. Therefore, your asking may need to extend to some conversation about possibilities and limitations, and how to deal with them together. When you get three people, you might share your idea with a church leader or with someone in your

community already involved in peacemaking. Don't give up easily. You'll have to ask a half dozen persons for every yes you get. I explain in *Journey into Peacemaking*[30] how to proceed, step by step. Your own church may have literature and help for proceeding, or an ecumenical group or peacemaking group in your community may.

5. Peacemaking groups also have an outward journey of a different sort than twelve-step groups. They connect with some ecumenical networks of information such as the following. You might want to do so yourself:

- Interfaith Impact, 110 Maryland Avenue NE, Washington, DC 20002; ecumenical, broad range of peacemaking, justice, and environmental issues.
- SANE/FREEZE: Campaign for Global Security, 1819 H Street NW, Washington, DC 20006; largest national peacemaking organization; provides legislative alerts.
- World Peacemakers, 2025 Massachusetts Avenue NW, Washington, DC 20036; based in Church of the Saviour and specializing in church peacemaker groups, but you need one of the other groups above for legislative alerts.
- Bread for the World, 802 Rhode Island Avenue NE, Washington, DC 20018; world hunger information and legislative alerts.
- Witness for Peace, 2201 P Street NW, Room 109, Washington, DC 20077; Latin American issues and some Middle East issues.
- Friends Committee on National Legislation, 245 Second Street NE, Washington, DC; broad range of peacemaking and justice issues; excellent newsletter.

9

Just Peacemaking Theory Is Already Emerging

The old bipolar order in which the two superpowers, the United States and the Soviet Union, along with their allies, dominated and defined power relations is dead. What the new order will be is now being shaped. Will it be an order of justice, polycentric pluralism, internationally agreed-upon common security, dominance by the United States, or chaos?

We will still have the threat of nuclear weapons, economic deprivation, ethnic nationalism, ecological erosion, and, as many nations see it, the threat of dominance by a regional power or by the one remaining military superpower. U.S. citizens will have a major opportunity to assist in fashioning a more just world order.

The United States will have a major responsibility, which it cannot carry out unilaterally; we will need global security, multilateral sharing, regular consultation with other nations, and greater attention to the United Nations. People will need to prod governments to pay attention to common security, human rights, and just peacemaking. We will need to do more than oppose war after these forces have brought us to the brink. We will need an international order of justice that encourages anticipation and prevention, attentiveness and listening, human rights and feeding the hungry.

We the people will need guidance in our peacemaking. Well-intended haphazard actions will not suffice. Nor can we do it alone. We will need help from our churches and peacemaker groups, linked together in information networks. To act together rather than merely as isolated individuals or isolated small groups, we need a just peacemaking theory. It will need to be clearly grounded in a biblical understanding of peacemaking and political wisdom, and clearly laid out in concrete steps so that we can agree on it, expect people to understand it, disseminate it, and use it to guide our own work and to prod, praise, or criticize governments.

In our journey together thus far we have seen that something like just peacemaking theory is emerging from biblical study and from many movements that give hope to people: environmental, peacemaking, human rights, children's rights, and twelve-step movements. It is not an esoteric idea. It is already in people's experience. It seems almost natural, like common sense. What it needs is to be named, so people can recognize it. According to the new constitution of Namibia, every person has a right to a name—a right that had been denied by the colonial administration. Just peacemaking theory is being born in our time. It has a right to a name.

Robert Jervis, the theorist of international relations, has applied the psychology of perception to the study of international relations. He shows that what we see depends on what we expect. People often fail to recognize a new reality around them until it is named. In one experiment playing cards were rapidly flashed on a screen. Some of the cards were strange—red spades and black diamonds. The subjects did not recognize what they were seeing. When they finally realized what was odd about one of them—"that's a red queen of spades!"—they were immediately able to recognize subsequent strange cards. Once having named the pattern, they could then see it occur again and again.[1]

Scientists often have failed to recognize what they were seeing until it was named. Thomas Kuhn is famous for pointing out example after example of this phenomenon in the history of science.[2] Jervis gives examples of six sightings of the planet Neptune and seventeen sightings of Uranus, all of which were written off as errors or as sightings of a fixed star rather than a moving planet because no one had yet identified a planet there.[3] Any astronomer who had thought to name what he or she saw could have become famous. None did, for generations, because they did not expect to see what they saw and so did not really see it.

During World War II, two British photo-intelligence experts were told to look for German rockets that might attack England. One expected the rockets to be huge and located next to a rail line. In some pictures from Peenemünde he saw only a vertical column. "Another analyst who expected that the rockets would be smaller and more mobile recognized that the 'column' was an upright rocket."[4]

General Short, who was in command of Pearl Harbor in 1941, had been having problems with sabotage attacks from guerrilla fighters on the island. When he received an official message that he should expect "hostile action" at any moment, meaning a bombing attack from Japan, he took precautions against sabotage and was totally unprepared for the massive, surprise bombing attack that destroyed a major part of the U.S. Navy, moored unprotected in the harbor. The message did not name clearly what pattern of attack he should look for.[5]

Just Peacemaking Theory Beginning to Emerge

Just peacemaking theory is already beginning to emerge. Its shape and ingredients need to be named so we can recognize it. One way to see it emerging is to review, briefly, statements by major denominations on the churches' calling to peacemaking. This can also serve as a review of our argument thus far.

The Presbyterians, with their emphasis on prevenient grace and practical-mindedness, preceded the others by adopting *Peacemaking: The Believers' Calling* (*Believers' Calling*) in 1980[6] and establishing an annual collection to support peacemaking initiatives and education. In 1983 the Catholic bishops adopted their pastoral letter, *The Challenge of Peace* (*Challenge of Peace*).[7] Then in 1985 the United Church of Christ adopted *A Just Peace Church* (*JPC*), declaring themselves cousins of the historic peace churches, but with their own tradition's emphasis on justice.[8] In 1986 the Methodist bishops adopted *In Defense of Creation* (*Defense of Creation*).[9] And in 1989 the historic peace churches (Mennonite, Friends, and Brethren), which had been uniting their efforts in the *New Call to Peacemaking,* together produced *A Declaration on Peace: In God's People the World's Renewal Has Begun* (*God's People*).[10] While several other denominations fashioned similar statements, for brevity's sake I focus on these five. (The above-stated abbreviations and page numbers identify citations.)

Four of the statements explicitly call for something like a just peacemaking theory. *JPC* begins with a dedicatory quote: "We now need to put as much effort into defining a just peace as we have done in the past in defining a just war" (page v; see also p. 134). The Catholic bishops issue a "call today to develop a theology of peace"; although the church's historic focus on just war theory and pacifism are still necessary, "limiting the resort to force" is not sufficient (*Challenge of Peace,* par. 23).

> A fresh reappraisal which includes a developed theology of peace will require contributions from several sectors of the Church's life: biblical studies, systematic and moral theology, ecclesiology, and the experience and insights of mem-

bers of the Church who have struggled in various ways to make and keep the peace in this often violent age. This pastoral letter is more an invitation to continue the new appraisal of war and peace than a final synthesis of the results of such an appraisal. (*Challenge of Peace,* par. 24)

The Presbyterians criticize Christian discussions of peace as inarticulate "concerning what it means to make peace" and much clearer about "the morality of participation in war." They conclude: "Christ, who wept over Jerusalem because it did not know the things that made for peace (Luke 19:41), might equally weep over a world— yes, even over a church—that seems not yet to be clear about the things that make for our peace" (*Believers' Calling,* p. 20).

The Methodists begin with a definition of *shalom* as "positive peace: harmony, wholeness, health, and well-being in all human relationships. It is the natural state of humanity as birthed by God. It is harmony between humanity and all of God's good creation." This definition rescues the biblical understanding of peace from being reduced to merely inner peace, or a peace that will be given in the last days, or merely the negative restraint of war. Biblical peace involves relationships with God, society, and environment (*Defense of Creation,* p. 24).[11] "In the roundedness of *shalom,* a just-war ethic is never enough; our churches must nurture *a new theology for a just peace*" (*Defense of Creation,* p. 13).

Although none of the statements names a "just peacemaking theory" with seven clear criteria, we can see its seven steps emerging in their thinking.

Affirm Our Common Security in Partnership with Adversaries

The Presbyterians clearly affirm the concept of common security: "We know that there can be no national security without global security and no global security without political and economic justice. . . . As God's people, we will seek the security of the whole human family—all for whom Christ died" (*Believers' Calling*, p. 5).

The Catholic bishops say sensible and successful diplomacy demands that we avoid an enemy image that fails to recognize our common interests (*Challenge of Peace*, paragraph 257). Furthermore, "Papal teaching of the last four decades . . . has supported the United Nations specifically. . . . We urge that the United States adopt a stronger supportive leadership role with respect to the United Nations" (par. 267–68).

They emphasize that love for the enemy includes the practice of contemplative prayer, which "fosters a vision of the human family as united and interdependent in the mystery of God's love for all people." And they remind us of the prayers for peace at the end of every Mass, encouraging us "to make the sign of peace at Mass an authentic sign of our reconciliation with God and with one another" (par. 294–95).

The Methodists give twenty guiding principles of a "theology for a just peace" (*Defense of Creation*, pp. 36–37). Eleven of the principles closely resemble our seven guidelines. The other nine are presuppositions for these concrete steps. They especially emphasize common security and the love of the enemy:

> Security is indivisible in a world threatened with total annihilation. Unilateral security is impossible in the nuclear age. . . . The transformation of our conflict-ridden nation-state system into a new world order of common security and interdependent institutions offers the only practical hope for enduring peace. . . . The gospel command to love enemies is more than a benevolent ideal; it is essential to our own well-being and even to our survival.

Take Transforming Initiatives

The Catholic bishops explicitly call for a strategy of initiatives:

> We believe the urgent need for control of the arms race requires a willingness for each side to take some first steps. . . . By independent initiatives we mean carefully chosen limited steps which the United States could take for a defined period of time, seeking to elicit a comparable step from the Soviet Union. . . .
> In 1963 President Kennedy announced that the United States would unilaterally forgo further nuclear testing; the next month Soviet Premier Nikita Khrushchev proposed a limited test ban which eventually became the basis of the U.S.-Soviet partial test ban treaty. Subsequently, both superpowers removed about 10,000 troops from Central Europe and each announced a cut in production of nuclear material for weapons. (*Challenge of Peace*, par. 204–6)[12]

Transforming initiatives are also clearly emphasized by *JPC:* "*Unexpected initiatives* of friendship and reconciliation can transform interpersonal and international relationships and are essential to restoring community" (*JPC*, p. 136; see also p. 75). Each local church should become "a community . . . willing to take surprising initiatives to transform situations of enmity" (*JPC*, p. 137). They reject doctrines of deterrence based primarily on the use or threat to use weapons of mass destruction, and they "also reject unilateral full-scale disarmament." Instead they advocate "new policies of common security, using a combination of negotiated agreements, new international institutions and institutional power, nonviolent strategies, unilateral initiatives to lessen tensions, and . . . policies which will make the global economy more just" (*JPC*, p. 142). They call upon the United States and the Soviet Union, and all nations, to take unilateral initiatives toward implementing a mutual nuclear weapons freeze and "toward dismantling their military arsenals, calling upon other nations to reciprocate" (*JPC*, pp. 142–43).

The Methodist bishops call for "independent US or Soviet initiatives," such as a moratorium on nuclear tests and on production of fissionable materials for bombs, a halt in flight tests, and a halt in MX or sea-launched cruise missiles, and transfer of the money saved to economic development. "Any such initiative would be an invitation to reciprocal national restraint . . . , a diplomatic strategy successfully used by Presidents Eisenhower, Kennedy, and Nixon." Recent Soviet initiatives "unfortunately have not met with positive US responses" (*Defense of Creation*, p. 77).

Talk: Seek Negotiations, Using Methods of Conflict Resolution

The Catholic bishops urge that "repeated, systematic discussion and negotiation of areas of friction" with potential adversaries, including regular summit meetings, "are too important to be regarded . . . as a concession or an event made dependent on daily shifts in international developments" (*Challenge of Peace*, par. 207). They quote Pope John Paul II, himself an experienced diplomat, reminding us that adversaries often use tactical and deliberate lies, sophisticated techniques of propaganda, and ideologies opposed to the dignity of the human person. For such adversaries, "dialogue is fixed and sterile. . . . However, even in what can be considered as an impasse . . . , the attempt to have a lucid dialogue seems still necessary in order to unblock the situation and to work for the possible establishment of peace on particular points." They comment: "The cold realism of this text, combined with the conviction that political dialogue and negotiations must be pursued, in spite of obstacles, provides solid guidance." Even in such a context talking has achieved important arms control agreements (par. 254–55).

All the other statements imply that we should be talking and negotiating arms reductions. *God's People* finds strong grounding for talking with our enemies in the New Testament insistence on bringing Gentiles and Jews into the same community: The church is "the topsy-turvy inclusion of Gentiles with the heirs of Sarah and Abraham."

Seek Human Rights and Justice for All, Especially the Powerless

The Presbyterians state forcefully that "peace cannot be achieved simply by ending the arms race unless there is economic and political justice in the human family" (*Believers' Calling,* p. 5). They lead us in confessing our awareness of economic disparities and political oppression, human suffering, and the juxtaposition of affluence and arms with poverty and oppression (p. 5 *et passim*).

Challenge of Peace says little about human rights for the poor and powerless (see par. 216). However, the Second Vatican Council put it clearly: "While extravagant sums are being spent for the furnishing of ever new weapons, an adequate remedy cannot be provided for the multiple miseries afflicting the whole modern world. . . . The arms race is an utterly treacherous trap for humanity, and one which injures the poor to an intolerable degree."[13]

The U.S. bishops speak eloquently in their pastoral letter, *Economic Justice for All:*[14]

> The hundreds of billions of dollars spent by our nation each year on the arms race create a massive drain on the U.S. economy as well as a very serious "brain drain." Such spending on the arms race means a net loss in the number of

jobs created in the economy, because defense industries are less labor-intensive than other major sectors of the economy. Moreover, nearly half of the American scientific and engineering force works in defense-related programs and over 60 percent of the entire federal research and development budget goes to the military.

Both documents strongly emphasize the rights of workers, and the human rights of all persons, including the poor and the powerless.[15]

The United Church of Christ defines its identity by affirming its special experience in the struggle for civil rights, Native American rights, and women's rights, as well as the "new winds of the Spirit" moving through the church and heard in voices of "women and African, Asian, Hispanic, and Native American men and women" (*JPC,* pp. 10–11). Thus we "seek human rights and justice for all, especially the powerless." "We start from the recognition that God's word of Just Peace today is heard most powerfully in the voices of those who have largely borne and still bear the burden of social, economic, and political oppression." The struggle includes "those who have to some extent enjoyed the fruits of privilege but who are now seeking liberation from their complicity in oppression and unjust privilege. To a certain extent, all people are caught in the bondage of violence and death that characterizes the structures of privilege and oppression" (*JPC,* pp. 39–40).

Thus the injustice of excessive military spending is strongly criticized (*JPC,* pp. 43, 73ff.). So is North American peace theology when it is based too much in the fear of war, instead of in the violence experienced every day in the life of the poor (pp. 65ff.). Human rights require that power be shared, limited, and criticized (pp. 75ff.).

Defense of Creation says, "Every policy of government must be an act of justice and must be measured by its impact on the poor, the weak, and the oppressed—not only in our own nation but in all nations."

God's People emphasizes the theme of justice in connection with the section on prophecy and the Messiah. It also emphasizes the Holy Spirit, who inspires the prophets to declare God's will for justice and to call us to repent of our injustice and idolatry. Justice is tellingly defined as "social structures marked by integrity and mutuality, which work on behalf of all people, and concern focussed on those marginalized by physical misfortune or social circumstances" (p. 10).

Realistically Acknowledge Our Captivity in Vicious Cycles and Our Need to Participate in a Realistic Peacemaking Process

The Presbyterians begin by acknowledging our bondage in alienating processes—"the continuing arms race and looming conflicts over diminishing energy resources as centers of power struggle for control" (*Believers' Calling*, p. 4—a prophetic acknowledgment ten years prior to the Gulf War of 1990–91). They confess, "Our fear for safety has led us to trust in the false security of arms; our sin of war has led us to take life; and now we are in danger of taking our own lives as well. Furthermore, economic systems fail to allow a quarter of the world's population full participation in their societies, creating recurrent patterns of starvation and famine in Asia and Africa" (ibid.).

The sense of bondage, the need for God's grace to deliver us, and the call to repentance ring true; they come from the heart of Presbyterian faith:

> It is a matter of praying and yearning. It is an inner response to God, who loves the whole world and whose Spirit calls for and empowers the making of peace. With repentance

and humility and the power of hope, let us tend to our task. . . .

In our confessions of faith the church has recognized this vocation, yet in our life we have been unfaithful to our Lord. We must repent. Our insensitivity to today's patterns of injustice, inequality, and oppression—indeed, our participation in them—denies the gospel. Christ alone is our peace. As part of his body in the whole church, we experience the brokenness of this world in our own life. Today we stand at a turning point in history. (*Believers' Calling,* p. 5)

In their statement, the U.S. Catholic Conference also confesses:

Because we are all capable of violence, we are never totally conformed to Christ and are always in need of conversion. . . .

The present nuclear arms race has distracted us from the words of the prophets, has turned us from peace-making, and has focused our attention on a nuclear buildup leading to annihilation. We are called to turn back from this evil of total destruction and turn instead in prayer and penance toward God, toward our neighbor, and toward the building of a peaceful world. (*Challenge of Peace,* par. 297–300)

The sense of participating in a biblically grounded, God-given drama of grace in our peacemaking is most clearly expressed by the historic peace churches' *God's People.* It is thoroughly grounded in the whole sweep of the biblical drama—the mission of Israel, the ministry of Jesus, and the mission of the church—not just a few select passages. It is Christ-centered and emphasizes the way of the cross, which includes nonviolence and peacemaking. It hears the biblical message as a call to commitment, obedience, discipleship, and participation in God's reign. *God's People* sees the biblical drama not only as revealing some ethical principles but also as describing the drama of God's reign, renewing the world, which is the drama in which the church, God's people, has its existence and mission. The broad biblical sweep and Christ-centered witness are intended as an invitation for all churches that take the biblical message as authoritative.

Instead of Making Judgmental Statements, Acknowledge to Others That We Have Caused Hurt and Want to Do Better

All the statements except *God's People* were written during the second Cold War, in the 1980s. Furthermore, the Catholic bishops especially were under attack from members of the government and political conservatives. That must have influenced them to be relatively silent on the sixth point (see *Challenge of Peace,* par. 245–51).

The Methodists are probably the clearest concerning our ideology of deterrence and its effect on our image of the enemy, and our need to repent and make amends. The chief author of their document, Alan Geyer, was especially aware of the need to confront this complex of problems. The Methodists emphasize that "repentance is a prerequisite of reconciliation for individuals, groups, nations, and churches. The churches' own implication in militarism, racism, sexism, and materialism requires a deeply penitent approach to peacemaking" (*Defense of Creation,* p. 37).[16]

All the seven steps of just peacemaking theory are articulated in *JPC.* There is a clear sense of acknowledging captivity, the need for forgiveness and repentance, and prayer (*JPC,* pp. 46–47, 85, 137–40, 144–45).

Participate in Groups with Truthful Information and a Voice in Policy-making

The Believers' Calling shines forth in its commitment to all sorts of group organization in the church for practical praying, learning, and acting on peacemaking. Fully half the statement is a mandate for the various groups in the church, at various levels from "local church peace fellowships and other community peace groups," to congregations, to synod task forces, to "all agencies of the General Assembly, seminaries, colleges, and other institutions," to the program agencies.

Challenge of Peace (par. 252) says "a glory of the United States is the range of political freedoms its system permits us. We, as bishops, as Catholics, as citizens, exercise those freedoms in writing this letter, with its share of criticisms of our government." The letter concludes with an extensive section on the role of clergy and women and men religious, educators, parents, youth, men and women in military service, workers in defense industries, scientists, public officials, and Catholics as citizens (par. 301–29). It favors cooperating with other Christians, Jewish and Islamic communities, and "all men and women of good will who seek to reverse the arms race and secure the peace of the world" (par. 329). It does not specifically mention either church-based or secular peacemaking organizations, except groups of physicians and scientists (par. 320). The emphasis is on the church itself teaching peacemaking.

JPC's special sense of the church as a just peace church and of the importance of organizing congregations and peacemaking groups is especially clear, since the statement is a dramatic declaration, after several years of discussion and refinement, of the United Church of Christ (UCC) as a just peace church (*JPC,* pp. 106–16, 137–38). The advocacy networks of the church are specially mentioned. The hunger, economic justice, and peacemaking advocacy networks of the UCC are known as a model for all other denominations to emulate.

Furthermore, the UCC states clearly that our theology of government should not be based primarily in coercion, as Paul Ramsey asserts, but in justice and consent of the people (*JPC,* p. 66).

The Methodists' emphasis on the sovereignty of God gives them a strong foundation for the independence of Christian churches and groups over against governments (*Defense of Creation*, pp. 24–29). The Bible has "a dual attitude toward political authority." Rulers' authority is provisionally from God, but when they become oppressive and lawless, "they are rightly subject to criticism, to correction, and, ultimately, to resistance." *Shalom* "indicates an alternative community—alternative to the idolatries, oppressions, and violence that mark the ways of many nations." Christians warn against the lies of the rulers and call for repentance and grace.

> The church of Jesus Christ, in the power and unity of the Holy Spirit, is called to serve as an alternative community to an alienated and fractured world—a loving and peaceable international company of disciples transcending all governments, races, and ideologies; reaching out to all "enemies;" and ministering to all the victims of poverty and oppression. . . . Loyalty to one's own government is always subject to the transcendent loyalty that belongs to the sovereign God alone. Such loyalty may be politically expressed either in support of or in opposition to current government policies. . . . Truthfulness is a necessary foundation of peacemaking. Lies tend to become tools of self-aggrandizement, weapons of hate, and acts of violence.

The study guide for *In Defense of Creation* begins with two chapters showing that the way to get started is to form peacemaking groups.[17]

God's People strongly emphasizes our seventh theme. Peacemaking is "not the calling of isolated individuals, nor of minority communities of the wider Church family. It is the vocation of the entire Church in its fullest sense of peoplehood" (p. 2). The church is to be an alternative to the world's way of doing politics, not a Constantinian marriage with the political establishment. There is greater trust in the grass roots, the base, the powerless, the practice of the people of God, than in the more hierarchical traditions. Hence the title chosen is *God's People.* "This people is by no means apolitical, acceding to any policy . . . , [but] allies itself with specific political powers only insofar as those powers are moving in the same direction as God's reign. . . . Sharing of wealth, broadening participation in policy-making, simplifying lifestyles in modesty—these are the seeds of peace. Failing to sow these, any people will perennially reap war" (pp. 47–49). Thus the statement "calls for positive but provisional political involvement."[18]

Needed: A Clear Picture of a Creative Pattern of Constructive Peacemaking

In sections III and IV of *Challenge of Peace* the people are given hope, guidance, and empowerment to take their own initiatives and not merely to watch passively. There, as well as in the last part of section II, numerous specific initiatives are advocated: a bilateral nuclear weapons freeze, bilateral deep reductions, a comprehensive test ban, removal of short-range and forward-based nuclear weapons (the Euromissiles), strengthening command and control, a strategy of independent initiatives, ongoing negotiations and summit meetings, negotiations to reduce conventional weapons and outlaw chemical and biological weapons, reduction of trade in military weapons, nonviolent means of conflict resolution and civilian defense, support for human rights and the United Nations. The bishops were able to be this specific because the Catholic tradition of moral theology believes in completing the task of spelling out concrete implications, and because *Challenge of Peace* was supported by extensive consultation with social scientists and experts both from the government and from the peace movement. These initiatives were being pushed by the peace movement, and the bishops' advocacy gave people great encouragement. However, most of the public and media discussion of the pastoral ignored these initiatives and focused on the part that rules out most uses of nuclear weapons but gives qualified, temporary approval to nuclear deterrence.

Why was more attention not given to the positive initiatives? Sandra Schneiders points out that the biblical basis in section I is never connected with the rest of the pastoral.[19] Instead just war theory in section I is connected with "limiting the resort to [nuclear] force" in section II. Hence section I builds the moral basis for focusing attention on the arguments for restraint in section II. Even the biblical section is still dominated by the debate between just war theory and pacifism; it primarily asks whether the Bible approves war or disapproves it. Thus neither the biblical nor the just-war part of section I builds the basis for an initiatives strategy in sections III and IV. What is needed is to develop a biblical basis, and a conflict resolution basis, for a constructive theology of peacemaking with transforming initiatives. The bishops clearly intend this. We can see it emerging throughout the pastoral. Once it is named and grounded in section I, the whole pastoral could become a unified, seamless web.

Similarly, *Believers' Calling*, which pioneered the way for the other statements, lacks the biblical grounding of specific steps in peacemaking. So when it turns to practical steps, there is a bumpy transition to "foreign policy subjects," "positions on many subjects related to peace and justice," "exercising our citizenship in the body politic to shape foreign policy," nurturing "changes in public attitude," and "specific foreign policy problems" (*Believers' Calling*, pp. 6–7). The language deals with "issues" without specific biblical or theological reference or a sense of what ethical insights, initiatives, or commitments we bring to these "issues."

In 1983 the Presbyterian General Assembly requested a

follow-up study. The response was a book, *The Peacemaking Struggle: Militarism and Resistance,* and a study paper for discussion, *Presbyterians and Peacemaking: Are We Now Called to Resistance?*[20] The book's preface explains that the work "was cast in the context of the ethics of a just peace." Edward Long writes that the ethics of pacifism and just war theory usually come into play "after the social and political situation is allowed to deteriorate and war seems to be the only possible outcome, . . . after discontent and conflict have intensified to the point where hostilities have broken out or where nations have amassed great capacities to destroy others."[21] We must find a new approach starting with the premise

> that justice is a social condition that contributes to harmony and order, that justice is less the system of restraints imposed by force than the condition of social well-being that makes conflict less likely to occur. Such a different way of thinking might be called the doctrine of a just peace. It directs attention to the needs, hopes, and aspirations of people, and is concerned to think how their needs can be cared for, their persons and communities respected, and their liberties cherished. In peace thinking, justice becomes the means of eliminating conflict before it erupts, of avoiding the conditions that lead to rancor and hostility if allowed to go uncorrected.
>
> There is afoot in our time, not least among thoughtful Christians, a still embryonic realization that such an innovative way of thinking is sorely needed.[22]

Yet the irony is that this beautiful description of the need was not followed by a development of the concrete steps of just peacemaking. Instead, the rest of the book is primarily a description of our society's bondage to the vicious cycles of destruction, and how to resist them with tax resistance, civil disobedience, withdrawal of cooperation, and critical thinking. There are many sharp insights, well worth reading. Yet unless people have a clear picture of a new pattern of constructive peacemaking in which they can engage, they are likely to feel powerless and without hope, to feel they are merely resisting a powerful status quo. Unless the new pattern has concrete steps that are biblically grounded and make sense in practice, church members are less likely to see it as essential to their mission as Christians. Hence the well-written study paper, a summary of the book, met strong resistance in the church—as its authors expected—and was not adopted.

The study paper began with a biblical section on the meaning of reconciliation in Colossians 1:15–20 and 2 Corinthians 5:16–21, and on the meaning of *shalom*. The definition of *shalom* is especially nicely done. The biblical work describes the content of peace and not the process of peacemaking, so the grounding for concrete steps of peacemaking is not yet developed.

The study process did lead, however, to extended discussion and the eventual adoption of *Christian Obedience in a Nuclear Age* in 1988. As with the other Presbyterian statements, it describes our bondage to idolatrous processes perceptively.[23] It agrees with the Methodists that "the moral case for nuclear deterrence, even as an interim ethic, has been undermined by unrelenting arms escalation." It says: "We agree with the report of the Episcopal Diocese of Washington (1987), which states that mutual vulnerability and the existing policy of nuclear deterrence are conditions that cannot immediately or easily be changed. . . . We must exercise our individual and corporate influence to effect a change in national policy as rapidly as possible."[24]

The Presbyterian statement continues:

> The church in the nuclear age must shift its energies from considerations of just war to the urgent and primary task of defining and serving a just peace. . . .
>
> Christian obedience demands that we move toward that peace in all possible ways: by extending the rule of law, ad-

vocating universal human rights, strengthening the organs
of international order, working for common security and
economic justice, converting industry to peaceful production, increasing understanding of and reconciliation with
those we identify as enemies, developing peacemaking
skills, constructing concrete manifestations of just peace
across barriers of conflict and injustice, and other means.[25]

By contrast with the study paper on resistance, *Christian Obedience in a Nuclear Age* celebrates the rights of
political advocacy in the United States and says "there is
a broad consensus in the Presbyterian church (U.S.A.)
that the primary course to be pursued . . . is the vigorous
and creative use of the ordinary and legal means available
to us as citizens," or in other words, "extraordinary use of
ordinary means."[26] Support is expressed for some whose
consciences lead them to practice tax resistance or civil
disobedience. But "negotiation is the alternative of choice
in the present situation"—negotiation of a comprehensive test ban, a nuclear weapons freeze, no first use of nuclear weapons, reductions and phased elimination of all
nuclear weapons, demilitarization of space, strengthening
of the Nonproliferation Treaty, and resolution of regional
conflicts.[27] The concept of common security is advocated
three times.[28] Church congregations are urged to form
"communities of dialogue and support in which the leading of the Holy Spirit can be discerned through 'study of
the Word, prayerful waiting on God, and searching moral
discourse with brothers and sisters in the faith.' "[29]

Thus most of the steps of the transforming initiatives
model are advocated in this document, though without
specific warrant in the central biblical passages we have
studied. The report received widespread support and was
adopted for official policy guidance.

The peace churches are biblically grounded if they are
anything. They describe the calling of God's people to
practice nonviolence, including the transforming initia-

tives taught by Jesus: love for our enemies, transforming initiatives toward those who hate us, blessing and praying for our persecutors (Luke 6). "Civil initiatives" are emphasized, such as civil disobedience, sanctuary for refugees, sharing wealth, and simplifying life-styles. They affirm the calling of the people of God to be the instrument of transformation of the world.

Yet *God's People* does not spell out specific practices of peacemaking as fully and clearly as one might expect from the historic peace churches, which have engaged their members in so many peacemaking initiatives. Nor is there help from the social sciences. If the biblical theology of the statement were explicitly joined with the seven-step transforming-initiatives model, it might lead to a more explicit emphasis on our own bondage in alienating processes, our need to practice repentance and forgiveness, and our need to participate in concrete grace-based peacemaking initiatives that are a faithful witness to Christ, as *God's People* clearly intends.

In all these church statements, surely something new is emerging. The time is already overdue for naming the constructive pattern of peacemaking, the pattern of transforming initiatives and just peacemaking theory, which is obligatory for all of us and for governments whose calling includes the common good and peace of their people.

Questions for Thought

1. Why do you suppose almost all major denominations produced extensive statements on peacemaking in the 1980s? Do you think it did any good?

2. Why do you suppose they agreed as much as they did?

3. All the church statements were seeking to support a process of peacemaking that would move us beyond the

Cold War era into a less dangerous, more just, and more peaceful era. Do you think this led them to anticipate the "turning" that happened in the end of the 1980s, and to begin to imagine a peacemaking ethic for the post–Cold War era?

4. In what ways can the emerging peacemaking ethic help us cope with a world with many centers of power, much economic deprivation and ecological deterioration, and a continuing nuclear threat?

5. The Catholic bishops argue that we should be talking regularly with potential adversaries even when they are ideologically rigid and propagandistic. Yet in recent years, the stated policy of the U.S. government has been to refuse to talk with Libya under Khadafi, Iran under the Ayatollah Khomeini, Cuba under Castro, Iraq under Saddam Hussein, the PLO (for many years), and terrorists. At the same time we have talked with many tyrannical dictators. With whom do you think we should talk, and with whom not? Why?

6. Are you convinced a new peacemaking model is emerging? Do you think the ingredients have been properly designated? What would you add or change? What reasons would you give?

10

Just Peacemaking, Just War, and Pacifism

No matter how well we do the work of just peacemaking, not all conflicts will be resolved. Some conflicts will lead to war, or the brink of war. We will need to debate whether to make war, and, if the political processes produce war, we will need to debate whether we ourselves should support or oppose it, participate in it or resist it. We will still need a theology of the restraint of war—*either pacifism or just war theory.*

Christian pacifism is based largely on the biblical passages we have studied as well as on other biblical passages that teach us to love our enemies and not to set ourselves violently against them. In addition, many pacifists argue that war has always been evil but is now a mega-evil because of the skyrocketing economic costs and destructive power of new weapons systems. Pacifism says Christians must never make war but instead should be peacemakers. John Howard Yoder has described something like twenty-seven varieties of pacifism in his book, *Nevertheless: The Varieties of Religious Pacifism.* In *Politics of Jesus* and other books he has made a strong and persuasive biblical argument for nonviolence as essential to the calling of the Christian.[1] Yoder's pacifism is not based on pragmatic arguments about the increasing destruction of war and the more efficient peaceful alternatives but on the essential characteristics of Christian discipleship, following Christ, and taking up our cross. Making war is the opposite of witnessing to Christ and following Christ.

Just War Theory and Just Peacemaking

Just war theory argues that some wars are just, and we are obligated to fight them; other wars are unjust, and we are obligated to oppose them. There are definite criteria for telling the difference. A just war must pass all the criteria; otherwise it is wrong to fight. Here is a short summary-interpretation of the criteria based on the U.S. Catholic bishops' definition in *Challenge of Peace*:

1. Probability of *success*: To kill and maim many people is wrong even for a just cause, if after all the deaths the cause will be lost anyhow.

2. Just *cause*: War may be fought only to protect innocent life, preserve conditions necessary for decent human existence, and secure basic human rights against a real and certain danger. The position of the side to be defended must be more just than the adversary's position.

3. Last *resort*: All peaceful alternatives must have been exhausted.

4. Just *authority*: War may be declared only by those with responsibility for public order. (The U.S. Constitution assigns this responsibility to Congress. In our interdependent global society, there should be international responsibility, such as the United Nations or a representative regional organization. A revolutionary war can be begun only by leadership truly representative of the people.)

5. Just *means*: War must not directly attack noncombatants but only military targets (discrimination). "Under no circumstances may nuclear weapons or other instruments of mass slaughter be used for the purpose of destroying

population centers or other predominantly civilian targets." Just means and cost/benefit proportionality apply both to the decision to make war and to conduct during the war.

6. *Cost/benefit proportionality*: The cost of the war to people and to the international community must not exceed the good expected if it is fought.

7. Just *intention*: The purpose of war may not be conquest, enslavement, revenge, or an ideological crusade but only the pursuit of peace and justice. Unnecessarily destructive acts or unreasonable conditions such as unconditional surrender must be avoided.

8. *Announcement*: The intention to make war and its just causes must be clearly announced by the legitimate authority, so that the adversary is aware of the seriousness of the situation and of what it must do to avoid war, and so that the people can judge its justice. (The bishops subsume this criterion under "Just Authority.")[2]

What can just peacemaking theory contribute to pacifism and just war theory?

First, it can give them time to work. Realism tells us that the forces of war build up so much momentum and are so powerful that they cannot be stopped by either pacifism or just war theory once we are at the brink of war. Only an overly optimistic rationalism can believe that moral arguments by pacifists and just war theorists in the church alone will stop many wars once war has become a front-page story. To raise issues of pacifism or just war theory as we approach the brink of war is almost always too late. In the case of the war against Iraq, many churches spoke clearly in December 1990 and January 1991, using just war theory to argue in favor of giving the sanctions time to work. However, insider interviews indicate the decision to make war and not wait for sanctions had already been made in October. Just peacemaking theory focuses attention on preventive and conflict-resolution measures early in a conflict, while there is still time to divert the forces that lead to war.

A second contribution of just peacemaking theory is that it gives the people and churches clearly articulated criteria to guide their own peacemaking initiatives and to measure whether the government is actually seeking peace as it claims. Thus it can empower the people to action and stimulate our independent and critical mindset. We are then more prepared to make the independent and critical judgments required by pacifism and just war theory.

Just peacemaking theory can help fill out the criteria of pacifism and just war theory. The more profound forms of Christian pacifism have always been biblically grounded and have always intended not merely a no to violence but a yes to a constructive way of life, with peacemaking initiatives such as work camps, exchange projects, visitation teams, Witness for Peace teams, service teams, alternative proposals, prayer services, vigils, rice meals, civil disobedience, nonviolent direct action, and committees on national legislation. Just peacemaking theory keeps pacifism from being narrowed down to simply saying no, as it is enticed to do in debates with just war theory. Pacifism also says yes to biblically grounded transforming initiatives of peacemaking. Pacifists are concerned about justice and human rights; just peacemaking theory strengthens that concern.

Just peacemaking also helps fill out the criterion of *last resort* in just war theory. The other resorts besides war are too seldom spelled out concretely. *The Challenge of Peace,* for example, has one paragraph regretting that nations often do not wait until the last resort, and one paragraph affirming the United Nations. But nations and ordinary people alike need help imagining what other possibilities must be tried. Just peacemaking theory does that: affirm valid interests, support institutions of common security, take transforming initiatives, negotiate, work on justice and human rights, acknowledge our own complicity, make amends, encourage the work of peacemaking groups.

In just war theory, *just intention* says we must seek to restore peace and reconciliation. Just peacemaking theory says we must pay attention to our adversary's valid security needs, to institutions of common security, and to justice and human rights as key ingredients of restoring peace.

Just authority depends on the people being accurately informed and not lied to; the seventh criterion of just peacemaking explicitly lifts up the dimension of truth for the people.

Just war theory may be based on the presumption against violence or on basic human rights.[3] Just peacemaking theory encourages it to develop its basis in human rights, as Michael Walzer does, as well as the presumption in favor of peacemaking initiatives. When assessing a new weapon, just peacemaking theory asks not only whether that weapon will discriminate between military targets and civilians but also whether its development will be a step toward arms control and reductions or a step away from arms control and toward escalation.[4] In the traditions of those who advocate pacifism and just war theory, there is much wisdom about how to make peace.[5] Just peacemaking theory lifts up that wisdom for notice.

Finally, just peacemaking theory makes clear that there are two questions, not just one. One asks what are the criteria for making peace, and the other, what are the criteria for restraining war. Paul Ramsey's criticism of the Methodist bishops wrongly assumes there is only one question: whether to make war. He argues there are only two possible answers: either you are opposed to participation in any war, or you have criteria that enable you to select some wars and oppose others. You are either a pacifist or a just war theorist. There is no third option. This

situation may be true if the only question regards participation in war. However, a second question might well be
based on a theology of peace—what initiatives are we to
take for the prevention of war? That question is less interested in whether you declare opposition to all wars or
some, than whether you are taking well-aimed initiatives
now, this week, to make peace. Nevertheless, just peacemaking theory does not allow us to do away with the question Ramsey is asking: whether to make war. Wars will
still happen. We will still need the question posed by just
war or pacifism. The two sets of questions should enrich
each other, not replace each other.

The Example of the Gulf War:
George Bush Versus Saddam Hussein

In the first chapter I mentioned a frustration shared by
many during the time before the Gulf War. We felt the
debate about whether to start war or to wait was inade-
quate. We wanted a third alternative, a debate about
peacemaking initiatives. We needed a model of just
peacemaking with definite criteria so public debate could
be focused, and so people could assess what the government was doing during the buildup. Let us now ask how
just peacemaking theory might have illuminated the aggression of Iraq against Kuwait and the subsequent war
against Iraq.

The war had a major impact on many people's values
and perceptions. For many in the United States, it was a
war not only against Iraq but also against the unhappy
memories of the Vietnam War. It was widely celebrated
because the military that had been ineffective against the
Vietcong guerrillas in the jungles of Vietnam was dramatically effective against the Iraqi army in the desert. Furthermore, Saddam Hussein had clearly committed
aggression and was a good enemy against whom to make

war. The cause was clearly just. The United States was more free of hate for the people of Iraq than for the enemy in most previous wars; animosity was aimed at Saddam Hussein, not at a caricature of the people of Iraq.

At least 200,000 human beings died. Their families were left with bitter grief.[6] Another quarter of a million human beings were wounded, and many permanently maimed. Greenpeace estimated the total of both civilian and military deaths during the war, plus those killed during the subsequent civil wars and those who died of epidemics and disease from the destruction of the water, food, and medicine supply, as well as electricity and transportation. Their calculation was that 225,000 to 245,000 had died by the end of May 1991.[7] They say more Iraqis died in this war with the United States than in their eight-year war with Iran. Allied cluster bombs and dumb bombs caused the majority of casualties during the war. The smart bombs we saw on television were not typical of the actual devastation. The Pentagon explained two weeks after the war ended that only 7 percent of the bombs dropped were smart bombs. Yet that is all we saw on the controlled television portrayal of the war. In any case, a nation was devastated. Two civil wars resulted (against the Kurds in the north and the Shiites in the south), killing many more people and disrupting the homes and lives of many others. Intense Arab resentments against the United States and the West were kindled.

The killing was far worse than television coverage led us to imagine; neither side's military allowed the reporters to televise the human side of the war.[8] It was a "nintendo war where no victims appear on the screen."[9] We have to exercise our own imagination and compassion to begin to feel what the war did to the dying and their families.

George Williamson, pastor of First Baptist Church in Granville, Ohio, visited Iraq shortly before the war broke out. He writes:

> I was taken to . . . a military parade done by a thousand or
> so Iraqi children dressed in mock fatigues. They were chant-
> ing, "Yes, yes, Saddam! No, no, Bush!"—their celebration
> of those who died in the long Iraq-Iran war whose day of
> celebration it was. Many of them are probably now dead.
> Shortly after my return home I was driving through Lancas-
> ter, Ohio, on Martin Luther King Day. I passed a demon-
> stration of U.S. children, approximately the same age,
> holding a large U.S. flag, chanting "Sack Iraq! Support the
> president!"—their celebration of America's greatest peace-
> maker. None of these children, whether in Baghdad or Lan-
> caster, had any idea of the meaning of their words or the
> reality in which they were participating. . . .
>
> The children I watched playing war in Baghdad and
> shouting their pro-Saddam, anti-Bush chant were as beauti-
> ful and attractive as any children. I had in my pocket some
> pictures of children from First Baptist Granville. I offered a
> few to the little mock warriors, who instantly gave up their
> war and surrounded me in a clamor for pictures. We made a
> shambles of the official military ceremony, but had a won-
> derful time for a mythical moment that held the war in sus-
> pension. When we parted, some of them clutching with
> obvious pride and joy the picture of children I know and
> love, the "Yes, yes, Saddam! No, no, Bush!" chant had been
> replaced by an antiphony between me and them: "I love
> you! I love you!"[10]

Many of those children are probably now dead. Many
of their fathers are surely dead, their families fatherless.
Had we been able to get Iraq out of Kuwait and stop Iraq's
military threat without such a destructive war, certainly
we would have preferred that. Could just peacemaking
have helped?

Affirm Valid Interests

Certainly, both sides failed miserably at *affirming one
another's valid interests.* For months, Iraq had been trying

to persuade Kuwait to listen to its interests. Kuwait was pumping much more oil than their OPEC (Organization of Petroleum Exporting Countries) quota, which had driven the price of oil much lower than the OPEC target price, with damaging consequences for Iraq.[11] Iraq was deeply in debt from its eight-year war with Iran and accused Kuwait of making economic war on Iraq. Iraq also claimed Kuwait had slant-drilled two and a half billion dollars worth of oil from Iraq's oil fields, under their border. Iraq also wanted to be able to use its only seaport, which was blocked by two small uninhabited Kuwaiti islands. Iraq expected Kuwait to forgive its debt incurred in the war against Iran on behalf of Kuwait and other Arab nations. "During the spring and summer, the Kuwaitis took an extremely hard line with Iraq. The Iraqi position is that Kuwait offered no significant concessions" on any of the issues. Crown Prince Hassan of Jordan said that "the entire Arab world had found Kuwait's defiant behavior toward Iraq in the months preceding the crisis incomprehensible."[12] One of the advisers of Jordan's King Hussein said, "The Kuwaitis were very cocky. They told us officially that the United States would intervene if there was trouble with Iraq."[13]

On Iraq's part, as Ze'ev Schiff has somewhat understated, Saddam "erred in his assessment that Washington would resign itself to his invasion of Kuwait."[14] He certainly did not affirm the valid interests of Kuwait or the United States. Without fuller discussion, we can at least conclude that the two sides failed to affirm one another's valid interests. And war resulted.

Harold Saunders is the highly respected Middle East expert who advised the Nixon, Ford, and Carter administrations and was the expert adviser in the Camp David talks—the one successful peace negotiation between Israel and an Arab country. Camp David achieved security for Israel's southern flank, returned the Sinai desert to

Egypt, and worked out a lasting peace between Israel and Egypt, although it did not achieve justice for the Palestinians. During the time of the sanctions against Iraq, Harold Saunders laid out a series of proposals for affirming the valid interests of the adversaries and thus making Iraqi withdrawal more likely without war:[15]

- Iraq should withdraw from all of Kuwait, with some security assurances of borders by a United Nations or Arab force.
- The question of slant-drilling of oil should be submitted to the World Court for a solution based on international law rather than aggression.
- The United Nations should station a peacekeeping unit on the uninhabited Kuwaiti islands to assure Iraq safe use of its seaport.
- An international Arab Bank for Reconstruction and Development should be created with contributions from oil producers to raise the incomes of have-not people in the Gulf.
- Iraq should negotiate its debts to its neighbors.
- The United States should announce its intention to seek to reconstitute the Arab-Israeli peace process. This would not be linked to Iraq's actions; it would be done because it was wise, prudent, and just. (It was in fact done *after* the war, without linkage.)

In addition to Saunders's proposals, it has become apparent that Iraq needs to be pressed to agree to international inspection of its nuclear research facility, as it agreed when it signed the Nonproliferation Treaty, and to agree to destroy its chemical weapons facilities and permit on-site inspection to verify this, as the United States and Soviet Union are agreeing to do. Such an agreement, backed up with inspections, can be more effective over the long haul than bombing those facilities. Bombing stops them for only a few years, as shown by the temporariness of the effect of the Israeli bombing of those facilities a few years ago. After the Gulf War, it became clear that war had failed to destroy either the chemical or the nuclear facilities. We were back to relying on the pressure of sanctions and international inspections to get rid of the facilities, as some of us had proposed before the war, based on just peacemaking theory.

As Cornel West points out, President Bush and Secretary Baker should be praised for their going to the United Nations to consult and organize international sanctions.[16] An essential part of common security in the new period is support for the United Nations and regular international consultation. The international community needs to use its diplomatic, political, and economic pressure to discourage aggression and to encourage human rights and conflict resolution. There were hundreds of consultations, and the United Nations organized the most effective trade embargo in memory. With some reluctance, the Bush administration agreed not to use its navy to enforce the embargo until the United Nations approved. It was a masterful beginning, and the Bush administration deserves praise, even if, as in all political actions, the motives were mixed.

Take Initiatives

Harold Saunders said, "A second component is essential to producing a political settlement. That is devising a scenario of political steps that could lead to changes in the situation."[17] He then described the strategy of independent initiatives.

In November, when the U.S. embassy in Kuwait was without water and fresh food, the Iraqi government took a surprising initiative—they sent food. In a press conference, President Bush said he did not know what this Iraqi initiative meant, but it was an interesting initiative. Then

President Bush, who had been prohibiting any talks with Iraq, announced that Iraq's foreign minister could come to Washington early in December, and Secretary Baker could go to Baghdad any time between December 15 and January 15—a U.S. initiative. Saddam Hussein then released the hostages he was holding—an Iraqi initiative. A series of independent initiatives was under way that was creating openings for talks. Unfortunately, the exchange broke down over the disagreement whether January 12 was too late for Secretary Baker to go to Baghdad.

On February 6, after the bombing had been going on for three weeks, Secretary Baker announced five pillars of settlement for after the war: a new security arrangement for the Gulf, an arms control agreement, a program of economic reconstruction for the have-nots in the Arab world including those in Iraq and Iran, a renewed effort to settle the Israeli-Palestinian and Arab-Israeli conflicts, and a comprehensive strategy for reducing U.S. dependence on imported oil. Initiatives to *actually begin organizing* some of these "pillars" could have been significant if they had been taken before the bombing, or even before the ground war. They were wise and right to do, war or no war. They could have decreased Arab resentment and given Saddam Hussein a somewhat more dignified way to retreat. They could have saved 200,000 lives.

Talk with the Enemy

Both sides failed to enter into serious talking, serious negotiations using methods of conflict resolution. For months, Iraq had been insisting Kuwait needed to listen to Iraq's complaints—a clear signal of trouble to come. Then on July 16 the senior Pentagon intelligence officer for the Mideast saw clear aerial photo evidence of an Iraqi buildup of tanks and artillery in preparation for a major attack.[18] The U.S. government said nothing to Iraq. On

July 25 the U.S. ambassador to Iraq, April Glaspie, met with Saddam Hussein at his request. He probed U.S. intentions, asking, "What can it mean when the United States says it will now protect its friends?"[19] She said, "We have no opinion on the Arab-Arab conflicts like your border disagreement with Kuwait." Glaspie has been criticized for not stating firmly that the United States would respond strongly to aggression. A review of several secret cables, especially Glaspie's summary of her meeting with Hussein, showed Hussein made a number of veiled threats that he might resort to force and that she and President Bush took a conciliatory approach rather than giving a firm warning.[20]

On July 30 the senior Pentagon intelligence officer for the Middle East said the evidence predicted Saddam would attack soon. The United States said nothing to Iraq. On August 1 at 6 A.M., the senior Pentagon intelligence officer for the Middle East reported unmistakable evidence Iraq was moving to attack. The United States said nothing. On August 1 at 9 P.M., Iraq attacked.

The admonition to talk when there is a problem between us does not mean only "soothing talk." There are times to confront. Surely this was a time to have confronted, firmly.

From the standpoint of just peacemaking, we can also suggest the United States should have affirmed valid interests on both sides and offered to consult, to mediate, or to urge Kuwait to submit the issues to arbitration. Not only firm warning, but also initiatives that get at the source of the anger are needed.

Some have the impression that there were negotiations with Saddam Hussein. The data paint a somewhat different picture. During the time of the sanctions, from August through early December, the U.S. government refused to talk with Iraq. Under great pressure, President Bush announced Secretary Aziz could come to Washington early in December (a satisfactory date was accepted) and Secretary Baker could go to Baghdad any time between December 15 and January 15. Baghdad agreed, setting January 12 as the date; but President Bush said that was too late. Eventually Secretary Baker, already in Geneva, talked with Aziz there on January 9. But it was Hussein in Baghdad he needed to see; Hussein made the decisions, and he was known to shoot members of his staff who brought him bad news. Throughout this time, Vice President Quayle and President Bush announced that there would be no negotiations, no concessions, no compromises; we would only present the ultimatum—get out of Kuwait or we will destroy you thoroughly. Secretary General Perez de Cuellar of the United Nations was told by the United States that he could do no more. Prime Minister Mitterand of France suggested that after Iraq got out, there could be a peace consultation concerning Israeli-Palestinian relations, but President Bush rejected that proposal immediately. This series does not exemplify talking, negotiating, using methods of conflict resolution. Until the last days before the beginning of the ground war, Saddam Hussein on his part did not talk seriously either. Jim Wallis concluded that "both sides were intransigent, both sides blocked potential solutions. . . . Saddam's belligerence caused him to miss many opportunities, and the United States snuffed out potential openings for a political settlement."[21]

Many experts, including the CIA, the Department of State, the chairman of the joint chiefs of staff, and Ambassador Bandar of Saudi Arabia, thought Iraq would withdraw at the last minute.[22] Several experts expected Saddam would withdraw *after* the January 15 deadline so as to do it on his schedule, not ours. Our military had left the public impression we would not be ready to attack until February. We began the bombing the first day after the deadline, at 7 P.M., January 16, earlier than almost anyone expected. Would Saddam have pulled out that week? We will probably never know.

In the last days before the ground war, President Gorbachev worked out an agreement for Iraq to get out of Kuwait without their previous unacceptable conditions. It could have been a serious opening to explore, but we did not explore it; we began the ground war. Jim Wallis wrote with anguish:

> Bush's rejection of the last-ditch Soviet peace effort was especially tragic. NBC commentator John Chancellor observed that Saddam Hussein had been trying to give up for five days. The Soviet proposal had secured the essentials of the U.N. resolutions: Iraq's withdrawal from Kuwait and subsequent restoration of Kuwaiti sovereignty.
>
> Each hour brought Iraq closer to the U.S. demands for the terms of withdrawal. But George Bush couldn't wait.[23]

For some readers, Wallis's description may overly personalize the impatience. But that is how President Bush's advisers repeatedly characterized his intense personal involvement and impatience.[24]

Seek Human Rights

In several ways, inattention to justice and human rights was a major cause of the war. Muhammad Muslih and A. R. Norton argue that the Gulf War was largely "the product of . . . the absence of democracy. . . . Had there been a minimum level of parliamentary activity and political consultation in Iraq, Hussein could not have blundered into a senseless eight-year war with Iran followed by a suicidal adventure in Kuwait." And had there been democratic processes of consultation in the Arab states allied against him, "a political solution could have been found to avert war."[25]

Among the Arab states there is one democracy—Egypt.

There are three semi-democratic constitutional monarchies with multiparty parliaments—Jordan, Algeria, and Tunisia. They did not cause the war and do not support terrorism. The war was caused by a dispute between a dictatorial national security state and an absolute monarchy—Iraq and Kuwait. Injustice causes wars.

"An increasing Arab popular will for democracy" is sweeping through the Middle East.[26] It is partly a reaction against autocracy and extreme economic inequality, partly an accomplishment of educational and economic development, and partly a result of Saddam's stirring up emotions. U.S. policies can encourage it and swim with it or align with the blocking forces. "The shining victory over Iraq will quickly tarnish if Washington aligns itself with stagnant diplomacy and a return to the status quo" of unjust and undemocratic governments.[27]

There were four reasons for the United States to support trends toward democracy and human rights during the conflict: to soften Saddam's appeal to the millions of oppressed Arabs; to give him an out so he could withdraw while pointing to new opportunities for justice to the people; to foster a more just, stable, and peaceful Middle East for the future; and to support what is right and just for the people, who have already suffered more than enough.

At the time of Iraq's invasion, Kuwait was an absolute monarchy, "a family enterprise quietly resented by commoners." While still in exile and trying to rally support from Western democracies, the emir announced his intention to allow elections for a meaningful parliament after he returned. President Bush could have jumped at the chance to focus world attention on the announcement and cement it in place as a firm commitment. Instead, the United States was passive, and after the war the emir spent months being vague about when and if elections might occur. Resentment built up. He faced "serious challenges to liberalize the political system from a newly assertive and increasingly militant opposition. . . . Old grievances have been rekindled by a new sense of contempt for the emir and his retinue, especially among Kuwaitis who stood their ground against Iraqi occupiers while the emir cooled his heels at the Saudi resort of Taif."[28] Arthur Waskow wrote that the Bush administration merely shrugged at democracy for Kuwait and rights for the Kurds.[29]

The war also unleashed reform forces in Iraq. Michael Lerner wrote that "the United States has turned its back on the reform forces, leaving them in the brutal hands of Saddam's regime. . . . As hundreds of thousands of Kurds flee their homes, desperately seeking refuge in Iran or Turkey, we are witnessing the creation of a new refugee population."[30] Rahab Hadi, a Palestinian reporter at the United Nations, wrote that "the United States ignored Saddam's gassing of the Kurdish population at Halabja in 1988 to crush their quest for self-determination; his torture of children; and his elimination of the democratic opposition. Why?" At that time the U.S. government supported Saddam against Iran, then our enemy.[31] After the Gulf War, the administration decided not to stop Saddam from slaughtering Kurds and causing their flight into hunger, cold, and disease. It did not want the revolt to split Iraq and disrupt the Middle East power balance. But the American people, seeing the suffering of the Kurds, demanded more attention to human rights. "Mr. Baker's visit, hastily arranged last week, is part of the Bush administration's effort to blunt criticism of its failure to help the Kurds militarily by focusing attention on American aid." Aid, however, was not enough, the Kurdish leaders told Mr. Baker. Action to ensure their safety was necessary so they could return home.[32]

Saddam Hussein roused up support among Arabs by claiming to be fighting for the rights of Palestinians. This was surely a ploy to try to split his Arab opposition. President Bush could have expressed strong concern for Palestinian rights, as well as for the rights of Jews to security, and begun consultations with Israeli, Palestinian and Arab representatives during the time of the sanctions, while he had leverage. Doing so would not have been linked to anything Saddam would do; it would have been simply wise, prudent, and just. Such an initiative could have weakened Saddam's appeal, as well as giving him a way out without war.

The war was also caused by "the alarming, incongruous distribution of wealth and population in the Arab world."[33] There is incredible wealth in the hands of a few ruling families and great poverty for the many who have no vote. Saddam Hussein's rebellion against wealthy and Western powers released resentments of the people over these injustices, in spite of his own dictatorial rule and despotic personality.[34]

Should the United States pay most attention to the enormous wealth and oil of the absolute monarchies, Saudi Arabia and Kuwait? The rulers of these states fear movements for democracy. They punish Jordan financially, which has moved toward a multiparty parliamentary democracy with a constitutional monarchy. How much should the United States push for human rights and how much follow the wishes of the economically powerful as it seeks common security arrangements in the Middle East?

Acknowledge Vicious Cycles

I do not want to seem to stand in judgment over the actions of my own government. Saddam Hussein was a despotic dictator who began two wars of aggression, who used poison gasses against his own country's Kurdish people, who was trying to develop nuclear weapons, and who stubbornly refused to retreat from Kuwait by the January

15 deadline. President Bush and Secretary Baker are to be commended for working so closely with the United Nations and for the remarkably successful worldwide trade embargo against Iraq. The efficiency of the weapons and the discipline of the armed forces who so devastated the Iraqi army was truly amazing. Our nation does need to get over the sense of shame that it received from the Vietnam War, the Watergate scandals of the Nixon administration, and the Iran-Contra scandals of the Reagan administration.

The Sermon on the Mount, as well as all of Jesus' ministry, seeks not to give people a guilt trip but to deliver them from the vicious cycles that cause our bondage to guilt, hostility, and injustice.

When I write of our need to "acknowledge realistically our captivity in vicious cycles and to participate in a realistic peacemaking process," I must admit my own captivity and not merely my government's; I must point to the processes of grace in which we can participate and not merely diagnose error; and I must do it realistically. At the same time, we need to acknowledge that a large portion of the American people thought we should delay the beginning of the war until later, and to recognize that the troops performed outstandingly well and deserve to be welcomed home.

I have thought for years that we needed a just peacemaking theory so that we would not find ourselves at such a brink, with a national debate limited to making war and doing nothing. I acknowledge that I have not done my part clearly and effectively enough.

What captivity to vicious cycles would it be healthy for us to acknowledge? Just as the German churches confessed for themselves, we have been suffering from the distortions of an enemy image. We led the coalition against the Soviet Union and developed an anti-ideology that served not only the purposes of containment but also our sense of rivalry, our self-righteousness, and our elite's economic interests in resisting needed reform. We cast the Soviet Union in the image of Hitler, and therefore missed some openings for conflict resolution. Then when the Soviet Union turned, we cast the Ayatollah Khomeini as the new Hitler and built up Saddam Hussein's army in its eight-year war against Iran. And then we cast Saddam as the new Hitler. Each enemy image had some objective truth in it; each enemy committed more than its share of injustice. But each enemy image was probably also part our projection; each caused us to misperceive some openings for peacemaking, and each caused much suffering for millions of people. Our nation too is part of that humankind of which the apostle Paul said, "There is no distinction, since all have sinned and fall short of the glory of God" (Rom. 3:22–23).

There are other vicious cycles that have affected our actions—our overdependence on oil, our overdependence on absolute monarchies, our self-righteousness,[35] the wish of many to demonstrate the potency of our military and thus combat the Vietnam syndrome and the declining military budget,[36] President Bush's political need to recover from sinking twenty points in the polls after congressional battles in which he seemed to stand for tax breaks for the wealthy and against the middle class.[37] Bob Woodward reported, based on hundreds of insider interviews with his top advisers, that President Bush's advisers were worried that his commitment to war against Saddam was overly intense personally and emotionally, and that he rejected recommendations of Joint Chiefs Chair Colin Powell, Secretary of State James Baker, Admiral Crowe, General Jones, General Schwarzkopf, and General Butler that they give the trade embargo time, saying to Powell, "I don't think there's time politically for that strategy."[38] Woodward does not indicate whether President Bush was thinking of coalition politics in the Gulf or partisan politics in the United States. John Sununu, President Bush's White House administrator, was quoted by aides as saying, before the war, that a quick, successful war would be political gold for the president.

There are obvious indications of Saddam's being caught up in vicious cycles of power aggrandizement, authoritarian isolation, personal resentments, animosities with Kuwait and Israel, economic debts from his war with Iran, and oppression of Kurds, Shiites, and others of his own people. Furthermore, there was surely much misperception and alienation caused by cultural barriers and ignorance of one another's history and values.

Avoid Judgmental Statements; Make Amends

Saddam's comments about us as the Great Satan did not motivate us to adopt a more mellow policy, and our *ad hominem* judgments about Saddam did not bring him closer to a solution. Harold Saunders's address to the World Affairs Council advocated an approach that "would have avoided personal name-calling, while firmly condemning aggression."[39]

Secretary Baker's "five pillars" for recovery after the war made great sense and dealt with the log in our own eye. His pillars would have established a process for building a new relationship with the people of the region, including Jordanians, Palestinians, Iranians, and Iraqis. Millions of Arabs developed intense resentments against the U.S. government, and some reconciling initiatives were much needed. Time would tell whether the pillars were mirages made of mere words or solid intentions to take significant action.

Sensitive to the threat of animosities and prejudices stirred up by the confrontation in the Gulf, the ecumenical Council on Peacemaking in Louisville, Kentucky, organized local trialogues between Muslims, Jews, and

Christians. The interest and participation were dramatic, and the results were highly significant. Large numbers of persons from the three faiths worshiped in each other's temples and mosques. They were taught the meaning of each other's art and symbols of history. Perhaps the most telling point was made by Egyptian American Dr. A. E. Bastawi: "We have to learn your history, your language, and how you think if we are to cope in this world. We wish you would learn just a bit of our history." So we studied. We found that Arabs were promised independence and self-determination if they would fight against the Ottoman Empire that ruled over them during World War I. However, after the war, the European powers carved up the territory as their colonies. Similar promises were made and broken after World War II, and again in the struggle for a homeland for the Palestinians. When the Holocaust against Jews is added to the story, the result is a gigantic log in the eye of the West. Not learning this history and not taking steps to heal it leaves us sounding arrogant and insensitive. A significant first step is to learn something of the history of the Middle East and of the practices and beliefs of Judaism and Islam. A good first step is to study Charles Kimball's book *Striving Together: A Way Forward in Christian-Muslim Relations.*[40] Another step is to begin your own dialogue or trialogue.

Gabriel Habib, general secretary of the Middle East Council of Churches, said it was very important to Christians in the Middle East that strong voices in the Western churches opposed the war. That "not only provided Middle East Christians with a sense of solidarity, but helped convey to Moslems that the war was not a Christian crusade."[41]

Work with Churches and Peacemaker Groups

We need churches and peacemaker groups to nourish independent Christian ethics, to help us guard against a jingoistic and self-righteous nationalism that can make it all too easy for us to get into other wars. I have a dream of thousands of such groups blossoming in churches, leading us toward our own "turning" toward just peacemaking. Jim Wallis tells how Brazilian Christians, blocked in their struggle for basic human rights, did not despair but saw it as a call "to go deeper." They began organizing small communities, groups of people doing Bible study and discussing what steps they could take within the limits they were given. Their efforts became the base community movement, and eventually they developed 100,000 small communities that revitalized Christian faith and worship and steadily pressed their government toward democracy and justice.[42] We too can organize small communities of Christians, doing Bible study, praying, and discussing what initiatives we can take for Christian peacemaking.

I hope the modest proposal of this book can be helpful for churches and peacemaker groups to guide them in their own peacemaking initiatives and to assist them in thinking critically and independently of the shifting winds of nationalism.

I hope this modest proposal can be discussed and debated, revised and refined, affirmed and adopted by others so that churches that seek to follow Jesus Christ can delineate the steps on the path that leads toward peace. I hope that in some form it can be helpful to churches and groups that want a tool for thinking faithfully, critically, and independently. I hope that it can point people toward taking small steps with their sisters and brothers that provide personal experience and empowerment in being peacemakers.

My hope is not that we have made a turning into an era where there will be perfect harmony and no wars. My hope is that we may be turning into a time when we have a clearer understanding of the processes that resolve conflicts, remedy injustices, and enable us to participate in the kind of peacemaking that delivers us from at least some of the vicious cycles in which we find ourselves.

My hope is not that governments will be perfect, or perfectly just. Nor that the people will be perfect. My hope is that we will have a stronger loyalty to the initiatives that make for peace.

I am not good at creating beautiful dreams. I am too much influenced by the realism of Reinhold Niebuhr. Too many dreams seem like sentimental hopes, without practical steps in the direction of the dreams. I want an ethic of practical steps.

I do, though, have a dream that three kinds of peace-and-war ethics will be widely understood: pacifism, just war theory, and just peacemaking theory. One can be either a pacifist or a just war theorist and a supporter of just peacemaking theory. Then when we have our next debate about making a war, the debate will not be between making war and doing nothing. It will be between making war and taking active peacemaking initiatives. We can debate which peacemaking initiatives should be taken and begin taking them.

The churches and the people will have a plumb line to place alongside the wall of the government (Amos 7:8), to measure that wall and determine whether it really is a wall of peace or is merely pretending to seek peace (Jer. 6:14). The people will blow their horns and circumnavigate that wall, and the wall will turn into a true wall of peace, or crumble and fall so people can step over it and make peace themselves (Josh. 6:1–16; Jer. 8:11–12).

If the governments do not change, at least the churches will be clear about their calling. My hope is not that the governments will be sinless but that the churches will hear Jesus' words and do them. At least, I hope they will take the first steps, plant the mustard seeds. They will know the things that make for peace. And they will practice the steps of peacemaking in their individual relations, families, churches, workplaces, and citizen advocacy. They will be the church of Jesus Christ. That is my dream.

"Blessed are the peacemakers, for they will be called children of God."

Questions for Thought

1. How much should the United States push for human rights and how much follow the wishes of the economically powerful as it seeks common security arrangements in the Middle East?

2. Is national unity so important that we should support whatever the president decides in wartime and in the months that lead up to war, or should we seek independence or separation between our faith perspective and governmental decision-making?

3. Once a war is over, what stance should we adopt?

4. Is peacemaking only relevant before the decision to go to war is made, or are efforts to settle the conflict with less killing called for even while the war is proceeding?

5. Can you try out the steps of just peacemaking in your own circle of acquaintances this week? Can you share your intentions and your results with a trusted friend or wise adviser to see what you can learn from discussion?

6. Look through the many books listed in the notes at the end of this book to find some you would like to take up for further information and help.

7. Can you find a group in your church or your community that you might help in its peacemaking efforts and/or from which you can receive some encouragement?

8. Might it be helpful to go back and read Matthew 5, Luke 6, and Romans 12 and give prayerful thought to their meaning for your life?

Notes

Preface

1. Jörg Swoboda, "Gifts and Gift-Giving, East and West," *The Christian Century* (July 25–August 1, 1990): 707.

Chapter 1

1. James William McClendon, *Ethics* (Nashville: Abingdon Press, 1986).

2. Jörg Swoboda, *Die Revolution der Kerzen: Christen in den Umwälzungen der DDR* (Wuppertal und Kassel: Oncken Verlag, 1990), p. 5. See also the special edition of *Der Spiegel,* entitled *Spiegel Spezial: 162 Tage Deutsche Geschichte: Das halbe Jahr der gewaltlosen Revolution* (1990), pp. 9ff., 13–15.

3. Intermediate Nuclear Forces Treaty. See chapter 5.

4. John P. Burgess, "Church-State Relations in East Germany: The Church as a 'Religious' and 'Political' Force," *Journal of Church and State* (Winter 1990): 17ff.

5. The Conciliar Process is called in English "Justice, Peace and the Integrity of Creation," but in German the word translated "integrity" is actually *Bewahrung,* literally "preservation." An excellent book in English translation resulting from the Conciliar Process in West Germany is Ulrich Duchrow and Gerhard Liedke, *Shalom: Biblical Perspectives on Creation, Justice and Peace* (Geneva: WCC Publications, 1989).

6. Max Stackhouse, *Creeds, Societies, and Human Rights* (Grand Rapids: Wm. B. Eerdmans Publishing Co., 1984).

7. Gottfried Zimmerman, in Swoboda, *Die Revolution der Kerzen,* p. 211.

8. Robert de Gendt, "Quels Concepts de Sécurité pour la Grande Europe?" *Recontre Internationale* (Brussels: February 23, 1990); Jens Langer, "New Germanies in a New Europe," *Christianity and Crisis* (June 18, 1990): 197.

9. See the writings of Robert Jervis, especially *The Meaning of the Nuclear Revolution: Statecraft and the Prospect of Armageddon* (Ithaca, N.Y.: Cornell University Press, 1989) and *The Illogic of American Nuclear Strategy* (Ithaca, N.Y.: Cornell University Press, 1984).

Chapter 2

1. Harvey McArthur has made the point best, summarizing twelve ways interpreters water down or block its applicability, in *Understanding the Sermon on the Mount* (New York: Harper & Row, 1960), chapters 3 and 4.

2. Quoted in Pinchas Lapide, *The Sermon on the Mount: Utopia or Program for Action?* (Maryknoll, N.Y.: Orbis Books, 1986), p. 3.

3. Rudolf Schnackenburg, *Die Bergpredigt: Utopische Vision oder Handlungsanweisung* (Dusseldorf: Patmos Verlag, 1982), pp. 41ff.

4. Schnackenburg, *Die Bergpredigt,* pp. 44–45. Gunther Bornkamm, *Jesus of Nazareth* (New York: Harper & Row, 1960), p. 224.

5. Lutheran theologian Hans-Richard Reuter has summarized much of the evidence for this conclusion in the following three works: "Die Bergpredigt als Orientierung unseres Menschseins Heute," *Zeitschrift für Evangelische Ethik* 23 (1979): 84–105; "Liebet eure Feinde!" *Zeitschrift für Evangelische Ethik* 26 (1982): 159–79; "Bergpredigt und Politische Vernunft," in Schnackenburg, *Die Bergpredigt,* pp. 60–80.

6. Martin Luther King, Jr., *Stride Toward Freedom* (New York: Mentor, 1958), pp. 96ff.; *Strength to Love* (Philadelphia: Fortress Press, 1963 and 1981), pp. 150ff.

7. Warren S. Kissinger, *The Sermon on the Mount: A History of Interpretation* (Metuchen, N.J.: The Scarecrow Press, 1975), p. 6.

8. Ibid., p. 35. See also the Schleitheim Confession.

9. Joachim Jeremias, *The Meaning of the Sermon on the Mount* (Philadelphia: Fortress Press, 1963), pp. 27, 32; Schnackenburg, *Die Bergpredigt,* p. 31; Samuel Sandmel, *A Jewish Understanding of the New Testament* (Cincinnati: Hebrew Union College Press, 1951), p. 150; Lapide, *The Sermon on the Mount,* p. 139.

10. Cf. Lapide, *The Sermon on the Mount,* p. 36.

11. Christian Wolf, "Die Bergpredigt—Stachel des Evangeliums," pp. 6–7, unpublished manuscript read at Eastern Union Conference, East Germany, April 26, 1985.

12. Isaiah 61 explains the difference between Luke's "blessed are the poor" and Matthew's "blessed are the poor in spirit": Matthew was trying to reflect the translation he had of Isaiah 61:1, which in the original means "poor" both in the socioeconomic sense and in the spiritual sense.

13. Robert Guelich, *The Sermon on the Mount* (Waco, Tex.: Word Press, 1982), pp. 37, 68, 71, 75, 111; Jacques Dupont, *Les Beatitudes,* vol. 2, *La Bonne Nouvelle* (Paris: H. Gabalda et Compagnie, 1969), pp. 106, 115, 122, et passim. See also Peter Stuhlmacher, "Jesu volkommenes Gesetz der Freiheit," *Zeitschrift für Theologie und Kirche* (1982): 283ff.; and W. D. Davies, "Ethics in the New Testament," in *Interpreter's Dictionary of the Bible,* vol. 2 (Nashville: Abingdon Press, 1962), p. 168. I want to indicate special gratitude to W. D. Davies, who was my teacher and who has influenced my approach to the Sermon on the Mount and the New Testament in ways I hope he can discern. He shared the text of "Ethics in the New Testament" with his students as he was completing it.

14. Guelich, *The Sermon on the Mount,* pp. 20, 28, 32.

15. Schnackenburg, *Die Bergpredigt,* pp. 24, 31.

16. Ibid., pp. 55–56.

17. Lapide, *The Sermon on the Mount,* p. 28; cf. W. D. Davies and Dale C. Allison, Jr., *A Critical and Exegetical Commentary on the Gospel According to St. Matthew,* vol. 1 (Edinburgh: T. & T. Clark, 1988), pp. 389ff.

18. Wolf, "Die Bergpredigt," pp. 7–8. Also Jack Dean Kingsbury, *Matthew as Story,* 2nd ed. (Philadelphia: Fortress Press, 1988), pp. 61–62.

19. W. D. Davies, "Ethics in the New Testament," p. 168.

20. See also Stephen Charles Mott, *Biblical Ethics and Social Change* (New York: Oxford University Press, 1982), pp. 82–83.

21. Stuhlmacher, "Jesu volkommenes Gesetz der Freiheit," pp. 291–92, 311; Guelich, *The Sermon on the Mount,* pp. 235–37; Schnackenburg, *Die Bergpredigt,* pp. 21–22; Georg Strecker, *The Sermon on the Mount* (Nashville: Abingdon Press, 1988), p. 61; Mott, *Biblical Ethics and Social Change,* chapters 4 and 5. See also chapter 3, below.

22. Jeremias, *The Meaning of the Sermon on the Mount,* pp. 30–31. See also Lapide, *The Sermon on the Mount,* pp. 36, 117; Schnackenburg, *Die Bergpredigt,* p. 24; and Davies, *Setting of the Sermon on the Mount* (Cambridge: Cambridge University Press, 1964), p. 96.

23. Carl G. Vaught, *The Sermon on the Mount: A Theological Interpretation* (Albany, N.Y.: State University of New York Press, 1986), p. 65.

24. Jeremias, *The Meaning of the Sermon on the Mount,* p. 32.

25. Sandmel, *A Jewish Understanding of the New Testament,* p. 150.

26. Closest is John Piper, who points out that "negative commands were always accompanied by a positive counterpart and here is where the emphasis fell"; *Love Your Enemies: Jesus' Love Command in the Synoptic Gospels and the Early Christian Paranesis* (Cambridge: Cambridge University Press, 1979), p. 17.

27. The consistency is so thorough that it raises the question, Why does number 3, on divorce, lack a transforming initiative? Consider what sort of transforming initiative might have fit Jesus' teaching—something like "Go, talk to your sister (wife), and seek to be reconciled, while there is still time." The context was one of inequality: Prior to the time of the Deuteronomic Reform, indicated in the teaching of Deuteronomy 24, men could divorce women at a whim and then later change their minds at another whim. Hence divorced women lived in limbo,

without defined status. Nor could women divorce men. The command to give a certificate at least established the status of divorced women and was a move toward *partial* equality, with some rights. Gradually divorce was made somewhat more difficult "in favor of the wife and an eventual salvaging of the endangered marriage," and the wife was given the right to seek a divorce in some cases. Jesus moved forward in the direction of equality and of peacemaking between husband and wife, as was the original intention of the Creator (Lapide, *The Sermon on the Mount,* pp. 64, 67–68). Jesus and his movement upset the status quo: He had women as disciples, he dialogued with them as equals, and he taught them as only men were to be taught. Many women had positions of leadership in the churches. This upset the patriarchal context of the early church (Elizabeth Schüssler Fiorenza, *In Memory of Her* [New York: Crossroad, 1983], pp. 143ff.).

By advocating the transforming initiative of talking and seeking reconciliation, Jesus would have been implying equality between men and women as well as commanding that we seek to make peace. This would have been uncomfortable for the patriarchal culture in which his teachings were handed on before Matthew wrote his Gospel. Hence it was "forgotten." No one claims the Gospels wrote down everything Jesus taught. Some was left out. "Go talk to your sister and seek to make peace" was a likely candidate for forgetfulness. If I were not afraid of being taken literally by some, I would jump at the chance to suggest that the triadic transforming initiatives pattern has enabled us to recover an original teaching of Jesus, forgotten for twenty centuries!

28. James A. Brooks and Carlton Winbery, *Syntax of New Testament Greek* (Washington, D.C.: University Press of America), p. 88. The usual translation of Matthew 5:48, not "all-inclusive" but "perfect," has overwhelming problems, as most every scholar agrees. If you put it in the context of its Old Testament background, it has a twofold meaning: (1) love with unlimited boundaries, universal, all-inclusive, and (2) undivided loyalty to God, whose love includes all. So a better translation is "all-inclusive." This translation also fits what Jesus has just been emphasizing, and it fits Luke's report of the same teaching: "Be

ye merciful, as your Father is merciful." See Davies and Allison, *A Critical and Exegetical Commentary,* pp. 560–63. Others suggest "wholeness," which is very close to "all-inclusiveness." In both contexts when Matthew uses *teleios* (Matt. 5:48; 19:21), he is pointing to all-inclusive loyalty to God and inclusion of enemies and the poor. Luke's word, "merciful," (toward enemies) also points to all-inclusiveness. For "wholeness," see Lapide, *The Sermon on the Mount,* p. 118; Guelich, *The Sermon on the Mount,* p. 235; and Schweizer, *The Good News According to Matthew,* p. 135. The translations and paraphrases in Table 2.1 are mine.

29. For example, Gunther Bornkamm's helpful essay, "Der Aufbau der Bergpredigt," *New Testament Studies* (1978): 419–32; Andrej Kodjak's *A Structural Analysis of the Sermon on the Mount* (Berlin: Mouton de Gruyter, 1986), which suffers from its lack of attention to previous scholarly discussion; Christoph Burchard, "The Theme of the Sermon on the Mount," in *Essays on the Love Commandment,* ed. Luise Schottroff (Philadelphia: Fortress Press, 1978); the summary of others' proposals and constructive proposal in Schnackenburg, *Die Bergpredigt,* pp. 19ff.; and the several discussions in Davies and Allison, *A Critical and Exegetical Commentary,* and Guelich, *The Sermon on the Mount,* which together I find most helpful.

30. Davies and Allison, *A Critical and Exegetical Commentary,* pp. 70, 86–87, 504ff., 625–27. Cf. Davies, *Setting of the Sermon on the Mount,* pp. 301, 307. As a Christian ethicist who respects careful biblical work, I am greatly indebted to New Testament specialists David Garland, Alan Culpepper, Gerald Borchert, and Walter Wink for their careful reading, helpful suggestions, and much-appreciated encouragement concerning this delineation of the structure and thrust of the Sermon on the Mount.

31. Quoted by Davies, *Setting of the Sermon on the Mount,* pp. 303–4.

32. The two hyperboles, "Pluck out your eye" and "Let not your left hand know what your right is doing," would be impossible if taken literally, of course. But they are memorable ways of saying we should remove ourselves from the source of temptation and should give in secret. These are eminently more doable

than pretending we are pure while walking purposefully into the situation of temptation.

Chapter 3

1. Pinchas Lapide, *The Sermon on the Mount: Utopia or Program for Action?* (Maryknoll, N.Y.: Orbis Books, 1986), pp. 23, 141–42.

2. Ernst Troeltsch, "The Significance of the Historical Existence of Jesus for Faith," in *Ernst Troeltsch: Writings on Theology and Religion,* ed. Robert Morgan and Michael Pye (Atlanta: John Knox Press, 1977), pp. 194ff.; *The Social Teaching of the Christian Churches,* vol. 1 (New York: Harper, 1960), pp. 43ff.

3. Kenneth Underwood, *Protestant and Catholic* (Boston: Beacon Press, 1957).

4. John Piper, *Love Your Enemies: Jesus' Love Command in the Synoptic Gospels and the Early Christian Paranesis* (Cambridge: Cambridge University Press, 1979).

5. W. D. Davies, *The Setting of the Sermon on the Mount* (Cambridge: Cambridge University Press, 1964), pp. 345–46, 353ff.; *Paul and Rabbinic Judaism* (London: SPCK, 1948 and 1955), pp. 136ff.

6. Victor Paul Furnish, *Theology and Ethics in Paul* (Nashville: Abingdon Press, 1968), pp. 53–54.

7. Dale Allison, "The Pauline Epistles and the Synoptic Gospels: The Pattern of the Parallels," *New Testament Studies* (1982): 1ff. For more on Luke's version, see my "The Politics of Jesus in the Sermon on the Plain," in the forthcoming *Radical Catholicity* (Grand Rapids: Wm. B. Eerdmans Publishing Co., 1992).

8. Davies and Allison, *A Critical and Exegetical Commentary,* pp. 543, 553; Furnish, *Theology and Ethics in Paul,* pp. 53–54; C. E. B. Cranfield, *A Critical and Exegetical Commentary on the Epistle to the Romans* (Edinburgh: T. & T. Clark, 1979), pp. 629, 640, 645, 677; Ernst Käsemann, *Commentary on Romans* (Grand Rapids: Wm. B. Eerdmans Publishing Co., 1980), p. 347; Allison, "The Pauline Epistles"; Charles Talbert, "Tradition and Redaction in Romans 12:9–21," *New Testament Studies* (1969): 87.

9. John Howard Yoder, *Reinhold Niebuhr and Christian Pacifism* (Scottdale, Pa.: Concern, 1955); and *Politics of Jesus* (Grand Rapids: Wm. B. Eerdmans Publishing Co., 1972), chapter 1.

10. Duane Friesen, *Christian Peacemaking & International Conflict: A Realist Pacifist Perspective* (Scottdale, Pa.: Herald Press, 1986); Ronald Stone, *Christian Realism and Peacemaking: Issues in U.S. Foreign Policy* (Nashville: Abingdon Press, 1988).

11. Clarence Jordan, *Sermon on the Mount* (Valley Forge, Pa.: Judson Press, 1952), pp. 56ff.

12. Francis A. Beer, *Peace Against War* (San Francisco: W. H. Freeman, 1981), pp. 239–40, 275ff.

13. Sam Keen, *Faces of the Enemy: Reflections of the Hostile Imagination* (San Francisco: Harper & Row, 1986).

14. Jordan, *Sermon on the Mount,* p. 57.

15. John R. Stott, *The Message of the Sermon on the Mount: Christian Counter-Culture* (Downers Grove, Ill.: Inter-Varsity Press, 1978), pp. 107, 110.

16. Walter Wink, *Violence and Nonviolence in South Africa: Jesus' Third Way* (Philadelphia: New Society Publishers, 1987), pp. 13ff. Wink documents this thoroughly in his presently unpublished manuscript, "Neither Passivity Nor Violence: Jesus' Third Way (Mt. 5:38–42 and parallels)." Cf. John Ferguson, *The Politics of Love: the New Testament and Nonviolent Revolution* (Nyack, N.J.: Fellowship of Reconciliation, 1979), pp. 4–5; Lapide, *The Sermon on the Mount,* p. 134. Some scholars, noticing the reference to a law court in Matthew 5:40 (but not in Luke), limit the meaning to not resisting in the law court. I believe this is too narrow a limitation, for the following reasons: (1) They assume the point is negative renunciation and don't emphasize positive initiative enough; (2) the "eye for an eye" teaching was designed to stop vengeful violence outside the law court (Eduard Schweizer, *The Good News According to Matthew* [Atlanta: John Knox Press, 1975], p. 129); (3) "Go the second mile" and "give to the one who begs" are outside the law court; (4) Luke puts these teachings in the context of violence outside the law court; (5) Jesus showed consistent concern for zealot-like violence against Roman oppressors and their collaborators—

outside the law court; and (6) I'm intentionally building on Romans 12 and Luke as well as Matthew, and they don't limit it to the law court. See also Lapide's argument from "careful translation back into Jesus' mother tongue," *The Sermon on the Mount,* pp. 130ff.

17. This is nicely explained by Walter Wink, *Violence and Nonviolence,* pp. 15ff.

18. Gerhard Lohfink, *Wem gilt die Bergpredigt?* (Freiburg: Herder, 1988), p. 44; Hans Weder, *Die "Reden der Reden": Eine Auslegung der Bergpredigt Heute* (Zürich: Theologischer Verlag Zürich, 1985 and 1987), pp. 128–29.

19. Luke may reverse the terms because he is thinking not of the law court but of robbery, and naturally a robber would take the coat or outer garment first. Luke is writing to a Gentile audience that would not understand the Exodus and Amos context and so gives it the context of robbery to make a similar point: Give what you were not asked for. Wink takes Luke to be the correct version and suggests the rich person is suing the poor person for his outer garment, or mantle or coat (p. 16, and see footnote 12). In that case the spirit of the law is even more clearly being violated by the one who is suing. But see Davies and Allison, *A Critical and Exegetical Commentary,* pp. 544ff. Wink, *Violence and Nonviolence,* p. 17, adds an important point: "Indebtedness was the most serious social problem in first century Palestine. Jesus' parables are full of debtors struggling to salvage their lives. The situation . . . was the direct consequence of Roman imperial policy."

20. Georg Strecker, *The Sermon on the Mount: An Exegetical Commentary* (Nashville: Abingdon Press, 1988), p. 84.

21. Lapide, *The Sermon on the Mount,* pp. 112–13.

22. Weder, *Die "Reden der Reden,"* p. 131.

23. Lohfink, *Wem gilt die Bergpredigt?* p. 45.

24. Davies and Allison, *A Critical and Exegetical Commentary,* p. 546.

25. William Klassen, *Love of Enemies: The Way to Peace* (Philadelphia: Fortress Press, 1984), pp. 119–20.

26. Ibid.

27. Peter Stuhlmacher, "Jesu volkommenes Gesetz der Freiheit," *Zeitschrift für Theologie und Kirche* (1982): 320–21.

28. The transforming initiatives interpretation agrees with Wink and Lapide. It was previously advanced in Glen Stassen, "The Time Machine," *Pulpit Digest* (August 1980), and *Journey into Peacemaking* (Memphis: Brotherhood Commission, Southern Baptist Convention, 1983 and 1987), chapters 5, 6, 9; Jürgen Moltmann and Glen Stassen, *Justice Creates Peace* (Louisville, Ky.: Baptist Peacemakers International Spirituality Series, 1988), pp. 17–32. Robert Guelich (*The Sermon on the Mount* [Waco, Tex.: Word Press, 1982], pp. 220, 252) and Georg Strecker (*The Sermon on the Mount: An Exegetical Commentary* [Nashville: Abingdon Press, 1988], p. 83) assume a compliance or renunciation-of-rights interpretation.

29. "When the *victim* determines how far to go, he or she has control—is no longer subjugated, is superior [or equal]" (Schweizer, *The Good News According to Matthew,* p. 130). See Wink's graphic description in *Violence and Nonviolence,* pp. 14–34.

30. Davies, *Setting of the Sermon on the Mount,* p. 308.

31. Elizabeth R. Achtemeier, "Righteousness in the Old Testament," *Interpreter's Dictionary of the Bible,* vol. 4 (Nashville: Abingdon Press, 1962), pp. 80ff.

32. Ibid.

33. Alan Richardson, "Righteousness," *A Theological Word Book of the Bible* (London: SCM, 1950); Gottfried Quell and Gottlob Schrenk, "Dikaiosyne," in *Theological Dictionary of the New Testament,* vol. 2, ed. Gerhard Kittel (Grand Rapids: Wm. B. Eerdmans Publishing Co., 1964), p. 195.

34. Achtemeier, "Righteousness," pp. 82–83; cf. Gerhard von Rad, *Old Testament Theology* (Edinburgh: Oliver & Boyd), p. 377.

35. Achtemeier, "Righteousness," p. 83.

36. Johanna W. H. Bos, "Out of the Shadows: Genesis 38; Judges 4:17–32; Ruth 3," in *Semeia 42: Reasoning with the Foxes: Female Wit in the World of Male Power,* ed. J. Sheryl Exum and Johanna W. H. Bos (Atlanta: Scholars Press, 1988).

37. Quell and Schrenk, "Dikaiosyne," pp. 195–96.

38. Benno Przybylski, *Righteousness in Matthew and His World of Thought* (Cambridge: Cambridge University Press, 1980), pp. 25, 58–59, 64–72, 99.

39. Michael H. Crosby, *House of Disciples: Church, Economics and Justice in Matthew* (Maryknoll, N.Y.: Orbis Books, 1988), pp. 180, 182, 187, 190–91.

40. Guelich, *The Sermon on the Mount,* pp. 235–36.

41. See John Howard Yoder, *Politics of Jesus* (Grand Rapids: Wm. B. Eerdmans Publishing Co., 1972); and Sharon Ringe, *Jesus, Liberation, and the Biblical Jubilee* (Philadelphia: Fortress Press, 1985).

42. Wolf, "Die Bergpredigt," pp. 15–16; Stuhlmacher, "Jesu volkommenes Gesetz der Freiheit," pp. 313–14; Lapide, *The Sermon on the Mount,* pp. 67ff.

43. Richard Barnet, *The Roots of War* (Baltimore: Penguin Books, 1973), chapters 3 and 5; see especially p. 51. See also Robert Jervis, *Perception and Misperception in International Politics* (Princeton, N.J.: Princeton University Press, 1976), chapter 4 and passim.

44. Martin Luther King, Jr., *Strength to Love* (Philadelphia: Fortress Press, 1981), pp. 47–48.

45. Lapide, *The Sermon on the Mount,* pp. 85ff. Davies and Allison, *A Critical and Exegetical Commentary,* pp. 549–50. It probably comes from the Qumran community (Davies, *Setting of the Sermon on the Mount,* p. 252) or from Matthew's desire to develop an antithesis to Jesus' teaching of love for the enemy and Leviticus 19:18 on love for the neighbor (Guelich, *The Sermon on the Mount,* pp. 226–27). And beyond that, we recognize it as a vicious cycle that seems almost universal in human experience.

46. Klassen, *Love of Enemies,* p. 7.

47. Schweizer, *The Good News According to Matthew,* p. 111.

48. Lapide, *The Sermon on the Mount,* p. 91; Piper, *Love Your Enemies,* passim.

49. Guelich, *The Sermon on the Mount,* p. 228. Cf. Davies and Allison, *A Critical and Exegetical Commentary,* pp. 551–52.

50. Lapide, *The Sermon on the Mount,* pp. 97–98.

51. Ibid., p. 116; see also the rabbinic citations on p. 120.

52. This comes immediately after Paul has asked us to bless (or pray for) our enemies, just as Matthew couples them in reverse order: "Love your enemies and pray for those who persecute you."

53. This anecdote was told me by my father, who was a member of Eisenhower's cabinet.

54. Christian Wolf, "Die Bergpredigt," pp. 11–13. Peter Stuhlmacher ("Jesu volkommenes Gesetz der Freiheit," p. 317) argues that "Enemy" should not be narrowed to mean only individual or private relationships; the term is comprehensive and includes political enemies.

55. See Davies and Allison, *A Critical and Exegetical Commentary,* pp. 554, 556. This point is repeated in Ephesians 5, 1 Peter 1, and 1 John 4.

56. Klassen, *Love of Enemies,* p. 85.

57. Matthew 10:12–13; Strecker, *The Sermon on the Mount,* p. 92; Davies and Allison, *A Critical and Exegetical Commentary,* p. 558; Guelich, *The Sermon on the Mount,* pp. 232–33.

58. Stott, *The Message of the Sermon on the Mount,* p. 119.

59. Cited in Davies and Allison, *A Critical and Exegetical Commentary,* pp. 616–17.

60. Ibid., pp. 588, 590.

61. Ibid., pp. 604–6.

62. For a partial description, see my *Journey into Peacemaking,* chapters 2 and 3, and my "Petitioning God for Peace," *Sojourners* (April 24, 1981): 23–24. See Walter Wink, "Waging Spiritual Warfare with the Powers," *Weavings* (March/April 1990): 32–41.

63. Davies and Allison, *A Critical and Exegetical Commentary,* pp. 668–69; Guelich, *The Sermon on the Mount,* pp. 350, 374–76.

64. Stuhlmacher, "Jesu volkommenes Gesetz der Freiheit," pp. 312–13.

Chapter 4

1. There is scholarly debate about how absolute and extensive the pacifism was, and how much it was opposition to the violence of military service or the idolatry of service to Caesar. See Roland Bainton, *Christian Attitudes Toward War and Peace* (Nashville: Abingdon Press, 1960); C. John Cadoux, *The Early Christian Attitude to War* (New York: Seabury Press, 1919 and 1982); Geoffrey Nuttall, *Christian Pacifism in History* (London:

Basil, Blackwell & Mott, 1958); John Helgeland, Robert J. Daly, and J. Patout Burns, *Christians in the Military* (Philadelphia: Fortress Press, 1985); the rebuttal to Helgeland by Mark Nation in *Radical Catholicity* (Grand Rapids: Wm. B. Eerdmans Publishing Co., 1992); Ronald G. Musto, *The Catholic Peace Tradition* (Maryknoll, N.Y.: Orbis Books, 1986), chapters 2, 3.

2. David Hollenbach, *Nuclear Ethics* (New York: Paulist Press, 1983), p. 75.

3. *Ökumenische Versammlung für Gerechtigkeit, Frieden und Bewahrung der Schöpfung* (Berlin: Aktion Sühnezeichen/ Friedensdienste, 1990), p. 40.

4. U.S. National Conference of Catholic Bishops, *The Challenge of Peace,* paragraphs 23–24, reprinted in *Catholics and Nuclear War,* ed. Philip J. Murnion (New York: Crossroad, 1983), p. 261.

5. John Howard Yoder, *He Came Preaching Peace* (Scottdale, Pa.: Herald Press, 1985), pp. 129, 136–37.

6. Alan Geyer, *The Idea of Disarmament!* (Elgin, Ill.: Brethren Press, 1985), pp. 172ff., 192; Edward Leroy Long, "The Mandate to Seek a Just Peace," *The Peacemaking Struggle: Militarism & Resistance,* ed. Ronald H. Stone and Dana Wilbanks (Lanham, Md.: University Press of America, 1985), pp. 29ff., and his *Peace Thinking in a Warring World* (Philadelphia: Westminster Press, 1983), chapter 1; and Ronald H. Stone, *Christian Realism and Peacemaking: Issues in U.S. Foreign Policy* (Nashville: Abingdon Press, 1988), p. 86.

7. Dieter S. Lutz, *Lexikon: Rüstung, Frieden, Sicherheit* (Munich: C. H. Beck, 1987), p. 291. Egon Bahr and Olaf Palme used the concept of common security in the latter seventies and early eighties. The Palme Commission brought it to international notice. Ibid., p. 132.

8. Lutz, *Lexikon,* p. 132; Dieter Senghaas, *Europa 2000: Ein Friedensplan* (Frankfurt am Main: Suhrkamp Verlag, 1990), pp. 17, 21–22. Randall Harvey translated Senghaas for me.

9. Schritte zur Abrüstung, *Von der Abschreckung zur Sicherheitspartnerschaft* (Bonn: n.p., May 1985), pp. 10–11; See also Theologische Studienabteilung beim Bund der Ev. Kirchen in der DDR und Aktion Sühnezeichen/Friedensdienste, *Sicherheits-Partnerschaft und Frieden in Europa* (Göttingen:

Steidl, 1983); Hartmut Lenhard, ed., *Versöhnung und Frieden mit den Völkern der Sowjetunion* (Gütersloh: Gerd Mohn, 1987), pp. 55–56.

10. Senghaas, *Europa 2000*, p. 47.

11. Elisabeth Raiser, Hartmut Lenhard, and Burkhard Homeyer, eds., *Brücken der Verständigung* (Gütersloh: Gerd Mohn, 1986), pp. 126–28.

12. *Ökumenische Versammlung für Gerechtigkeit*, pp. 23, 39, 89, 90, 98–99, 103, 105, 195.

13. Ibid., p. 51. The term "two-thirds world" in the East German document refers to what is usually called the Third World. It explains that the people who live in the developing lands of Asia, Africa, and Latin America under conditions of unjust deprivation compose at least two-thirds of the world's population.

14. Ibid., pp. 89–95.

15. Charles E. Osgood, *An Alternative to War or Surrender* (Urbana, Ill.: University of Illinois Press, 1962).

16. Schritte zur Abrüstung, *Von der Abschreckung zur Sicherheitspartnerschaft*.

17. *Ökumenische Versammlung für Gerechtigkeit*, pp. 21, 92–93, 97–98, 196.

18. Schritte zur Abrüstung, *Von der Abschreckung*, pp. 10–11.

19. Hans-Richard Reuter, "die Bergpredigt und politische Vernunft," in *Die Bergpredigt: Utopische Vision oder Handlungsanweisung*, ed. Rudolf Schnackenburg (Düsseldorf: Patmos Verlag, 1982), pp. 69, 74. Reuter refers us to the results of peace research described in H. Afheldt, *Verteidigung und Frieden* (München-Wien, 1976).

20. Readable introductions are Roger Fisher and Harold Urey, *Getting to Yes* (New York: Penguin Books, 1983); Fisher, *International Conflict for Beginners* (New York: Harper, 1969); and Kathleen and James McGinnis, *Parenting for Peace and Justice* (Maryknoll, N.Y.: Orbis Books, 1988).

21. *Ökumenische Versammlung für Gerechtigkeit*, pp. 39–40, 96, 113ff.

22. Ibid., pp. 22, 34. See also Senghaas, *Europa 2000*, for a similar assessment on these several points, pp. 21–23, 26–31, 38–42.

23. Ted Gurr, *Why Men Rebel* (Princeton, N.J.: Princeton

University Press, 1970), which won the annual award of the American Political Science Association.
24. Senghaas, *Europa 2000*, pp. 31ff.
25. *Ökumenische Versammlung für Gerechtigkeit*, p. 35.
26. Ibid., pp. 52–65.
27. Ibid., pp. 72–86.
28. Ibid., pp. 33–34.
29. Ibid., pp. 87–89.
30. Hans Bethe, Kurt Gottfried, and Robert S. McNamara, "The Nuclear Threat: A Proposal," *New York Review of Books* (June 27, 1991): 48ff.
31. Ibid.
32. Raiser, Lenhard, and Homeyer, *Brücken der Verständigung*, pp. 15ff.
33. *Ökumenische Versammlung für Gerechtigkeit*, pp. 20–25.
34. Raiser, Lenhard, and Homeyer, *Brücken der Verständigung*, p. 11.
35. *Ökumenische Versammlung für Gerechtigkeit*, pp. 22–23f.
36. Sidney Drell, "The Impact of a U.S. Public Constituency on Arms Control," in *Breakthrough*, ed. Anatoly Gromyko and Martin Hellman (New York: Walker & Co., 1988).
37. See Dietrich Bonhoeffer, *Ethics* (New York: MacMillan Publishers, 1965), pp. 110ff., 317, 327, 333, 358–60.

Chapter 5

1. From 1981–1982, as a member of the International Task Force of the Freeze Campaign, I represented the Freeze to the coordinating meetings of the European peace movement. For the next three years I served on the Freeze Strategy Committee, and eventually I served as its co-chair, and also chaired the subcommittee that developed the Freeze overture to Mr. Andropov and Mr. Reagan, explained below.
2. Lothar Rühl, *Mittelstreckenraketen in Europa: Ihre Bedeutung in Strategie, Rüstungskontrolle und Bündnispolitik* (Baden-Baden: Nomos Verlagsgesellschaft, 1987), p. 247; cf. pp. 289ff.
3. Strobe Talbott, *Deadly Gambits* (New York: Alfred A. Knopf, 1984), pp. 56–58.

4. Ibid. Actually, the Euromissile buildup may have been stimulated by Helmut Schmidt in the first place. In the 1977 Alastair Buchan Memorial Lecture before the International Institute for Strategic Studies, October 28, 1977, he declared that Soviet military superiority in Europe was impairing the security of Western Europe "if we do not succeed in removing the disparities of military power in Europe parallel to the SALT negotiations." He pointed to disparities in conventional weapons and in tactical (as opposed to long-range) nuclear forces. He said there were two ways of establishing balance: "a massive build-up of forces and weapons systems" by the West or negotiated mutual reductions to "achieve an overall balance at a lower level. I prefer the latter" (*Survival* [January/February 1978]: 3ff.). The U.S. government pointed to this address as the stimulus for its proposal to build up medium-range nuclear missiles on the ground in Western Europe. In our Freeze strategizing, we knew he said he preferred mutual reductions, and we were looking for whatever opening we could find to avoid what we assessed as a highly dangerous and destabilizing buildup.

5. Talbott, *Deadly Gambits,* pp. 56–57. The difference of perspectives is reflected in the language. In the original German it was called "the zero solution" (*die Null-Lösung*), but the U.S. government demoted it to merely "the zero option." Since it originated in Germany and has become not merely an option but the solution, I'll call it consistently by its original name. NATO's 1979 "double-track decision" was a decision to build new missiles for deployment in Europe, while simultaneously pursuing a negotiations track. The negotiations were to concern *how many* should be installed: "The document stated quite clearly that . . . the zero solution . . . was definitely not envisioned in December 1979. Quite the contrary." The plan was to deploy the U.S. missiles "even in the unlikely event that the specific threat of the SS-20s disappeared" (Talbott, *Deadly Gambits,* pp. 38–39).

6. Helmut Schmidt, "The 'Zero Option'—a Western Idea," *World Press Review,* July 1987—originally published in *Die Zeit*; Talbott, *Deadly Gambits,* p. 56; letter from Prof. Dr. Dieter Mahncke to Glen Stassen, April 27, 1988; and Lothar Rühl, *Mittelstreckenraketen in Europa,* pp. 289ff.

7. A pamphlet I wrote in 1982 for Clergy and Laity Concerned, *Pershing II and Cruise Missiles: Spreading Chaos,* was used widely in the peace movement to explain the dangers of the Euromissiles and to argue for a freeze and reductions.

8. Lynn E. Davis, "Lessons of the INF Treaty," *Foreign Affairs* 66, no. 4 (Spring 1988): 722: "The Soviets were obviously determined to prevent the U.S. from deploying *any* INF missiles in Europe."

9. Since then Talbott's book (*Deadly Gambits*) has verified this assessment.

10. Telephone conversation with General von Baudissin July 14, 1987. The above account has been verified by von Baudissin in a letter to me of March 7, 1989.

11. *Viernheimer Tageblatt,* October 28, 1981, p. 1; *The Economist* (October 31–November 6, 1981): 557; *Nuclear Disarmament News* (October 1981): 2–3.

12. David Cortright, "The Zero Option and the European Peace Movement," in a forthcoming book.

13. *The Washington Post,* October 22, 1981.

14. Talbott, *Deadly Gambits,* p. 60.

15. Ibid., pp. 59–65, 73–74.

16. *Pravda,* October 27, 1983. See also *The Washington Post,* October 27, 1983, article by Dusko Doder.

17. Elizabeth Drew, "A Reporter in Washington," *The New Yorker* (April 15, 1985); "Letter from Washington," *The New Yorker* (July 28, 1986): 68–73; "Letter from Washington," *The New Yorker* (October 27, 1986): 124–25.

18. Drew, "Letter from Washington," (October 27, 1986): 124–25.

19. Strobe Talbott, "We Meet Again," *Time* (December 14, 1987): 30.

20. Lynn E. Davis, "Lessons of the INF Treaty," pp. 722–23.

21. Schritte zur Abrüstung, *Die Chance nutzen!* (Nürnberg und Arnoldshain: 1987), pp. 2–4.

Chapter 6

1. See Tamar Jacoby, "The Reagan Turnaround on Human Rights," *Foreign Affairs* 64 (Summer 1986): 1066ff. Jacoby

shows how people and Congress caused a major reversal of presidential policy, paralleling the role of people and Congress in achieving the INF Treaty.

2. For example, the World Alliance of Reformed Churches' book *A Christian Declaration of Human Rights* (Grand Rapids: Wm. B. Eerdmans Publishing Co., 1977) refers to the origin of human rights in the Enlightenment on pp. 49, 55, and 129.

3. Wolfgang Huber and Heinz Eduard Tödt, *Menschenrechte: Perspektiven einer menschlichen Welt* (Stuttgart: Kreuz Verlag, 1977), p. 8.

4. Austin Woolrych, "The English Revolution: An Introduction," in *The English Revolution, 1600–1660,* ed. W. W. Ives (New York: Harper & Row), pp. 1–33.

5. See Michael Walzer, *The Revolution of the Saints: A Study in the Origins of Radical Politics* (New York: Atheneum, 1969), for a stimulating account of the role of religion and political theory in the more established Presbyterian and Anglican sectors of the revolution. There are many other fascinating accounts, a few of which will be mentioned in the following footnotes.

6. William Haller, *Tracts on Liberty in the Puritan Revolution, 1638–1647,* vol. 1 (New York: Columbia University Press, 1933), p. 111.

7. Richard Tuck, *Natural Rights Theories: Their Origin and Development* (Cambridge: Cambridge University Press, 1979 and 1981), pp. 147–50.

8. Joseph Frank, *The Levellers* (Cambridge: Harvard University Press), p. 39; G. E. Aylmer, *The Levellers in the English Revolution* (Ithaca, N.Y.: Cornell University Press, 1975), pp. 18, 55; W. L. Lumpkin, *Baptist Confessions of Faith* (Philadelphia: Judson Press, 1959), pp. 97ff.

9. H. N. Brailsford, *The Levellers and the English Revolution* (Stanford, Calif.: Stanford University Press, 1961), p. 50.

10. It is printed in B. Evans, *The Early English Baptists,* vol. 1 (London: J. Heaton & Son, 1862), pp. 254–56.

11. The Short Confession of Faith of John Smyth and his congregation in 1610, and their 1612 Confession, had both emphasized these themes. They can both be found in Lumpkin, *Baptist Confessions.*

12. Lumpkin, *Baptist Confessions,* p. 124.

13. Richard Overton, *New Lambeth Fair* (London: R.O. & G.D., 1642), p. A3. Quotations from Overton are adapted to fit present-day spelling and punctuation. I give thanks for the remarkable collections of seventeenth-century manuscripts and the friendly assistance to be found in the rare book libraries of Union Theological Seminary and Harvard University.

14. Ibid., p. B1.

15. Ibid., pp. A3–4.

16. Brailsford, *The Levellers and the English Revolution,* p. 52.

17. W. K. Jordan, *The Development of Religious Toleration in England,* vol. 4 (London: G. Allen & Unwin, 1940), pp. 190–91; William Haller, *Liberty and Reformation* (New York: Columbia University Press, 1955), pp. 176–78. Some of the same assumptions can still be seen in the more recent writings of Aylmer (*The Levellers in the English Revolution,* pp. 18–19) and Frank (*The Levellers,* pp. 41–42), although the more recent the scholar, the less the tendency. Winthrop Hudson criticizes this secularizing error perceptively in his essay, cited below.

18. Sandra Harding, *The Science Question in Feminism* (Ithaca, N.Y.: Cornell University Press, 1986), pp. 219–22, 240–42; W. Van den Daele, "The Social Construction of Science," in *The Social Production of Scientific Knowledge,* ed. E. Mendelsohn (Dordrecht: Reidel, 1977).

19. Brailsford, *The Levellers and the English Revolution,* pp. 52–53. Cf. Christopher Hill, *The World Turned Upside Down* (New York: Viking, 1972), p. 139.

20. Haller, in *Liberty and Reformation,* clearly recognizes the equalitarian and democratic implications of Overton's argument.

21. Richard Overton, *Arraignment of Mr. Persecution* (London: April 1645), pp. 4–6. The manuscript is reprinted in William Haller, ed., *Tracts on Liberty,* vol. 3, pp. 203–56.

22. It had a tradition: John Murton had made the wheat and tares the central text for his earlier mock trial in *Persecution for Religion Judged and Condemned.* For publishing such heresy Murton was jailed. His fellow believers sent him a jug of milk each morning, stopped with paper. He wrote on the paper with milk and smuggled it out with the empty bottle the next morn-

ing. It was heated with a candle, turning the milky writing brown, and thus was published his next pamphlet, *The Humble Supplement.* (See Leon McBeth, *The Baptist Heritage* [Nashville: Broadman Press, 1987], p. 75.)

23. Glen Stassen, "Anabaptist Influence in the Origin of the Particular Baptists," *Mennonite Quarterly Review* (October 1962): 322–48.

24. Richard Overton, *The Ordinance for Tithes Dismounted* (London: December 1645), pp. 13, 21–23 (italics added). Next, in *Divine Observations Upon the London-Ministers' Letter Against Toleration . . .* (London: January 24, 1646), he argues for religious liberty and against persecution, repeating arguments from *Arraignment.*

25. Haller, *Tracts on Liberty,* vol. 1, p. 111.

26. Richard Overton, *A Remonstrance of Many Thousand Citizens* (London: July 7, 1646), reprinted in ibid., vol. 3, pp. 353ff.

27. Richard Overton, *An Appeal . . . to the Free People* (London: July 17, 1647), reprinted in D. M. Wolfe, *Leveller Manifestoes of the Puritan Revolution* (New York: T. Nelson & Sons, 1944), pp. 154ff.; here quoting p. 182. See also A. S. P. Woodhouse, *Puritanism and Liberty* (Chicago: University of Chicago Press, 1951), pp. 323ff.; Aylmer, *The Levellers in the English Revolution,* p. 48; Hill, *The World Turned Upside-Down,* p. 31.

28. Winthrop Hudson, "John Locke: Heir of Puritan Political Theorists," in *Calvinism and the Political Order,* ed. George L. Hunt (Philadelphia: Westminster Press, 1965). Hudson's study focuses on religious liberty but includes the concept of natural rights as well as the emphasis on peace (pp. 117, 119, 125). He emphasizes the contribution of Overton's colleague, Roger Williams, but all the same arguments are in Overton as well, and Williams and Overton repeatedly cited each other as allies.

29. David Hollenbach, *Justice, Peace and Human Rights: American Catholic Social Ethics in a Pluralistic World* (New York: Crossroad, 1988), p. 88. Similarly, Heinz Eduard Tödt and Wolfgang Huber, *Menschenrechte: Perspektiven einer menschlichen Welt* (Stuttgart: Kreuz Verlag, 1977), p. 52, point out that in Germany the jurist Georg Jellinek made a breakthrough discovery in 1895: The source of human rights is not the

French Revolution but the U.S. Bill of Rights, which developed out of the demand for religious liberty. On the latter point, where James Madison and Baptists in Virginia played perhaps the key role, see William Lee Miller, *First Liberty* (New York: Alfred A. Knopf, 1986), parts 1 and 2.

30. Hollenbach, *Justice,* p. 89. Hollenbach's earlier book, *Claims in Conflict: Retrieving and Renewing the Catholic Human Rights Tradition* (New York: Paulist Press, 1979), tells the history of the development more fully. Chapter 4 emphasizes the importance of pluralism and the conflict between interest groups in contemporary society.

31. Hollenbach, *Justice,* p. 91. Cf. also Tödt and Huber, *Menschenrechte,* pp. 55–59.

32. Hollenbach, *Justice,* p. 91.

33. Ibid., p. 92.

34. Ibid., p. 96.

35. Ibid., p. 90.

36. H. Richard Niebuhr, "The Ego-Alter Dialectic and the Conscience," *Journal of Philosophy* 42 (1945): 352ff. James William McClendon, Jr., in "How Can a Christian Be a Law Librarian?" (manuscript), argues that Christians must be selective about the practices they engage in, must experience the counterpractice of an alternative community such as a church, and "must learn to make the intersection of these two the basis of a challenge to the standing order."

37. Hollenbach, *Justice,* pp. 108ff.

38. Ibid., p. 123.

39. Hollenbach, *Claims in Conflict,* p. 98.

40. Ibid., p. 95; also Tödt and Huber, *Menschenrechte,* pp. 80ff. In *Claims in Conflict,* chapter 5, Hollenbach presents a helpful discussion of priorities among the dimensions of rights, which is missing in the later book.

41. Tödt and Huber, *Menschenrechte,* pp. 15ff., 33–34; Hollenbach, *Justice,* pp. 113–14.

42. Monika Hellwig, "The Quest for Common Ground in Human Rights—A Catholic Reflection," in *Human Rights in the Americas: The Struggle for Consensus,* ed. John Langan, S.J., and Alfred Hennelly, S.J. (Washington, D.C.: Georgetown University Press, 1982), pp. 160ff.

43. Max Stackhouse, *Creeds, Society, and Human Rights* (Grand Rapids: Wm. B. Eerdmans Publishing Co., 1984).

44. Ibid., pp. 53–72. In his later book, *Apologia* (Grand Rapids: Wm. B. Eerdmans Publishing Co., 1988), Stackhouse reacts more strongly against pluralism than I would.

45. See the insightful essay by Riffat Hassan in *Human Rights in Religious Traditions,* ed. Arlene Swidler (New York: Pilgrim Press, 1982).

46. Tödt and Huber, *Menschenrechte,* pp. 69ff., 158–75.

47. Ronald Stone, *Christian Realism and Peacemaking: Issues in U.S. Foreign Policy* (Nashville: Abingdon Press, 1988), p. 75.

48. Tödt and Huber, *Menschenrechte,* pp. 39–40, 45–46, 51, 72, 151ff., 168ff. See also David P. Forsythe, *Human Rights and World Politics* (Lincoln, Neb.: University of Nebraska Press, 1983), pp. 98 et passim.

Chapter 7

1. See especially *Why Men Rebel,* by Ted Gurr (Princeton, N.J.: Princeton University Press, 1970). See also Francis A. Beer, *Peace Against War* (San Francisco: W. H. Freeman, 1981), and Michael Walzer, *Just and Unjust Wars* (New York: Basic Books, 1977).

2. Ronald Stone, *Christian Realism and Peacemaking: Issues in U.S. Foreign Policy* (Nashville: Abingdon Press, 1988), especially chapter 4, "Realism, Human Rights and U.S. Foreign Policy," although chapters 6 and 7 are important as well.

3. Marian Wright Edelman, *Families in Peril* (Cambridge: Harvard University Press, 1987), p. 22.

4. Children's Defense Fund, *Children 1990: A Report Card, Briefing Book, and Action Primer* (Washington, D.C.: Children's Defense Fund, 1990).

5. "Vaccine Shortages Causing Immunization Crisis," *CDF Reports* (May 1991): 3.

6. Phyllis Freeman and Anthony Robbins, "An Epidemic of Inactivity," *New York Times,* July 10, 1991.

7. Kathleen A. Guy, *Welcome the Child: A Child Advocacy*

Guide for Churches (Washington, D.C.: Children's Defense Fund, 1991), p. 67.

8. Children's Defense Fund, *Children 1990,* pp. 23ff.

9. Edelman, *Families in Peril,* p. 4.

10. Daniel Patrick Moynihan, *Family and Nation* (San Diego: Harcourt Brace Jovanovich, 1986, 1987), pp. 8, 186ff.

11. Edelman, *Families in Peril,* p. 24.

12. Children's Defense Fund, *Adolescent Pregnancy: An Anatomy of a Social Problem in Search of Comprehensive Solutions* (Washington, D.C.: Children's Defense Fund, 1987), p. 3.

13. Ibid., pp. 3–6.

14. Ibid., p. 7.

15. Children's Defense Fund, *Welfare and Teen Pregnancy: What Do We Know? What Do We Do?* (Washington, D.C.: Children's Defense Fund, 1986), pp. 5–7; Edelman, *Families in Peril,* pp. 65, 71. Two studies cited by *Welfare and Teen Pregnancy* did find a small correlation between being on welfare in the year after birth of the first child and repeat pregnancies. But studies by Bane, Ellwood, and Wilson cited by *Families in Peril,* p. 71, indicate "that welfare is not to blame for out-of-wedlock births."

16. Edelman, *Families in Peril,* p. 55.

17. Ibid., p. 10.

18. Ibid.

19. Children's Defense Fund, *Tackling the Youth Employment Problem* (Washington, D.C.: Children's Defense Fund, 1989), p. 5.

20. Children's Defense Fund, *S.O.S. America! A Children's Defense Budget* (Washington, D.C.: Children's Defense Fund, 1990), pp. 101ff.

21. J. Patrick Lavery, M.D., Georgia Chaffee, Shirley Martin, R.N., et al., "Pregnancy Outcome in a Comprehensive Teenage-Parent Program," *Adolescent and Pediatric Gynecology* (1988): 34–38.

22. Edelman, *Families in Peril,* p. 59.

23. Ibid., p. 88.

24. Children's Defense Fund, *Tackling the Youth Employment Problem,* p. 6; see also p. 13.

25. Children's Defense Fund, *A Vision for America's Future* (Washington, D.C.: Children's Defense Fund, 1989), p. 87.

26. Ibid., p. 85.

27. Edelman, *Families in Peril,* p. 89.

28. Children's Defense Fund, *A Vision for America's Future,* pp. xvii, 80.

29. Charles Murray, *Losing Ground* (New York: Basic Books, 1984), pp. 227–33.

30. Children's Defense Fund, *A Vision for America's Future,* p. 24.

31. "Recession May Trigger Large Jump in Child Poverty," *CDF Reports* (May 1991): 5. See also ibid., pp. 17–19.

32. Children's Defense Fund, *A Vision of America's Future,* pp. 22–24.

33. Ibid., p. 100.

34. Edelman, *Families in Peril,* p. 96.

35. Ibid., p. 16.

36. "Congress Moves to Help Neediest Americans," *CDF Reports* (November 1990): 1.

37. Marian Wright Edelman, "We Must Attack and Defeat Child Poverty," *CDF Reports* (January/February 1991): 1.

38. Children's Defense Fund, *The State of America's Children* (Washington, D.C.: Children's Defense Fund, 1991), pp. 9–12.

39. Quoted in Children's Defense Fund, *The State of America's Children,* p. 1.

Chapter 8

1. Patrick McCormick, C.M., *Sin as Addiction* (New York: Paulist Press, 1989); Dietrich Bonhoeffer, *Ethics* (New York: Macmillan Publishing Co., 1965), pp. 17ff.; see also any of Reinhold Niebuhr's books. See also James W. McClendon, Jr.'s, critique of decisionism in ethical method, in his *Ethics* (Nashville: Abingdon Press, 1986), pp. 56ff., whose critique relates closely to the work of the international relations theorists in the following note.

2. John Steinbruner, *The Cybernetic Theory of Decision: New Dimensions of Political Analysis* (Princeton, N.J.: Princeton University Press, 1974), pp. 25ff. et passim; Graham Allison, *Essence of Decision* (Boston: Little, Brown & Co., 1971); Robert Jervis, *The Logic of Images in International Relations* (Princeton, N.J.: Princeton University Press, 1970) and *Perception and*

Misperception in International Politics (Princeton, N.J.: Princeton University Press, 1976); Richard E. Neustadt and Ernest R. May, *Thinking in Time: The Uses of History for Decision-makers* (New York: Free Press, 1988).

3. McCormick, *Sin as Addiction,* p. 181.

4. *Al-Anon's Twelve Steps & Twelve Traditions* (New York: Al-Anon Family Group Headquarters, 1988), p. 7.

5. Jael Greenleaf, "Co-Alcoholic/Para-Alcoholic: Who's Who & What's the Difference," in *Co-Dependency: An Emerging Issue* (Pompano Beach, Fla.: Health Communications, Inc., 1984), pp. 6–11.

6. Wayne Oates, *Confessions of a Workaholic* (Nashville: Abingdon Press, 1971).

7. Sharon Wegscheider-Cruse, "Co-Dependency: The Therapeutic Void," in *Co-Dependency: An Emerging Issue,* p. 2. Especially persons in helping professions should read *When Helping You Is Hurting Me: Escaping the Messiah Trap,* by Carmen Renee Berry (New York: Harper & Row, 1989).

8. *Al-Anon's Twelve Steps & Twelve Traditions,* pp. 13ff.

9. Ibid., p. 21.

10. *Alcoholics Anonymous,* 3rd ed. (New York: Alcoholics Anonymous World Services, 1976), p. 25.

11. Janet Geringer Woititz, "The Co-Dependent Spouse," in *Co-Dependency: An Emerging Issue,* p. 90.

12. Robert Subby, "Inside the Chemically Dependent Marriage: Denial and Manipulation," in *Co-Dependency: An Emerging Issue,* p. 27; Robert Subby and John Friel, "Co-Dependency: A Paradoxical Dependency," in ibid., p. 36.

13. Sarah Frances Hines, in a lecture at the annual seminar of the Christian Life Commission of the Southern Baptist Convention, March 12–14, 1990, where an earlier form of this chapter was also presented.

14. *Al-Anon Faces Alcoholism* (New York: Al-Anon Family Group Headquarters, 1988), p. 220.

15. *The Dilemma of the Alcoholic Marriage* (New York: Al-Anon Family Group Headquarters, 1984), pp. 31ff.

16. Roger Fisher and William Ury, *Getting to Yes* (Harrisonburg, Va.: Penguin Books, 1983), pp. 31–32.

17. Oates, *Confessions of a Workaholic,* chapter 9.

18. Vernon Johnson, *I'll Quit Tomorrow,* rev. ed. (San Francisco: Harper & Row, 1980), chapter 5.

19. *Dilemma of the Alcoholic Marriage,* pp. 56–57.

20. For example, see David K. Switzer, *The Minister as Crisis Counselor,* rev. ed. (Nashville: Abingdon Press, 1986), pp. 138–42.

21. *Dilemma of the Alcoholic Marriage,* pp. 36–37.

22. *Al-Anon Faces Alcoholism,* pp. 134–35.

23. Angela Elwell Hunt, "Camp Transformation," *Fundamentalist Journal* (February 1987): 24–25.

24. Robin Norwood, *Women Who Love Too Much* (New York: St. Martin's Press, 1985).

25. Melody Beattie, *Codependents' Guide to the Twelve Steps* (New York: Prentice Hall/Parkside, 1990), pp. 119ff. This may be the best of the how-to books that I have cited.

26. *Alcoholics Anonymous,* pp. 60ff.

27. *Al-Anon's Twelve Steps & Twelve Traditions* recommends writing down what comes in meditation at the fourth step, the moral inventory, as well as at the eighth, which explicitly calls for a list.

28. *Dilemma of the Alcoholic Marriage,* pp. 12–13.

29. *Al-Anon Faces Alcoholism,* pp. 165ff.

30. See Glen Stassen, *Journey into Peacemaking* (Memphis: Brotherhood Commission, 1983 and 1987), for a step-by-step how-to description of such groups. Your denomination's headquarters probably has suggestions appropriate to your church tradition. Whatever your affiliation, you may write Baptist Peace Fellowship of North America, 499 Patterson Street, Memphis, TN 38111, for the pamphlet *How to Start a Peacemaker Group.*

Chapter 9

1. Robert Jervis, *Perception and Misperception in International Politics* (Princeton, N.J.: Princeton University Press, 1976), p. 150.

2. Thomas Kuhn, *The Structure of Scientific Revolutions* (Chicago: University of Chicago Press, 1962 and 1970).

3. Jervis, *Perception and Misperception,* p. 157.

4. Ibid., p. 163 et passim.

5. Ibid., pp. 206ff.

6. General Assembly, *Peacemaking: The Believers' Calling* (New York: The General Assembly of the United Presbyterian Church in the United States of America, 1980).

7. U.S. National Conference of Catholic Bishops, *The Challenge of Peace* (Washington, D.C.: United States Catholic Conference, 1983).

8. Susan Thistlethwaite, ed., *A Just Peace Church* (New York: United Church Press, 1986).

9. United Methodist Council of Bishops, *In Defense of Creation* (Nashville: Graded Press, 1986).

10. Douglas Gwyn, George Hunsinger, Eugene F. Roop, and John Howard Yoder, *A Declaration on Peace: In God's People the World's Renewal Has Begun* (Scottdale, Pa.: Herald Press, 1991).

11. A biblically realistic understanding of *shalom* makes clear that harmony between all of God's creatures will not be achieved this side of the fulfillment of the eschaton, but we are given mustard seeds of peace and justice in this time and are adopted as children of God when we participate in God's peacemaking now. Here I concur with some of Paul Ramsey's criticism that the Methodists are overly optimistic about achieving harmony in this history. However, Ramsey tends to relegate God's delivering grace to a transhistorical realm and then to spiritualize Jesus' teachings so they have no reference to Jesus' and our sociopolitical contexts. He needs a subtler eschatology than that. See Paul Ramsey and Stanley Hauerwas, *Speak Up for Just War or Pacifism* (University Park, Pa.: Pennsylvania State University Press, 1988), pp. 34–35, 39, 43ff.

12. President Kennedy's courageous and successful initiative to halt above-ground nuclear testing, rightly praised by the bishops, was actually first taken by President Eisenhower; it was reciprocated by the Soviet Union and lasted for two and a half years, until just before President Kennedy's election. See Harold Stassen, *Eisenhower: Turning the World Toward Peace* (St. Paul: Merrill-Magnus, 1990).

13. *Pastoral Constitution on the Church in the Modern World* (par. 81), reprinted in David J. O'Brien and Thomas A. Shan-

non, eds., *Renewing the Earth: Catholic Documents on Peace, Justice and Liberation* (Garden City, N.Y.: Doubleday, 1977), pp. 263–64.

14. U.S. National Conference of Catholic Bishops, *Economic Justice for All* (Washington, D.C.: United States Catholic Conference, 1986), par. 148; cf. par. 249.

15. See ibid., pp. 12, 45ff., 60, 69ff., 126.

16. They renounce the use of nuclear weapons and strongly criticize the ideology of deterrence (pp. 14–15 et passim). Paul Ramsey seems to miss the point of the bishops' criticism of deterrence as an idolatrous ideology. He says "the point of nuclear deterrence always was only nuclear war prevention and nuclear peacemaking" (*Speak Up for Just War or Pacifism*, p. 62). As Ramsey knows, the principal author of the Methodist bishops' statement is Alan Geyer; three chapters of his book, *The Idea of Disarmament* (Elgin, Ill.: Brethren Press, 1982 and 1985), are devoted to showing that deterrence is not a morally pure idea and does not mean merely a redundant collection of weapons. It is an ideology used to justify hundreds of billions of dollars worth of military buildup. It needs to be understood as it actually functions in its concrete political, military, economic, and ideological context.

17. "How to Get Started: Form a Small Group," and "John Wesley and the 'United Societies': Small Groups in Methodist Tradition," in Heidi Hilf, ed., *Peace with Justice in the Local Church* (Washington, D.C.: General Board of Church and Society, n.d.), pp. 9–11.

18. Howard John Loewen, "Reflections on Three Peace Statements" (manuscript, March 17, 1990), p. 2, commenting on *In God's People*.

19. Sandra M. Schneiders, "New Testament Reflections on Peace and Nuclear Arms," in *Catholics and Nuclear War*, ed. Philip J. Murnion (New York: Crossroad, 1983), pp. 91ff.

20. Ronald H. Stone and Dana W. Wilbanks, eds., *The Peacemaking Struggle: Militarism and Resistance* (Lanham, Md.: University Press of America, 1985) and Stone and Wilbanks, *Presbyterians and Peacemaking: Are We Now Called to Resistance* (New York: Advisory Council on Church and Society, 1985).

21. Edward Long, in Stone and Wilbanks, *Presbyterians and Peacemaking,* pp. 36–37.
22. Stone and Wilbanks, *Peacemaking Struggle,* p. 38. The study paper includes the same quote (p. 43).
23. The 200th General Assembly, Presbyterian Church (U.S.A.), *Christian Obedience in a Nuclear Age* (Louisville, Ky.: The Office of the General Assembly, 1988), pp. 3–5.
24. Ibid., p. 7.
25. Ibid., p. 8.
26. Ibid., pp. 2, 9, 11.
27. Ibid., p. 8.
28. Ibid., pp. 8, 21, 22.
29. Ibid., p. 17.

Chapter 10

1. John Howard Yoder, *Nevertheless: The Varieties of Religious Pacifism* (Scottdale, Pa.: Herald Press, 1971); *The Original Revolution: Essays on Christian Pacifism* (Scottdale, Pa.: Herald Press, 1971 and 1977); *The Politics of Jesus* (Grand Rapids: Wm. B. Eerdmans Publishing Co., 1972); *The Priestly Kingdom* (Notre Dame: University of Notre Dame Press, 1984); *He Came Preaching Peace* (Scottdale, Pa.: Herald Press, 1985).
2. U.S. National Conference of Catholic Bishops, *The Challenge of Peace* (Washington, D.C.: United States Catholic Conference, 1983), par. 85–109, 147. I have arranged the criteria in an unusual order as an aid to memory, as suggested by one of my less respectful students. It forms an acronym: SCRAM CIA.
3. See Ralph Potter, *War and Moral Discourse* (Richmond, Va.: John Knox Press, 1969), and Michael Walzer, *Just and Unjust Wars* (New York: Basic Books, 1977).
4. See chapter 5, above, and U.S. National Conference of Catholic Bishops, *The Challenge of Peace.*
5. To cite two outstanding examples from an earlier decade: Theodore R. Weber, *Modern War and the Pursuit of Peace* (New York: Council on Religion and International Affairs, 1968), and American Friends Service Committee, *Peace in Vietnam* (New York: Hill & Wang, 1967). For more recent examples, see Duane Friesen, *Christian Peacemaking and International Conflict*

(Scottdale, Pa.: Herald Press, 1986), and Ronald Stone, *Christian Realism and Peacemaking: Issues in U.S. Foreign Policy* (Nashville: Abingdon Press, 1988).

6. "Military officials in Riyadh, Saudi Arabia, were quoted . . . as estimating that the Iraqi dead totaled 100,000" (*New York Times,* March 23, 1991, p. 4). Jim Wallis reports that "Saudi and European figures now put the number at 100,000 people killed in six weeks," that standard estimates put the wounded at about two and a half times those killed, and that this many casualties in six weeks makes the loss of life in the Gulf War "the most intensive toll since World War II," in "Where Do We Go from Here?" *Sojourners* (May 1991): 4.

7. "Greenpeace Estimates Greater than 200,000 Casualties," Greenpeace press release, Washington, D.C., May 29, 1991. See also William M. Arkin, Damian Durrant, and Marianne Cherni, *On Impact: Modern Warfare and the Environment: A Case Study of the Gulf War* (Washington, D.C.: Greenpeace, 1991).

8. Jay Rosen, "From Slogan to Spectacle; How the Media and the Left Lost the Gulf War," *Tikkun* (May/June 1991): 22ff.; Mark Hertsgaard, "The War and the Media: Palace Court Mentality," *Christianity and Crisis* (March 18, 1991): 79–80.

9. Wallis, "Where Do We Go from Here?" p. 4.

10. George Williamson, *Who Is God in the Heat of War, in the Hope for Peace?* (Memphis: Baptist Peace Fellowship of North America, 1991), pp. 15–16.

11. Milton Viorst, "The House of Hashem," *The New Yorker* (January 15, 1991): 42.

12. Ibid., pp. 42ff.

13. Ibid., pp. 43–44.

14. "Israel after the War," *Foreign Affairs* (Spring 1991): 32.

15. Harold H. Saunders, address before the Middle East Institute of the World Affairs Council, Washington, D.C., January 17, 1991.

16. Comments by Cornel West in "Roundtable," *Tikkun* (May/June 1991): 28.

17. Saunders, address, pp. 6ff.

18. Bob Woodward, *The Commanders* (New York: Simon & Schuster, 1991), p. 205. See also pp. 211–12, 216, 219ff. for what follows.

19. Ibid., pp. 211ff.

20. *New York Times,* July 13, 1991, pp. 1, 4.

21. Jim Wallis, "A Neither Just Nor Holy War," *Sojourners* (April 1991): 11.

22. Woodward, *Commanders,* pp. 346, 350ff.

23. Wallis, "A Neither Just Nor Holy War," p. 11.

24. See Woodward, pp. 226, 229, 241, 260ff., 277, 282, 350–51; and Jack Nelson, "Bush Out to Get Hussein, President's Advisers Say," *Los Angeles Times,* February 17, 1991. Both are based on insider interviews with President Bush's closest advisers.

25. Muhammad Muslih and A. R. Norton, "The Need for Arab Democracy," *Foreign Policy* (Summer 1991): 4.

26. Charles Kimball, "The Case for Diplomacy," *Sojourners* (February-March 1991): 19.

27. Ibid., pp. 4–5.

28. Brewster Grace, "The Gulf: The View from Jordan," *Christianity and Crisis* (November 12, 1990): 350; Milton Viorst, "The House of Hashem," passim; Muslih and Norton, "The Need for Arab Democracy," passim.

29. Muslih and Norton, "The Need for Arab Democracy," p. 14.

30. Ibid., pp. 9, 11.

31. Arthur Waskow, "Jews and the Gulf War: The View from 'In Between,' " *The Nation* (May 27, 1991): 697.

32. "Editorial: After Iraq," *Tikkun* (May/June 1991): 5

33. Rabab Hadi, "Palestinian Blood and Gulf Oil," *Christianity and Crisis* (November 12, 1990): 348.

34. *New York Times,* April 9, 1991, pp. 1, 4. See also comments of Cornel West and Senator Paul Wellstone in "Roundtable," *Tikkun,* pp. 29–30.

35. William Sloane Coffin, "The Gulf: Self-Righteousness (and Oil)," *Christianity and Crisis* (November 12, 1990): 342: "We love our enemies not by countenancing their sins but by remembering our own. It is the only way to avoid the self-righteousness that is the bane of both interpersonal and international relations."

36. Michael Klare, "Big Victory—for the Wrong Policy," *Christianity and Crisis* (March 18, 1991): 81–83.

37. Woodward, *Commanders,* pp. 226, 229, 241, 260–62, 277, 282, 301, 350–51.

38. Ibid., pp. 41–42, 299–300, 308, 310–11, 313, 331–32, 342.

39. Saunders, address, p. 4.

40. Charles Kimball, *Striving Together: A Way Forward in Christian-Muslim Relations* (Maryknoll, N.Y.: Orbis Books, 1991).

41. Leon Howell, "The War: Rhetoric, Reasons, Results," *Christianity and Crisis* (May 13, 1991): 140.

42. Wallis, "Where Do We Go from Here?" p. 5.